Innovative Funding and Financing for Infrastructure

Investment in infrastructure is critical to economic growth, quality of life, poverty reduction, access to education, good-quality healthcare – that is, a dynamic economy. Yet amid scarce public capital, heavily indebted governments, and increased demands on government resources, infrastructure projects often suffer from investment shortfalls and inadequate maintenance. These challenges merit renewed efforts at finding additional sources of funding. *Innovative Funding and Financing for Infrastructure* focuses on innovative approaches to financing as well as debt and equity from new sources and structures. It provides critical methods to increase the capital available for infrastructure, reduce fiscal liabilities, and improve leverage of scare public resources. Designed for students and specialists in the fields of investment planning and finance, this book offers a survey of creative approaches from around the world, resulting in a practical guidance for policymakers and strategists on how governments can enable and encourage innovative funding and financing.

Jeffrey Delmon is a senior infrastructure finance specialist at the World Bank. He is the author of numerous books, articles, and blogs, including *Private Sector Investment in Infrastructure: Project Finance, PPP Projects and PPP Programs*, 4th ed. (2021), *A Decision-Makers Guide to Public Private Partnerships in Airports* (2020), and *Public-Private Partnership Projects in Infrastructure: An Essential Guide for Policy Makers*, 2nd ed. (2017). He is an adjunct associate professor at the National University of Singapore, lectures at the Singapore Management University, and is a member of the International Advisory Panel of the Climate Impact Exchange.

Innovative Funding and Financing for Infrastructure

Addressing Scarcity of Public Resources

JEFFREY DELMON

Shaftesbury Road, Cambridge CB2 8EA, United Kingdom

One Liberty Plaza, 20th Floor, New York, NY 10006, USA

477 Williamstown Road, Port Melbourne, VIC 3207, Australia

314–321, 3rd Floor, Plot 3, Splendor Forum, Jasola District Centre, New Delhi – 110025, India

103 Penang Road, #05–06/07, Visioncrest Commercial, Singapore 238467

Cambridge University Press is part of Cambridge University Press & Assessment, a department of the University of Cambridge.

We share the University's mission to contribute to society through the pursuit of education, learning and research at the highest international levels of excellence.

www.cambridge.org
Information on this title: www.cambridge.org/9781009340205
DOI: 10.1017/9781009340182

© Jeffrey Delmon, 2024

This publication is in copyright. Subject to statutory exception and to the provisions of relevant collective licensing agreements, no reproduction of any part may take place without the written permission of Cambridge University Press & Assessment.

First published 2024

A catalogue record for this publication is available from the British Library

A Cataloging-in-Publication data record for this book is available from the Library of Congress

ISBN 978-1-009-34020-5 Hardback
ISBN 978-1-009-34017-5 Paperback

Cambridge University Press & Assessment has no responsibility for the persistence or accuracy of URLs for external or third-party internet websites referred to in this publication and does not guarantee that any content on such websites is, or will remain, accurate or appropriate.

Ad majorem dei gloriam

Contents

List of Figures	*page* xiii
Preface	xv
Acknowledgments	xvii

1 Introduction and Summary	1
1.1 *Innovative Sources of Funding*	3
1.2 *Innovative Sources of Finance*	9

PART I FUNDING

2 Land Value Capture	15
2.1 LVC Instruments	17
2.1.1 *Land for Cash*	17
2.1.2 *Land as Public Contribution*	18
2.1.3 *Land as Collateral*	18
2.1.4 *Developer Exactions and Impact Fees*	18
2.1.5 *Land Pooling/Readjustment*	19
2.1.6 *Betterment Levies/Special Assessments*	20
2.1.7 *Density Bonus*	21
2.1.8 *Upzoning*	21
2.1.9 *Transferable Development Right*	22
2.1.10 *Joint Ventures*	22
2.2 *Bringing Forward LVC Funding*	22
2.3 *Lessons Learned*	23
2.3.1 *Consultation with Property Owners, Developers, and Other Stakeholders*	23
2.3.2 *Setting Appropriate Charges on Owners/Developers*	24
2.3.3 *Consultation with Community*	24
2.3.4 *Administrative Capacity*	24

	2.3.5 Legal Framework	25
	2.3.6 Land Controls, Cadaster or Land Registry, Technology, and Data Systems	25
	2.3.7 Dynamic Real Estate Market	25
	2.3.8 Transparent Land Sales	26
	2.3.9 Readiness of Financial and Capital Markets	26
	2.3.10 Fiscal Mandates and Powers of Enforcement	26
	2.3.11 Need for Accurate and Complete Data	26
	2.3.12 Risk of Overreliance	27
	2.3.13 Managing Corruption and Perceptions Thereof	27
	2.3.14 Avoiding Excessive Gentrification	27
3	Commercial Value Capture	28
	3.1 Introduction to CVC	29
	3.2 Implementing CVC Systematically	32
	3.3 CVC in Different Sectors	34
	3.3.1 Transport	34
	3.3.2 Power	36
	3.3.3 Water and Wastewater	38
	3.3.4 Solid Waste Management	39
	3.3.5 Urban Redevelopment	41
	3.3.6 Government Offices	43
	3.3.7 Public/Low-Cost Housing	44
	3.3.8 Historic and Cultural Sites	45
	3.3.9 Hospitality and Tourism	46
	3.3.10 Health	47
	3.3.11 Education	49
	3.4 A CVC Menu	50
	3.4.1 Advertising and Marketing	51
	3.4.2 Naming Rights	51
	3.4.3 Residential Space	53
	3.4.4 Government Office Space	56
	3.4.5 Retail Space	56
	3.4.6 Parking	61
	3.4.7 Hospitality and Tourism	65
	3.4.8 Vehicle, Logistics, and Other Sector Services	69
	3.4.9 Development Rights	70
	3.4.10 Infrastructure Sharing	74
	3.4.11 Cost Reductions	76
	3.4.12 Additional Offtake from the Facility	78
	3.4.13 Beneficiary Contributions, Prepurchase of Services, and Congestion Pricing	80
	3.5 Emissions Reduction Credits/Offsets	82
	3.6 Lessons Learned in Implementing Innovative Funding	86

Contents ix

  3.6.1   Think Outside the Box   87
  3.6.2   Don't Try to Be Too Clever   87
  3.6.3   Community Engagement   87
  3.6.4   Maintain Focus on Service Delivery   87
4   Programmatic Value Capture: Transit-Oriented Development   90
 4.1   TOD Principles   94
 4.2   Challenges When Delivering TOD and Best Practices   98

PART II   FINANCING

5   Principles of Finance   105
 5.1   Sources of Financing   109
  5.1.1   Equity Contributions   109
  5.1.2   Debt Contributions   109
  5.1.3   Mezzanine/Subordinated Contributions   111
  5.1.4   Securitization and Syndication   113
  5.1.5   Value for Money   114
 5.2   Financiers   115
  5.2.1   Local Commercial Banks   116
  5.2.2   Global Commercial Banks   117
  5.2.3   Development Financial Institutions   117
  5.2.4   Institutional and Retail Investors   117
  5.2.5   Debt Capital Markets   118
  5.2.6   Equity Investors   119
 5.3   Key Risks   120
  5.3.1   Completion   120
  5.3.2   Force Majeure and Change in Law   120
  5.3.3   Political Risk   121
  5.3.4   Environmental and Social Risk   121
  5.3.5   Currency Exchange Risk   122
  5.3.6   Interest Rate Risk   122
 5.4   Key Investor Concerns   123
  5.4.1   Importance of Project   123
  5.4.2   Project "Champion"?   124
  5.4.3   Project Approvals   124
  5.4.4   Demand Levels   124
  5.4.5   Source of Demand   125
  5.4.6   Revenues   125
  5.4.7   Government Creditworthiness   126
  5.4.8   Project Configuration   126
  5.4.9   Time for Construction/Implementation   127
  5.4.10   Materials/Inputs Required   127
  5.4.11   Access to Skilled Staff   127
  5.4.12   Cost and Revenue Risk   128

		5.4.13 Security Structure	128
		5.4.14 Foreign Exchange Risk	129
		5.4.15 Minimum Service-Level Obligations	129
		5.4.16 Government Obligations	129
		5.4.17 Reliability of Courts and Arbitration	129
		5.4.18 Program/Pipeline	130
		5.4.19 Open, Transparent, and Fair Procurement	130
	5.5	Project Finance	130
		5.5.1 Off-Balance Sheet	131
		5.5.2 Limited Recourse and Sponsor Support	131
		5.5.3 Bankability	133
		5.5.4 Taking Security	135
		5.5.5 Financial Ratios	137
		5.5.6 Refinancing	140
6	Climate Finance		141
	6.1	Financing Instruments	143
	6.2	Sources of Climate Finance	147
		6.2.1 Public Sources	149
		6.2.2 Private Sources	149
		6.2.3 Green Blended Finance	150
	6.3	Identification of Climate Finance Sources	151
	6.4	Roles of the Public and Private Partners	153
	6.5	Transaction Characteristics	153
	6.6	Compliance with Climate Finance Standards and Requirements	155
	6.7	Verification of Compliance	156
	6.8	Barriers to Accessing Climate Finance	157
7	Islamic Finance		159
	7.1	Overview of Islamic Finance Structures	161
	7.2	Sale and Leaseback	165
	7.3	Sukūk	168
		7.3.1 Sukūk Structure	169
		7.3.2 Sukūk – Asset Backed and Asset Based	170
	7.4	Islamic Climate Finance	171
	7.5	Islamic Finance Institutions	172
	7.6	Legal Issues and Documentation	173
8	Blended Finance		176
	8.1	Blended Finance Instruments	178
		8.1.1 Desire for Lower Income, Bias toward Middle Income	179
		8.1.2 Who Is Whom?	179
		8.1.3 When to Blend?	179
		8.1.4 Need for Commercially Viable Projects	181
	8.2	The Community of Practice around Blended Finance	181
	8.3	Drivers of Blended Financing	182

Contents

8.4	Blended Financing Funds and Facilities	183
8.5	Implementing Blended Finance Funds	186
	8.5.1 Functionality	186
	8.5.2 Fund Structure	187
	8.5.3 A Few Challenges	188
8.6	Core Recommendations for Blended Finance	191
	8.6.1 Is It Necessary?	191
	8.6.2 Manage Expectations	192
	8.6.3 Get the Incentives Right	193
	8.6.4 Impact	193
	8.6.5 Address Capacity Constraints	193
	8.6.6 Get the Structure Right	195

Glossary 197
Index 223

Figures

2.1	The basic TIF model	page 23
3.1	Global ERC markets	85
5.1	Sources of private financing for infrastructure	107
6.1	Accessing climate finance	142
7.1	*Istiṣnā'* structure	162
7.2	*Ijārah* structure	162
7.3	*Murābaḥah*	163
7.4	*Mushārakah*	164
7.5	*Mudārabah*	164
7.6	*Ijārah wa iqtina*	166
7.7	Madinah Airport PPP	167
7.8	Doraleh container project	174
8.1	BFF structure	188

Preface

This book is about how to mobilize more money for infrastructure, how to earn more revenue ("funding") for and from infrastructure investments, and how to borrow more ("financing"), in order to develop new or better infrastructure. More money for infrastructure means more investment, more jobs, better quality of life, and more economic growth.

Chapter 1 sets the scene and provides a summary of the topics covered by this book.

Part I ("Funding") looks at innovative sources of revenues. While more financing is important to enable infrastructure development, to the extent that new infrastructure does not generate sufficient revenues (e.g., through user fees), government must fill the resulting financial gaps. More funding reduces government liabilities and makes infrastructure more self-sustainable. This book will discuss some of the more innovative methods for mobilizing funding for infrastructure.

In particular, infrastructure investments tend to increase the value of land around the infrastructure assets or in the service delivery catchment area. Chapter 2 discusses land value capture (LVC) and the mechanisms to capture some of this increased value, the windfall that landowners may receive thanks to the infrastructure investment, and the use of part of that windfall to help fund the infrastructure investment that creates the value.

Infrastructure investments also create opportunities to generate economic activities and commercial revenues. The infrastructure investment can be structured so as to capture some of these commercial activities and/or the revenues generated by them to fund the infrastructure investment (commercial value capture or CVC). Chapter 3 describes various types of CVC used in different sectors and in countries around the world, sharing best practices and seeking to inspire planners, developers, and financiers alike to pursue and benefit from CVC. Chapter 4 discusses programmatic efforts to mobilize LVC and CVC, using the example of transit-oriented development and investments in transit infrastructure, which create transit corridors or areas, provide an opportunity to drive economic opportunities, and create a more livable context in the urban space. By embedding LVC and CVC into development policies like transit, government can generate innovative sources of revenues more consistently and efficiently.

Some very creative and innovative approaches have been adopted when mobilizing financing for infrastructure. Financing is a very complex topic, so Part II ("Financing") starts with a general overview of key issues. Innovative financing does not alter the fundamental nature of financing; hence Chapter 5 reviews these fundamental issues. Then Chapters 6–8 explore three important types of innovative financing that offer a new dynamic when mobilizing financing for infrastructure: climate finance, Islamic finance, and blended finance.

Acknowledgments

I have had the pleasure and privilege of working with some of the global experts in different fields, who have kindly provided their advice and guidance over the years. I can name only a few of them here, so please forgive me if I have missed anyone.

I would like to thank my colleagues from the World Bank (past and present) who helped review certain parts of this text and provided essential advice and support, in particular (in alphabetical order): Aijaz Ahmad, Abhijit Baumik, Bhavna Bhatia, Tim Brennan, Chalida Chararnsuk, Zhuo Cheng, Will Dachs, Victoria Rigby Delmon, Arnaud Dornel, Marc Forni, Katharina Gassner, Neeraj Gupta, Kirsten Huttner, Tim Irwin, Alex Jett, Ellis Juan, Teuta Kacaniku, Justina Kajange, Angelina Kee, Joel Kolker, Laszlo Lovei, Cledan Mandri-Perrott, Hanna Messerli, Komal Mohindra, Mark Moseley, Michel Noel, Paul Noumba Um, Fida Rana, Paul Reddel, Zak Rich, Heinz Rudolf, Dhruva Sahai, Valery Santos, Lucila Serra, Maria Penas Sierra, Sara Sigrist, Chandra Sinha, Sophie Sirtaine, John Speakman, Fiona Stewart, Satheesh Sundararajan, Nozomi Tokima, Chengyu Wang, Alex Weber, Roland White, and George Wolf. I would also like to thank Fred Ottavy, Falko Sellner, Trevor Taylor of Biwater, Richard Drummond of Export Credits Guarantee Department, and Scott Jazynka and my erstwhile colleagues at Allen & Overy, in particular Graham Vinter, John Scriven, Nigel Pritchard, Tom Levine, Steven Blanche, Fahad Doha, Dan Cocker, Leah Horstmann, Philippa Smart, Roy Freke, and Helen Sonnenthal.

And most importantly, my thanks to Vicky, Alex, and Natasha ... to piglet, tigger, and roo.

The findings, interpretations, and conclusions expressed herein are those of the author and should not be attributed in any manner to anyone mentioned above, nor to the World Bank, its affiliated organizations, or to the members of its board of executive directors or the countries they represent. This text does not constitute legal advice and does not substitute for obtaining competent legal counsel (readers are advised to seek the same) when addressing any of the issues discussed in this text.

1

Introduction and Summary

The world is a messy place, and while we do our best when developing and financing infrastructure projects to identify, mitigate, and manage risks, we are beset by challenges – climate change, natural disasters, war, political upheavals, economic crises (e.g., exchange rate shifts, inflation, commodity price variations), global pandemics, rising sovereign and corporate debt levels, and the foibles of the human condition. A more fundamental concern relates to project management and efficiency. Infrastructure projects must be well managed, well planned, technically and technologically robust, economically impactful, effectively delivered, efficiently managed, and financially sustainable, and they must deliver good-quality services. The complexity of infrastructure straddles public and private mandates and capacities; a partnering arrangement, whether by contract or regulation, is best placed to deliver efficient and sustainable infrastructure.

Even assuming perfect foresight and an ability to manage risk, the level of investment needed for infrastructure far exceeds available public resources. Developing countries are constrained in funding of public infrastructure by tighter fiscal space, increased national debt from a costly pandemic response, and a prevailing global economic slowdown characterized by higher inflation and higher fuel and commodity prices, which are worsened by geopolitical conflicts that confuse logistics and complicate sourcing of inputs. In 2021, public debt had increased by more than 10 percent of gross domestic product in most developing East and Asia-Pacific countries compared to prepandemic levels and by more than 20 and 30 percent in the Philippines and Fiji, respectively.[1] Given the need for capital in developing countries

---

[1] World Bank, *World Bank East Asia and Pacific Economic Update (Spring 2022): Braving the Storms* (World Bank, 2022), DOI: 10.1596/978-1-4648-1858-5. License: Creative Commons Attribution CC BY 3.0 IGO.

and the creativity required to make projects in the developing world attractive to private capital, this book gives particular focus to developing country investments.

Public funding and financing are not enough; the need for infrastructure investment necessitates commercial funding and private finance as well as public support. This text specifically differentiates funding and financing. Financing is the debt and equity used to develop infrastructure assets, which may come from public or private sources, can have many different characteristics, and can be sourced through different instruments. Funding is the revenues earned by the project, from users or other beneficiaries, from commercial activities, or from public contributions. The two are fundamentally linked – more funding means better terms for financing.

Funding (revenues) for infrastructure is tricky. For example:

- Demand for infrastructure can be uncertain, driven by alternate service provision, new technology, economic cycles, and the ability of users to pay.
- Willingness of users to pay for services and the need to protect users from (sudden) price increases (e.g., inflation, foreign exchange risk, interest rates) make user fees risky, politically sensitive, and in some cases unreliable.
- Government sources of capital (whether local or national) are often used as project revenue to offset capital investment and to fill the gaps – for example, capital contributions during construction (often called viability gap funding) and/or availability payments.[2] These sources may include general fiscal revenues, dedicated taxes, and central government transfers. While government capital shows commitment to the project, it is also a drain on public resources and can cause friction with the population and with future governments, increasing the likelihood of future governments trying to unwind or renegotiate a deal due to its fiscal cost.

Finding additional, commercial, sources of funding can make the project more sustainable, better able to adapt to changes in costs (e.g., inflation), better connected to the local community through services delivered and jobs created, and less of a burden on fiscal resources and therefore less likely to be a target for future governments seeking to reduce fiscal burdens.

Part I of this book focuses on "funding," on the revenue streams that are the lifeblood of any infrastructure project. Finding innovative sources of funding not only improves the financial viability of the project, earning more profits and allowing lower user fees and fiscal contributions on the back of these funding sources, but will also make more finance available. Lenders will be comforted by a more robust financial foundation of the project and by the diversity of risk that innovative commercial revenue streams can provide.

---

[2] For further discussion of project financial structuring, see Jeffrey Delmon, *Public–Private Participation Projects in Infrastructure: An Essential Guide for Policymakers*, 2nd ed. (Cambridge University Press, 2017).

1.1 Innovative Sources of Funding

Part II introduces finance and key innovative financing models. Innovative sources of financing can provide an important advantage for infrastructure projects: mobilizing more capital on better terms from a more diverse set of financiers. Three interesting types of innovative finance will be discussed here:

- Climate finance – where financiers seek to support investments with positive climate externalities;
- Islamic finance – whose financiers follow Islamic tenants, which place specific restrictions on the characteristics of the financing structure; and
- Blended finance – where development finance (financiers seeking to achieve developmental impacts – often with lower interest rates or grant funds) is mixed with commercial finance to combine their respective advantages.

While innovative finance provides an important opportunity for infrastructure finance, the fundamentals of finance are still fundamentals, and mobilizing innovative finance will still follow the basic principles of financing and concepts of bankability.

1.1 INNOVATIVE SOURCES OF FUNDING

The more revenues a project can mobilize and the more robust the sources of revenues, the more sustainable the project is and the more likely it is to survive economic crises, changes in government, political upheaval, and other systemic risks.

There are two main sources of revenues for infrastructure projects:

- **User payments** – Charges are collected from the users of the infrastructure or service. The level of user charges allowed is generally defined by an agreement with the contracting authority and/or by the sector regulator. User fees need to be kept affordable and are generally ill suited to responding to sudden increases in inflation or input costs. Charges must be affordable to all potential users, and the demand for the services must be sufficient to ensure the anticipated revenues. Users may need to be disconnected for failure to pay, which may not be legal or practical for core services – for example, disconnecting underprivileged users from water, solid waste, or sewerage services can be unpopular and even dangerous.
- **Government payments** – The project company is paid a fee (an "availability payment") by the contracting authority (or some other public source) to make specified infrastructure or services available for use. This approach is used where the contracting authority itself is the main user (e.g., paying the private partner for providing a building or facility), where the contracting authority is itself collecting charges from users (e.g., where the contracting authority collects solid waste charges from households and pays the private partner for services), or where users cannot be charged directly at all (e.g., where a contracting authority pays the project company to provide street

lighting). The contracting authority may prefer to retain responsibility for collecting charges where placing collection risk on the project company is not efficient or practical (e.g., where people are less likely to pay charges to a private entity, where collection risk is too high for the project company to manage, or where it is illegal for the project company to collect user charges directly). Some projects may receive additional support in the form of grants from national government and/or external donors or agencies and in the form of capital grants to offset initial construction costs. The purpose of such support is usually to plug gaps in the projects' finances and/or to reduce the cost of services to users. But government payments are not necessarily the most sustainable sources of funding; as fiscal capacity evolves and political will shifts, such demands on budget can elicit resentment.

Infrastructure practitioners are often so accustomed to designing projects around user payments and government funding that we do not provide incentives for private investors to mobilize innovative funding. Often, we are so cautious about private sector focus on profit that incentives to be creative around revenues might seem contrary to a focus on infrastructure services. While the focus on service delivery is critical when planning and developing infrastructure projects, government should look to mobilize funding from a variety of sources. For example:

- *Land value capture* – The development of infrastructure assets will often result in an increase in land values adjacent to the project site or in the catchment area of infrastructure services; for example, the construction of a new public market can result in a significant increase in the value of the land around the market, where commercial activities will develop to respond to opportunities created by the market. Connecting a neighborhood to electricity or to fiber broadband can increase land values in that neighborhood. But these are windfall land value increases, and the landowner has done nothing to merit such increases; in fact taxpayers have funded the infrastructure investment that generates the windfall. It would be appropriate for such landowners to share in the land value increase only to help fund the investment in infrastructure that will create or has created the increase. The government has a number of methods available to capture part of this land value increase to help fund its investment (land value capture or LVC).[3] This topic is discussed in great detail in sector literature. This book will introduce and summarize the topic in Chapter 2, as a first step to understanding key concepts and issues. For a more detailed understanding of LVC, sector literature is referenced liberally in chapter footnotes.
- *Commercial revenues* – Often, an infrastructure project will have the potential to generate commercial revenues from part of, or in some way that is

---

[3] For further discussion of LVC, see "Module 16: Harnessing Land Value Capture," World Bank Municipal PPP Framework, www.worldbank.org/ppplrc. For further discussion of CVC, see https://ppp.worldbank.org/public-private-partnership/Innovative_Revenues_for_Infrastructure.

1.1 Innovative Sources of Funding

related to, the public infrastructure or service it delivers. The contracting authority can use the public assets or rights that it provides to the project company as part of the project – for example, concession, land, and access rights – to specifically enable the project company to leverage more additional revenues from commercial activities such as advertising, parking, office space, residential space, and retail facilities (commercial value capture or CVC). CVC is described in greater depth in Chapter 3.[4]

Governments often perceive investment needs, in particular infrastructure, solely as a public service, a cost center. In fact, such investments may also create commercial prospects, providing opportunities for higher value and more or new commercial activities. Such commercial activities can provide additional advantages to the community: more and better commercial services, economic growth, and jobs. CVC links the infrastructure with the community more completely, leveraging synergies. A project with well-developed CVC should be more sustainable, through diversified demand risk and revenue sources but also due to its links with the community; future governments should be less likely to seek to renegotiate or unwind the project.

Infrastructure can provide a useful mechanism to mobilize CVC to fund public services.[5] For example:

- A public market may not be able to attract sufficient revenues from letting space in the market to vendors to cover costs, but the project may offer other commercial activities in or near the market to generate needed revenues and offer additional services, such as residential or office space.
- Bus or truck terminals may not generate enough revenue from fees charged to buses or trucks, but they often provide an opportunity for retail activities, selling goods and services to passengers and the public, including parking, advertising, retail, and hospitality.
- Government offices normally do not generate revenues, outside of government lease payments, but in some circumstances they can be developed as mixed-use space, with commercial office and retail facilities, to generate additional revenues.

Chapter 3 provides a more detailed description of a few of the key commercial activities that can be adopted into infrastructure projects to mobilize CVC, including the following:

- Advertising and marketing – The project may be able to take advantage of user and other traffic and the space available on and around an infrastructure asset for advertising.

[4] For further discussion of CVC, see "Module 17: Capturing Commercial Value," World Bank Municipal PPP Framework, https://ppp.worldbank.org/public-private-partnership/municipal-and-subnational/municipal-public-private-partnership-framework and https://ppp.worldbank.org/public-private-partnership/Innovative_Revenues_for_Infrastructure.
[5] Delmon, *Public–Private Partnerships*.

- Naming rights – Where an infrastructure asset is iconic, like a stadium, companies may be willing to sponsor the structure for the right to display their names on that structure and for their names to be associated with it.
- Residential space (including low cost) – Housing can be built above or around the infrastructure to generate additional revenues. For some forms of infrastructure, such as transport, the asset may increase the value of housing and allow for mixed-use facilities that provide a further cross-subsidization of low-cost housing.
- Parking (above and/or below ground) – The space above, below, and around the infrastructure can be used for commercial parking facilities, to earn new revenues and to address congestion.
- Hospitality (e.g., hotels, restaurants, cafes, catering) and tourism – The location of the infrastructure might make hospitality facilities more attractive; for example, convention centers are often developed with hotels, sporting facilities with restaurants and cafés.
- Medical services (e.g., clinics, imaging, consultants, pharmacy) – Often developed alongside hospitals, specialist medical services provide additional services to the community and also leverage new revenues from high-value services.
- Logistics facilities (e.g., cargo handling, warehousing, chillers, dry ports) – Ports, airports, and other transport infrastructure can often provide an opportunity for logistics facilities, to improve the general transport offering of the country and the facility, but these high-value services can also cross-subsidize the large-scale infrastructure that creates the opportunity for logistics facilities.
- Vehicle services (e.g., petrol, mechanics, truck/bus parking) – Where vehicles use the infrastructure or where the infrastructure offers large amounts of space outside of congested urban areas, commercial revenues can be extracted from vehicle services in and around such infrastructure.
- Retail and commercial space – While other more specific examples of retail and commercial activities are listed here, the variety of such activities that might be appropriate for a given infrastructure investment is vast; hence, a catch-all category is included to encourage thinking outside of the box, looking at all activities that might be appropriate for the project and community in question.
- Development rights – Investments in infrastructure can increase the demand for additional property development, for example, more square footage, additional floors, and rezoning for different uses; these development rights can be sold at a premium that reflects the additional value of the property.
- Repurposing or adaptive reuse of idle assets – In some cases existing buildings or facilities may be linked to the infrastructure investment. By commercializing these assets, government addresses the challenge of disused or underused assets and creates new revenue streams at the same time.
- Infrastructure sharing (internally and externally) – An infrastructure project may also provide an opportunity for other infrastructure; for example,

1.1 Innovative Sources of Funding

road and rail projects require large rights of way that can also be used for telecoms, power, and water transmission infrastructure; central heating and cooling or similar services developed for one purpose can be expanded to provide services for a larger population, providing an additional public service and diversifying demand and sources of revenue.
- Usage of facilities during off-hours or off-seasons – Some infrastructure is used intensively only at certain times, for example, sporting facilities, convention centers, educational facilities, and school dormitories; these facilities can be used for revenue-generating purposes during off-periods.
- Cost reductions – An infrastructure investment may (or may be designed to) reduce the costs of the contracting authority; rather than structure payments to the project based on usage or availability, the payment stream may be linked to cost reductions achieved by the project. The revenues can be ring-fenced from allocations for costs that are reduced by the project.
- Additional offtake from the facility – The infrastructure can be used to create other forms of offtake; for example, methane captured from solid waste projects and sludge processed from wastewater treatment plants can be commercialized or processed to produce additional offtake.
- Beneficiary contributions and prepurchase of services – There may be large users of services who wish to enable project development. In some cases, these large users may need to provide contributions to capital costs; for example, large mines located along a new road corridor will have a specific interest in providing capital to improve their time to market, reduce wear and tear on vehicles, and so on and may therefore contribute to capital costs of the road. Future large users may be willing to prepurchase services, for example, universities prepurchasing bandwidth from a fiber-optic project.

When identifying potential infrastructure projects and performing prefeasibility and feasibility studies to assess and validate each project, the contracting authority should assess the possibility of CVC. The focus on commercial revenues must never take the focus off the public services to be provided by the infrastructure. For example, a public market looking for higher-value commercial space might be tempted to reduce the space made available for low-cost vendors. A low-cost housing project looking to mobilize commercial revenues through mixed-use space might be tempted to reduce the number of low-cost units developed.

Increasing commercial activities can place more pressure on public service requirements. For example, a parking garage that mobilized CVC by leasing office space developed above it will need to provide additional parking to address the needs of the tenants of the office space. A bus terminal mobilizing CVC by offering additional commercial services might need to be designed for increased foot traffic, as passengers remain in the terminal longer than normal to benefit from the commercial services and other customers come to the terminal who are not otherwise bus passengers.

Emission Reduction Credits

Other innovative sources of revenue come from services that an infrastructure asset can provide only if designed and managed accordingly; for example, as companies and governments seek to deliver on net-zero greenhouse gas emissions, they are, under various mechanisms, allowed to purchase the emissions reductions delivered by others. A well-designed infrastructure project can deliver such emissions reductions, get those reductions certified, and sell those emissions reductions around the world. These emissions reduction credits have to comply with different requirements and standards but can offer a significant new source of revenues for a project and at the same time certify the project's green credentials, which can also open the door for other forms of financing.

Turning Innovative Sources of Funding into a Programmatic Solution

A project should maximize sustainable revenues from all potential beneficiaries, and therefore the contracting authority should use the following hierarchy of revenue sources when designing a project:

First, infrastructure projects should maximize sustainable revenues from service beneficiaries. Those who receive a service, or a better service, should pay for it. Sustainable means that the tariffs are progressive in nature and affordable for users and the contracting authority and that the users are willing and able to pay the proposed tariffs.

Second, infrastructure projects should capture part of the land value increase resulting from the infrastructure.[6] This can be achieved through taxation, property development levies, contributions, and a number of other mechanisms.

Third, infrastructure projects should maximize sustainable commercial revenues. Infrastructure should be used to create additional economic opportunities and improve existing economic activities.

Finally, only after the first three revenue sources have been explored should public money be used as project revenue or public guarantees to enhance project viability, and only where that public support represents value for money for the government, the community, and the economy.

The project will be vulnerable if the private partner makes too little profit or makes too much. The public–private partnership (PPP) agreement needs to address payment risk, demand risk, and sharing of superprofits (when the project performs significantly better than the forecast at the time of bidding).

---

[6] Rana Amirtahmasebi, Mariana Orloff, Sameh Wahba, and Andrew Altman, *Regenerating Urban Land: A Practitioner's Guide to Leveraging Private Investment*, Urban Development Series (World Bank, 2016), DOI: 10.1596/978-1-4648-0473-1.

1.2 Innovative Sources of Finance

Transit-Oriented Development
Other approaches to infrastructure planning and design can be used as a vehicle for embedding innovative sources of funding into projects at an early stage and to approach project planning systematically to ensure the best generation of innovative sources of funding. Transit-oriented development (TOD) provides an excellent opportunity to leverage LVC and CVC consistently, and in fact in certain countries LVC/CVC is synonymous with TOD. Chapter 4 describes TOD as a generator of LVC and CVC.

1.2 INNOVATIVE SOURCES OF FINANCE

Finance is capital provided to develop an infrastructure asset, generally seeking to be repaid with the possibility of upside in the form of interest to be paid or a share of profit to be earned. Finance comes in the form of equity and debt.

- Equity funds are invested in the project company as share capital and other shareholder funds. They hold the lowest priority of the contributions; for example, debt contributors will have the right to project assets and revenues to meet debt service obligations before the equity contributors can obtain any return or, on termination or insolvency, any repayment, and equity shareholders cannot normally receive distributions unless the company is in profit.
- Debt contributions have the highest priority among the invested funds (e.g., senior debt must be serviced before most other debts are repaid). Repayment of debt is generally tied to a fixed or floating rate of interest and a program of periodic payments. Debt generally receives no upside; if the project is particularly profitable, the lenders will not receive a share of those profits but will only be paid the agreed debt service.
- Mezzanine/subordinated contributions (e.g., subordinated loans and preference shares) fall somewhere between equity and debt, with lower priority than senior debt but higher priority than equity. Mezzanine contributors will be compensated for the added risk they take either by receiving higher interest rates on loans than the senior debt contributors or by participating in the project profits or the capital gains achieved by project equity.

Infrastructure must be financially sustainable to attract private financing; its revenues need to be resilient and able to cover all operating expenses, including debt servicing, and provide shareholders with reasonable dividends. Lenders will be concerned about ensuring that the project is able to pay interest and repay the principal. They will have a conservative view on assumptions such as traffic forecasts and impose specific requirements (maintenance funds, reserve fund for debt service, minimum revenue guaranteed) to provide them with additional protections, which will have financial implications. Chapter 5 provides an introduction to the fundamentals of finance.

The decision as to which type of financing to adopt will depend on government fiscal position, the market availability of financing, and the willingness of lenders to bear certain project risks or credit risks according to their view of how the market is developing and changing and of their own internal risk management regime.

The most common types of financing are:

- *Government financing* – where the government borrows money and provides it to the project through on-lending, grants, or subsidies or where it provides guarantees of indebtedness. The government can usually borrow money at a lower interest rate but is constrained by its fiscal space (in particular its debt capacity) and will have a number of worthy initiatives competing for scarce fiscal resources. The government is also generally less able to manage commercial risk efficiently.
- *Corporate financing* – where a company borrows money against its proven credit position and ongoing business and invests it in the project. The size of investment required for an infrastructure project and the returns that such companies seek from their investments may result in a relatively high cost of financing and therefore can be prohibitive for the contracting authority.
- *Project financing* – where nonrecourse or limited recourse loans are made directly to a special purpose vehicle. Lenders rely on the cash flow of the project for repayment of the debt; security for the debt is primarily limited to the project assets and future revenue stream. By using such techniques, investors can substantially reduce their equity investment (through debt leverage) and exposure to project liability, thereby reducing the total project cost. This said, project financing requires a complex structure of contracts, subcontracts, guarantees, insurances, and financing agreements in order to provide lenders with the security they require and the risk allocation necessary to convince them to provide funding. This complexity requires significant upfront investment of time and resources by the contracting authority in project development. Further, project financing may increase the overall costs of debt for the project.[7]

Generally speaking, a sovereign government will be able to obtain financing at a lower cost than the sponsors or the project company.[8] The cost-effectiveness of government financing will depend on the credit profile of the government in

---

[7] Project financing is discussed in more detail in Chapter 5.

[8] Lower interest rates obtained by a government reflect the contingent liability borne by taxpayers. Michael Klein, "Risk, Taxpayers and the Role of Government in Project Finance," World Bank Policy Research Working Paper 1688 (World Bank, 1996). Thus, the risk that results in higher private finance interest rates reflects the actual project risk and is subsidized by taxpayers to achieve the lower public finance interest rates. Since the private sector is best placed to manage most of the commercial risk in infrastructure projects, it is argued that private finance is the most efficient method of financing infrastructure; the inherent subsidy of public finance is more appropriately used in other areas.

1.2 Innovative Sources of Finance

question (as reflected in its credit rating) and any other restrictions that apply to that government in relation to assuming new debt obligations. However, government financing is often rendered less efficient by public procurement processes, failure or unwillingness to implement incentive mechanisms to achieve greater efficiency, and failure to control changes and other risks that result in higher construction and operation costs. Private sector financing may therefore prove – in certain circumstances – less expensive, less time-consuming, and more flexible to arrange or more practical than public sector financing. The private sector can provide new sources of finance (in particular where fiscal space or other constraints limit the availability of government financing), impose clear efficiency incentives on the project, bring new technologies, and invigorate local financial markets.

The overall interest rate applicable to projects financed using corporate financing must take into consideration the minimum level of return on investment (ROI) demanded by sponsors to forego other investment opportunities. The corporate entity in question will borrow funds to finance the project, but it will compare the return earned from such financing against its other commercial activities where it would invest these funds if it did not invest them in the project (the "opportunity cost" of the project). This minimum ROI (which represents the cost of corporate financing) will normally significantly exceed the cost of project financing or government financing. Corporate financing is also less project specific than project financing and therefore may fail to implement the project-specific efficiencies and discipline generally mandated by project-specific limited recourse financing.

Project financing tends to attract a higher rate of interest than government financing, since the lenders take an element of commercial risk, but lower than corporate financing where the returns need to justify its diversion of investment funds from other opportunities. In particular, project financing offers a lower weighted cost of capital,[9] mixing cheaper limited recourse debt with more expensive private equity capital.

Financing that appears on the balance sheet of either the host government or the project sponsor will have implications for other transactions undertaken by the government or the project sponsor in that further financing will be more difficult and more expensive to obtain. By placing the debt on the balance sheet of a special purpose vehicle in a manner that is not (or is only to a limited extent) consolidated onto the project sponsors' balance sheet or the government's liabilities, the debt becomes "off-balance sheet." For this reason, the actual cost of on-balance sheet financing may be greater than perceived. Project financing may enable the government and the project sponsor to finance the project off-balance sheet and therefore avoid these costs and risks.

The implications of project financing on a government or a project sponsor will depend on the accounting treatment, and therefore the accounting

---

[9] See Section 5.2.

standards, applied. Also, it should be noted that keeping debt off-balance sheet does not reduce the actual liabilities for the government and may merely disguise government liabilities, reducing the effectiveness of government debt monitoring mechanisms. As a matter of policy, the use of off-balance sheet debt should be considered carefully and protective mechanisms should be implemented accordingly.[10]

---

[10] Timothy Irwin, "Controlling Spending Commitments in PPPs," in Gerd Schwartz, Ana Corbacho, and Katja Funke (eds.), *Public Investment and Public-Private Partnerships: Addressing Infrastructure Challenges and Managing Fiscal Risks* (Palgrave Macmillan, 2008), pp. 105–117.

PART I

FUNDING

2

Land Value Capture

Public investments can have significant impact on land values; for example, climate resilience is highly valued by tenants and property developers.[1] Infrastructure investment can have a significant and beneficial impact on adjacent land value. "Land value capture" (LVC) mobilizes some or all of the land value increases resulting from actions other than the landowner's, such as public investments in infrastructure, climate resilience investments, or administrative changes in land use norms and regulations, for the benefit of the community at large.[2] The objective of LVC is to draw on publicly generated land value increases to enable local administrations to improve their land use management practices and to help them fund infrastructure and service provisions.[3]

A good example of LVC is property tax, which requires landowners to share a percentage of the land value with the government (see for example Box 2.1). The amount of property tax paid increases as the value of the land increases

---

[1] Anthony Flint, *Return on Investment: Research Links Climate Action with Land and Property Value Increases* (The Lincoln Institute, 2022).

[2] For example, the principle may exist at law that no citizen should accumulate wealth that does not result from his or her own efforts, known as "unjust enrichment" in both civil and common law traditions. Martin Smolka, *Implementing Value Capture in Latin America Policies and Tools for Urban Development* (Lincoln Institute of Land Policy, 2013), www.lincolninst.edu/sites/default/files/pubfiles/implementing-value-capture-in-latin-america-full_1.pdf.

[3] Rana Amirtahmasebi, Mariana Orloff, Sameh Wahba, and Andrew Altman, *Regenerating Urban Land: A Practitioner's Guide to Leveraging Private Investment*, Urban Development Series (World Bank, 2016), DOI: 10.1596/978-1-4648-0473-1; George E. Peterson and Olga Kaganova, "Integrating Land Financing into Subnational Fiscal Management (English)," Policy Research Working Paper No. WPS 5409 (World Bank, 2010), http://documents.worldbank.org/curated/en/173371468149668444/Integrating-land-financing-into-subnational-fiscal-management; Flint, *Return on Investment*; *Unlocking Infrastructure Investment: Innovative Funding and Financing in Regions and Cities*, OECD Report for the G20 Infrastructure Working Group (OECD, 2021).

> **Box 2.1 Property tax reform in Mexicali, Mexico**
>
> The city of Mexicali stopped assessing a composite property tax on land and permanent structures and started taxing only the value of the land, requiring major changes in tax administration including changes in land assessment. During the first period of implementation the new taxing system allowed the city to double property tax revenue, prompting other municipalities to implement similar reforms.[4]

(no matter the cause of the increased value). However, property taxes are generally ill suited to capture the value created by public investments, as they focus on the factual value of the land with improvements. Property tax should aim to differentiate tax burden based on "windfall" benefits of unimproved land location, physical characteristics, and neighboring uses, incentivizing improvement of underused sites by making land idling and holding prime lands for speculation a burdensome option for landowners. This is not an easy transition to make. Property tax reforms can increase the complexities of tax administration, necessitate additional technical capacity for maintaining advanced land cadaster and land reassessment systems, and require that fiscal powers be devolved so that local governments can structure and impose such taxes.[5]

There is huge potential in LVC. It represents a more equitable sharing of the cost of public investment, enables government to mobilize more capital to deliver investments, and incentivizes efficient use of public capital and public investments that create real value. For example, for the development of the Canary Wharf Crossrail station in East London, LVC policies yielded more than USD 1.2 billion of the USD 23 billion capital costs for the rail network, also known as the Elizabeth line.[6]

In practice, the successful implementation of LVC requires access to significant data and specific management skills to engage with diverse stakeholders and understand land market conditions; implement comprehensive property monitoring systems; achieve a fluid dialogue among fiscal, planning, and judicial entities; and engage the political resolve of local government leaders.[7] Land value increases are captured more successfully from landowners and other stakeholders who perceive they are receiving greater benefits from a public intervention than those accruing from business as usual.[8]

---

[4] Ibid.
[5] "Land Value Capture: Investment in Infrastructure," City Resilience Program, 2018.
[6] Flint, *Return on Investment*.
[7] Smolka, *Implementing Value Capture in Latin America Policies*; Lourdes Germán and Allison Ehrich Bernstein, *Land Value Return: Tools to Finance Our Urban Future* (Lincoln Institute of Land Policy, 2013), www.lincolninst.edu/publications/policy-briefs/land-value-return.
[8] Smolka, *Implementing Value Capture in Latin America Policies*.

2.1 LVC Instruments

Moreover, LVC can improve the sustainability of a project, embedding it with the local community and ensuring that local landowners will benefit from the project in real terms. Projects embedded with the community are more likely to survive changes in government, changes in circumstances, and crises that may arise from time to time.

There is an emerging body of knowledge documenting LVC practices.[9] LVC is a government policy approach to increase land value and promote equal and sustainable development. It also helps cities finance urban infrastructure by borrowing against property taxes and other LVC revenues. LVC has been well developed by analysts and practitioners.[10] This chapter will focus on presenting an introduction to LVC and will provide references to facilitate readers seeking an in-depth study.

2.1 LVC INSTRUMENTS

A number of LVC instruments and approaches have been adopted globally, to meet local needs and to achieve the desired impact, as LVC is extremely context specific. This section will describe some of the key instruments and the lessons learned globally when implementing LVC.[11]

2.1.1 Land for Cash

Excess/underutilized public assets (e.g., land or property) can be disposed (through sale or lease) for cash, which is reinvested in infrastructure.

---

[9] Hiroaki Suzuki, Jin Murakami, Beth Chiyo Tamayose, and Yuhung Hong, *Financing Transit-Oriented Development with Land Values: Adapting Land Value Capture in Developing Countries (English)*, Urban Development Series (World Bank, 2015), p. xxii; OECD, "Building a Global Compendium on Land Value Capture," 2020, www.oecd.org/cfe/cities/land-value-capture.htm#:~:text=About%20the%20Global%20Compendium%20on,are%20important%20for%20systematic%20adoption; AHURI, "What Is Value Capture? Understanding Value Capture and How It Can Fund Infrastructure Projects," 2017, www.ahuri.edu.au/research/ahuri-briefs/what-is-value-capture; Maria Hart, "Developing Cities Need Cash. Land Value Capture Can Help," World Resources Institute, 2020, www.wri.org/insights/developing-cities-need-cash-land-value-capture-can-help; RICS, "Land Value Capture: Attitudes from the House-Building Industry on Alternative Mechanisms," 2020, www.rics.org/globalassets/rics-website/media/knowledge/research/research-reports/rics0094-land-value-capture-research-report.pdf; and Smolka, *Implementing Value Capture in Latin America Policies*.

[10] A few key texts include: "Land Value Capture: Investment in Infrastructure"; Smolka, *Implementing Value Capture in Latin America Policies*; German and Bernstein, *Land Value Return*; Rohit Sharma and Peter Newman, "Land Value Capture Tools: Integrating Transit and Land Use through Finance to Enable Economic Value Creation," *Modern Economy* 11, no. 4 (2020): 938–964; OECD and Lincoln Institute, "Global Compendium of Land Value Capture Policies," 2021; Lawrence C. Walters, *Land Value Capture in Policy and Practice* (Brigham Young University, 2013).

[11] Rana et al., *Regenerating Urban Land*.

> **Box 2.2 The city of Ahmedabad, India, opens up Sabarmati riverfront**
>
> The Sabarmati riverfront in Ahmedabad was a blighted urban space with large informal settlements, lack of accessibility, and a shortage of new commercial investment or jobs created. The city undertook to support residential redevelopment through USD 17 million of upfront public investment, including a twenty-two-kilometer promenade, slum resettlement, sewage upgrade, environmental rehabilitation, and land reclamation. The result was a well-serviced and walkable waterfront, river access open to public, 202 hectares of land made available for modern development, reduced erosion and exposure of the city to flood risk, and 30 hectares of reclaimed land for sale.[12]

The disposition can require the investor to make additional investments, deliver public goods/services, or carry out other restructuring of the asset. See, for example, Box 2.2 on using abandoned riverfront property for development.

2.1.2 Land as Public Contribution

The public sector "invests" its land (e.g., as an equity contribution into a public–private partnership, joint venture, or other structured arrangement) and the private sector provides capital investment. The public entity captures the value of the land through delivery of public services and its share in project profits.

2.1.3 Land as Collateral

Value can be captured through the sale or lease of publicly owned land whose value has been enhanced by public investment. For example, for a port project, a government can transfer the land surrounding the port to a public–private development corporation. The private entity can then borrow against the land as collateral, to finance the port construction, and repay the debt by selling or leasing the land whose value had been enhanced because of access to the new port.

2.1.4 Developer Exactions and Impact Fees

Developers may be obliged to fund part or all of the costs of infrastructure needed to deliver public services to the site. For example, developer exactions may include the following:

---

[12] "Land Value Capture: Investment in Infrastructure."

2.1 LVC Instruments

- *Dedication of land for public use,* for example, reserving a certain percentage of land for parks or other public space;
- *Construction of public improvements,* for example, the developer constructs a public road to connect the proposed development with the existing public road network or trunk lines that deliver water and remove wastewater to the neighborhood; or
- *Funding,* for example, the developer provides a financial contribution toward the cost of a section of highway, a new bus stop, or a light rail train station.

It can be technically cumbersome to estimate appropriate exactions to be imposed on a landowner.[13] With the exception of some robust real estate markets, imposing an extra levy can at times have the effect of discouraging, rather than incentivizing, private sector investment. Any government discretion regarding assessment amounts can create perceptions of corruption and can also result in (expensive) legal challenges, testing whether there is a direct relationship between the project proposed and the exaction required (the "essential nexus" test) and whether the exaction is roughly proportional to the impact created by the project.[14]

2.1.5 Land Pooling/Readjustment

Landowners or occupants voluntarily contribute part of their land for infrastructure development and for sale to cover some project cost. In return, each landowner receives a serviced plot of smaller area with higher value within the same neighborhood. Landowners' consensus can be difficult to obtain, especially if projects fully rely on voluntary participation. This mechanism requires strong project management and technical capacity, particularly in negotiation and building consensus with landowners; it can also result in disputes, resentment, and legal challenges over participation and the plots allocated as compensation. As an example, land readjustment has been used in Japan since the late nineteenth century for urban expansion, urban development or renewal, disaster prevention, and reconstruction. It was formalized in 1954 by the Land Readjustment Act. Land readjustment needs approval from prefectures and the consent of at least two-thirds of involved landowners and leaseholders. Newly readjusted areas generally include publicly owned plots for sale, which are used to recover development costs. Typically, 30–40 percent of readjusted plots are reserved for public improvements such as infrastructure and utilities.[15]

---

[13] Julie Kim, "CePACs and Their Value Capture Viability in the U.S. for Infrastructure Funding," Working Paper WP18JK1 (NewCities Foundation, 2018).
[14] Ibid.
[15] OECD and Lincoln Institute, "Global Compendium of Land Value Capture Policies."

2.1.6 Betterment Levies/Special Assessments

Instead of value-based property taxes, a betterment levy requires property owners to contribute based on the specific benefit their property receives from public improvements.[16] Levies can be charged to support a specific project or can be charged periodically against a program of investments (see the example from Chile, in Box 2.3).

For example, in Johannesburg, South Africa, property owners in city improvement districts (CIDs) agree to pay for supplementary services and improvements, such as security measures, infrastructure upgrades, litter collection, and upkeep of public spaces. A CID can be formed when a petition is filed by at least 51 percent of the property owners in a geographic area and then approved by the municipality. The CID levy is compulsory and is calculated based on the value of the individual property and applied pro rata. Other common terms used for CIDs around the world include special assessment districts, benefit assessment districts, local improvement districts, and business improvement districts.[17]

While levies can be imposed by the government, there is an opportunity to use the levy to engage with the local business community, to get them involved in the planning and decision processes, to ensure that infrastructure investments fit well with community needs, and to encourage local economic growth and job creation. Local property owners might consider betterment levies as disguised taxes and demand a public vote, with the legal and institutional complexity that entails.[18] Approaches that bundle projects citywide have proven more successful.

Box 2.3 Development in Chacabuco, Chile

In late 1990s Santiago metropolitan region started expanding north in the Chacabuco province with fourteen major real estate projects approved (primarily housing), adding 40,000 new households to the metro region, in an area lacking urban infrastructure services or connectivity to Santiago's urban core. A twenty-one-kilometer radial highway connecting to central Santiago was to be built with additional forty-one kilometers of byways and interchanges under a concession model, comprising 39 percent government funding and 61 percent developer impact fees levied per buildable housing unit based on each project's impact on the road network.[19]

---

[16] Oscar Borrerro Ochoa, "Betterment Levy in Colombia: Relevance, Procedures and Social Acceptability," *Land Lines*, Lincoln Institute of Land Policy, April 2011; Kim, "CePACs and Their Value Capture Viability."
[17] Sharma and Newman, "Land Value Capture Tools."
[18] William B. Fulton and Paul Shigley, *Guide to California Planning* (Solano Press Books, 2012); Kim, "CePACs and Their Value Capture Viability."
[19] "Land Value Capture: Investment in Infrastructure."

2.1 LVC Instruments

2.1.7 Density Bonus

The government can permit a developer to increase the maximum allowable development (e.g., floor area or height or buildings), or to change the nature of development, on a site in exchange for funds and/or in-kind support. This works best in cities in which market demand is strong and land availability is limited or for projects or sites in which the developer financial incentives outweigh alternative development options. These additional development rights may require investment that fits with the infrastructure plan, which in turn may improve the leverage effect of infrastructure investment and the additional development rights.

2.1.8 Upzoning

Another approach to LVC using development rights is to change the zoning in and around the infrastructure development to allow for higher value (e.g., from industrial to residential) or more dense use (e.g., increasing allowable floor area ratio). As with density bonuses, upzoning can be successfully deployed as a kind of financing tool for urban regeneration only when sufficient market demand exists and where the system for enforcing zoning regulations and collecting fees/taxes associated with zoning provide sufficient income (see, for example, the up-zoning program in Brazil described in Box 2.4).

Box 2.4 Porto Maravilha urban waterfront revitalization, Rio de Janeiro, Brazil

This project involved the revitalization of about 1,250 acres of underutilized and mostly government-owned Guanabara Bay waterfront. It was home to 35,000 residents and is to become a mixed-use mixed-income community of more than 100,000. The development plan includes complete reconstruction of local water, sanitation, and drainage systems, extensive streetscaping and landscaping, installation of three sanitation plants, historic preservation, at least 3,000 social housing units, and cultural and education facilities. The program commenced in 2009 and is to be completed by 2025.

Infrastructure has primarily been financed through Certificates of Additional Construction Potential bonds (CEPACs) – development rights for upzoning sold to developers to raise funds to finance infrastructure construction. More than four million square meters of additional density was sold via CEPACs during 2011–2013, generating USD 1.8 billion in upfront infrastructure funding (the initial purchaser of CEPACs was a state-owned financial bank, which then sold the CEPACs at a profit to private real estate developers as demand rose).[20]

---

[20] Ibid.

Upzoning does not allow as much direct control of development investments as density bonuses but may be easier to implement for government.

2.1.9 Transferable Development Right

A transferable development right (TDR) uses a similar concept to upzoning or density bonuses to direct new developments away from historic landmarks and other sensitive sites needing preservation to areas that are looking to promote more concentrated developments. One of the key concerns identified around TDRs has been poor planning of additional infrastructure needs to accommodate the incremental development density. For this reason, TDRs must be integrated into comprehensive master development plans.[21]

2.1.10 Joint Ventures

A joint venture can be set up between private investors and government to deliver investments. For example, local businesses and industries may band together to develop specific infrastructure that will benefit their commercial interests and the community, while government provides approvals, permits, and land. The asset developed will be available to and delivered in accordance with the needs of the community. This model has been used in particular for rail and other transport development.[22]

2.2 BRINGING FORWARD LVC FUNDING

In many cases LVC mechanisms provide additional revenues to government only after the fact, that is, after the land value has increased. Yet, governments need to mobilize these resources in advance to fund the investments that create the land value increase. Various financing mechanisms have been developed to borrow against future LVC. For example, under tax increment financing (TIF), government issues a bond on the capital markets to borrow against anticipated increases in tax receipts that accompany successful urban redevelopment.[23] The tax revenues, which exceed the taxes that would have been collected without the redevelopment, constitute the "tax increment," and the TIF captures that gain to pay the bond holders, borrowing against the future anticipated increase in tax revenues generated by the project (see Figure 2.1).

---

[21] Kim, "CePACs and Their Value Capture Viability."

[22] For example, the first private rail projects in the United Kingdom in the 1840s and the Pacific Railroad Act of 1862 in the United States, under which the government provided land grants, 400-foot rights-of-way plus ten square miles for every mile of track built, for the construction of the transcontinental railroad. Sharma and Newman, "Land Value Capture Tools."

[23] Sharma and Newman, "Land Value Capture Tools."

2.3 Lessons Learned

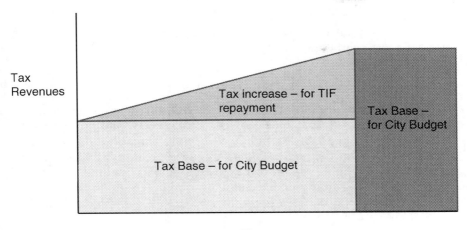

FIGURE 2.1 The basic TIF model
Source: Author

The performance assessments of TIFs have been mixed. In some cases, TIFs have been overleveraged, diverting significant property tax revenues from other taxing entities.[24] The tendency has been to overinflate the incremental revenue projections to help secure the upfront financing, which frequently results in large and mounting TIF debts for local governments, in excess of the actual tax revenues generated.[25]

2.3 LESSONS LEARNED

As discussed in the earlier sections, LVC has been implemented under a number of different structures and using instruments appropriate to the context and conditions in which it is implemented. It is a powerful financing and planning tool, but the risks of overreliance, corruption, and gentrification should be carefully addressed. This section shares a few best practice lessons learned from LVC design and implementation.

2.3.1 Consultation with Property Owners, Developers, and Other Stakeholders

Land value increments are captured more successfully when communication channels with landowners and stakeholders exist and the benefits from a

---

[24] George Lefcoe and Charles W. Swenson, "Redevelopment in California: The Demise of TIF-Funded Redevelopment in California and Its Aftermath," *National Tax Journal* 67, no. 3 (2014): 719–744.
[25] Kim, "CePACs and Their Value Capture Viability."

proposed public intervention are clearly laid out. Providing opportunities for dialogue between affected owners and the government is important to share information and garner public support.

2.3.2 Setting Appropriate Charges on Owners/Developers

Clear legislation concerning LVC, its processes, the determination of fees and taxes, institutional mandates, affected landowners, and procedures for resolving disputes can reduce conflict, elicit public support, and bring LVC to the political mainstream. Developers are usually receptive to such charges (which are generally passed on to buyers and tenants) as long as approval and other processes are streamlined and decision processes do not carry too much risk.

2.3.3 Consultation with Community

The nature of LVC can make it difficult for the average citizen to understand. It can appear as though government is providing opportunities to property developers and large financiers and/or can look like tax-like impositions on citizens, without an understanding of the advantage received by the government and the community. This is of particular concern in countries where land is a particularly sensitive issue or where communities suffer from the denial of services to certain areas, races, or ethnicities, spatial segregation, or social stratification. In other cases, communities may object out of a desire to avoid change, a "not in my backyard" or NIMBY response, or, more seriously, resistance to resettlement or other more fundamental changes to the community that the government believes are essential. Legal proceedings against the use of LVC instruments are common.[26] A robust public consultation process is critical. The community can also help identify key risks that require mitigation and challenges that need to be managed, which might not be obvious to those outside of the community. But consultation can also be tricky. The LVC structure is often negotiated/implemented as the development takes shape. Consultation processes will need to adjust as the LVC evolves. Some information will be commercially sensitive, and the government will not want to give away its plans too early to avoid giving property developers too much leverage.

2.3.4 Administrative Capacity

Spatial planning frameworks should clearly define the roles of different levels of government in preparing plans and land use regulations that serve as the baseline for LVC administration. Local governments are mostly responsible

[26] OECD and Lincoln Institute, "Global Compendium of Land Value Capture Policies."

2.3 Lessons Learned

for sound planning and land use principles, managing land assets, identifying affected landowners and negotiating with them, setting fees and contributions, and engaging with the community on development plans and terms, among other items. Local governments may face huge challenges delivering on these responsibilities, where they suffer from institutional capacity limitations. Central governments need to provide support to local government, including administrative capacity, policy guidelines, and accurate cadaster and land transaction data for LVC implementation.

2.3.5 Legal Framework

Land value capture structures require the certainty of a legal framework that protects the rights of all parties and allows flexibility in the kind of instruments used to deliver LVC. Avoiding weaknesses in the legal framework, including in enforcement and access to justice for all stakeholders, is critical for a robust LVC framework. Lower-income countries tend to give less discretion to local government officials to implement LVC than do higher income countries, but central governments may have more difficulty implementing LVC.[27]

2.3.6 Land Controls, Cadaster or Land Registry, Technology, and Data Systems

Even where the legal framework is robust, data can be difficult to obtain, and registration of the rights created under an LVC program needs to be formalized, for example, through a land registry or cadaster. In many developing countries these are difficult mechanisms to implement well, but improvements in data generation (through satellites and drones) and software tools have improved significantly the access of developing countries to these mechanisms.

2.3.7 Dynamic Real Estate Market

As LVC leverages the increase in property value, it works best in dynamic real estate markets, that is, in areas that are most responsive to infrastructure upgrades (urban core, waterfront, etc.), where the highest land value differential is achieved. Where timing of disposal of land or capturing land value is important to the LVC model, government may not have the experience or capacity to act in a timely manner. Current spending can become dependent on unrealistic expectations of future land price increases. Given the uncertainty of LVC, it is critical that proceeds be used for infrastructure investment and not for operating budgets.

---

[27] Ibid.

2.3.8 Transparent Land Sales

Transparent and competitive land auctions can greatly enhance revenues – in some cases increasing the realized land price per square meter by a factor of ten or more. Direct negotiations with land developers are tempting; they seem easier and faster than auctions but generally result in inferior financial and developmental results.

Transparent public accounting of the use of proceeds can help to manage perceptions of corruption or bureaucratic capture. In an effort to maximize LVC, governments may be tempted to use restrictive zoning to drive up land values or abuse developer exactions. This practice can harm the local economy, unduly raise real estate prices, and distort urban development patterns.

2.3.9 Readiness of Financial and Capital Markets

Access to finance for infrastructure developments can benefit from local financial markets that are able to manage and absorb the kind of investment vehicles used for LVC, in particular allowing for borrowing against future LVC revenues like TIFs. Local financial markets may be shallow (not have much available liquidity), short (able to provide debt only over short tenors), or lacking sophistication (where the available types of financial instruments are limited and those working in the industry are not familiar with many of the models discussed here). Regulatory reform in local financial markets can help, as can partnering with global financiers to help local financiers gain experience with LVC instruments.

2.3.10 Fiscal Mandates and Powers of Enforcement

Land value capture may rely on tax or other regulatory functions to define and enforce LVC principles. If a government's fiscal mandate is not clear or where fiscal obligations cannot be or are not enforced effectively, this may undermine the LVC program. Those holding mandates to set and enforce rules around LVC also need the capacity to implement their mandates well. This may also be a question of perception; investors need to have the confidence that the tax and other regulatory functions will be implemented.

2.3.11 Need for Accurate and Complete Data

An inventory of land assets owned by government agencies can identify current land use and determine its market value. Access to such a pool of data, to the extent it is complete and accurate, improves government's ability to obtain best price and identify issues/challenges in advance to address them when they arise and to improve the value of the property to the market. The government can then decide which land parcels would be more beneficial to urban development

2.3 Lessons Learned

if sold, determine the kind of additional services or investments that purchasers should be required to deliver, and identify the potential purchasers of such land to allow the government to prepare and get maximum value from it. This exercise often leads governments to discover they own far more undeveloped land than they had realized.

2.3.12 Risk of Overreliance

Overreliance on LVC exposes projects to excessive market risk. While a robust real estate market and rising land prices are good for LVC, projects should estimate the revenue to be generated from LVC schemes based on cautious and realistic assumptions, given the unpredictability of the real estate market. Governments should prepare contingency plans in case revenues are lower than projected.

2.3.13 Managing Corruption and Perceptions Thereof

In general, in many developing countries, the public has a negative perception of government disposal of land, the assumption being that the buyers will be the elites and those with connections. To secure public support, government should implement transparency in decision processes, monitoring, and evaluation. It should raise public awareness of the chosen scheme and its objectives, principles, rules, and regulations. It is also important for governments to involve civil society organizations in planning and project development activities. Probably the most important way to prevent potential corruption is to require transactions to follow market pricing, based on an independent assessment. Transparent information systems will also help prepare future LVC schemes, by making the relevant market data available.

2.3.14 Avoiding Excessive Gentrification

Property developers under LVC schemes often displace low-income households by increasing property values and pricing out low-income communities. LVC should not just create economically efficient and environmentally friendly urban spaces, it should also address urban poverty and deprivation. Where possible, government should pursue affordable housing and provide developers with incentives to ensure that affordable housing is built close to transit stops. A density bonus for constructing social housing can be included in LVC agreements.

3

Commercial Value Capture

Conventional approaches to funding public infrastructure are not bringing in sufficient revenue to fund the growing infrastructure gap. The most common mechanisms governments use to pay for infrastructure investments are (a) user pays, in which the operator collects tariffs for the service from the end-user, and (b) government pays, in which the government allocates tax revenues through fiscal budgeting for funding the investment. The user pays, to the extent affordable and to the extent it is politically acceptable to charge tariffs on users. This latter point is tricky. For example, in many countries, even though agriculture is a viable and popular economic activity, governments are not able to charge farmers for the water they use or indeed impose any incentive for farmers to conserve water. Even though farmers can and should pay for water, it is not politically acceptable for the government to charge farmers for such resources. Where users cannot or will not pay, the government normally makes up the difference, providing subsidies or grants to cover construction and/or operating costs of infrastructure.

Economic planners and financial managers in government are looking for creative ways to pay for public infrastructure. Public spending could leverage more private capital through investment planning reforms to encourage planners to create public infrastructure services that in addition to providing core services also create places and spaces that enable commercial value creation and then capture a fair share of that commercial value to fund capital investments. It is common to perceive investment needs, in particular infrastructure, solely as a public service, a cost center for government, whereas, in fact, such investments may also create commercial opportunities. These opportunities not only provide a new source of revenue for the investment but can also anchor innovative sources of financing.

Commercial activities around infrastructure investments often result in significant profits for the private sector, providing opportunities for higher value for money and more or new commercial activities (for ease of reference, the term "commercial value capture" or "CVC" will be used here[1]).

For example, the operator of a bus rapid transit system can be allowed to develop space in, around, and above bus stations for retail letting, office space, or other commercial activities to generate income and improve project revenues. The scale of CVC may not be sufficient to fully fund public infrastructure, and projects should not become overly focused on such revenue generation. This said, CVC can usually make a material contribution to the overall project economics and so can substantially increase project viability. This chapter provides a brief introduction to CVC and how those planning or designing infrastructure projects can avail those projects of CVC.

As a fundamental step, governments can apply a comprehensive planning approach to identify the broader needs of users and beneficiaries within a community that creates commercially driven demand for integrated solutions. Stable funding sources make projects more bankable as financiers perceive lower risk of default.[2]

3.1 INTRODUCTION TO CVC

Governments tend to look for revenues for infrastructure projects from users of the infrastructure (e.g., consumers of water, drivers on a motorway, or passengers on a light rail trains [LRTs]). If users cannot (or will not) afford tariffs or fees high enough to fund the infrastructure in question, then the government will make up the difference through capital contributions against construction or availability payments during operations.[3] This narrow focus misses various sources of funding (revenues) for infrastructure, in particular CVC.

Public infrastructure often creates places and spaces that can provide opportunities for higher value and more or new commercial activities that generate new or additional revenue streams. Most often it is the private sector that takes advantage of these opportunities and disproportionately increased profits. However, governments are instrumental in creating the places and spaces where

---

[1] "Commercial value capture" was introduced as a concept for generating additional commercial revenues to governments for funding infrastructure in "Module 17: Capturing Commercial Value," World Bank Municipal PPP Framework, 2019. CVC will be the primary focus of this chapter as there is relatively limited published knowledge on CVC mechanisms. The concept of commercial value capture was introduced in "Module 17: Capturing Commercial Value," World Bank Municipal PPP Framework, https://ppp.worldbank.org/public-private-partnership/sites/ppp.worldbank.org/files/2020-02/World%20Bank_Municipal%20PPP_Module%2017_Content.pdf. For further discussion of CVC, also https://ppp.worldbank.org/public-private-partnership/Innovative_Revenues_for_Infrastructure.

[2] "Innovative Infrastructure Financing through Value Capture in Indonesia," ADB, 2021, www.adb.org/news/speeches/innovative-infrastructure-financing-value-capture-indonesia-bambang-susantono.

[3] For further discussion of government capital grants, viability gap funding, availability payments, and other mechanisms, please see Jeffrey Delmon, *Private Sector Investment in Infrastructure: Project Finance, PPP Projects and PPP Programs* (Kluwer Law International, 2021).

these commercial activities occur and therefore should capture a fair share of the value created to fund the infrastructure that creates the value. Such commercial revenues can be mobilized for many infrastructure projects, alongside or linked to public services; for example, CVC may be available in various ways:

- A public market project that may not be able to attract sufficient revenues from vendor fees to cover operating costs, much less depreciation or initial capital investment, may include other commercial activities to generate the needed revenues and offer additional services, for example, retail, residential, or office space (see Box 3.9[4]).
- Bus or truck terminals provide an opportunity for retail activities, selling goods and services to passengers and passersby (see Box 3.12[5]).
- Government offices can be developed with commercial office space and mixed-use facilities to reduce costs to government (see Box 3.8[6]).
- Convention centers are often developed with hotels because revenues from convention centers are generally insufficient to cover costs but they attract customers for hotels and retail services.

Thus, CVC can be a way for governments to increase revenues to fund improvement of facilities, expansion of services, and/or asset maintenance without increasing taxes, creating fiscal liabilities, or charging user fees. Governments can apply a comprehensive planning approach that creates commercially driven demand for integrated solutions by identifying the broader needs of users and beneficiaries.

Commercial activities around infrastructure investments often result in commercial gain for the private sector, providing opportunities for more or new commercial activities of higher value. In some cases, tax regimes capture a share of this profit for the government to help fund the infrastructure. For example, property tax captures increase in land values, and business tax captures increase in business activity. However, in many cases, the taxation systems are insufficiently dynamic or tax recovery is too low. Therefore, other mechanisms are needed to capture some of the commercial opportunities generated by infrastructure investments to help fund those investments. Also, by designing infrastructure accordingly, governments can encourage such commercial opportunities and help to increase commercial investment, multiply jobs, and improve the economic impact of infrastructure.

As a fundamental step, governments can apply a comprehensive planning approach to identify the broader needs of users and beneficiaries within a community that creates commercially driven demand for integrated solutions. When considering an infrastructure project, the contracting authority should

---

[4] Global Platform for Sustainable Cities, World Bank Municipal PPP Framework, 2019, Project Summary No. 25.
[5] Global Platform for Sustainable Cities, Project Summary No. 5.
[6] Global Platform for Sustainable Cities, Project Summary No. 30.

3.1 Introduction to CVC

assess the possibility of CVC, by considering (a) commercial activities under, above, or around the project facilities and (b) commercial activities delivered from the project facilities, but it should always ensure that the project focuses on the public services that form the core of the project.

In a comprehensive planning approach to innovative funding sources, thinking outside of the box to identify new funding solutions for infrastructure is probably the most challenging for many governments, where new ideas or approaches may be perceived as risky.

Where property prices are high, air rights over a public asset can have significant value. For example, Washington, DC, United States, developed low-cost housing and refurbished a library and a fire station in exchange for the right to build condominiums (see Box 3.6).[7] The same approach can be used for other developments, such as parking garages and bus terminals. Also in Washington, DC, a stretch of highway that runs through the center of the city was built with residential, office, retail, and parking facilities, including public spaces. This project revitalized a large area of the downtown.[8]

The space under public facilities may also provide opportunities for commercial activities. An example would be the parking area under Rivera Navarrete Avenue in San Isidro, Peru. The municipal government wanted to address the constant congestion problems of Lima's financial center and, at the same time, to reduce the estimated deficit of 10,600 parking spaces in the area. A three-story parking facility was developed underground, under the main avenue (see Box 3.18).[9]

The space around a public asset may also provide opportunities for new revenue streams. As an example, the facilities in Oyster School in Washington, DC, property development paid for the cost of school refurbishment (see Box 3.5).[10]

Sometimes the project facility itself can be used for commercial purposes as well as public services. For example, when redeveloping the Mandaluyong City Market in the Philippines, the usual subsidized space for low-cost vendors was combined with high-value business and entertainment space, that is, department stores, a bowling alley, and a movie theater. The high-value space produces sufficient revenue to subsidize the low-cost vendor facilities (see Box 3.9).[11] In Danli, Honduras, the municipality built a modern bus terminal to replace its outdated and disorganized bus terminal. The new bus terminal provided retail facilities, warehousing, and meeting rooms within the bus terminal (as well as around and above) (see Box 3.12).[12] These facilities

---

[7] Global Platform for Sustainable Cities, Project Summary 48.
[8] Global Platform for Sustainable Cities, Project Summary 50.
[9] Global Platform for Sustainable Cities, Project Summary 27.
[10] Global Platform for Sustainable Cities, Project Summary 58.
[11] Global Platform for Sustainable Cities, Project Summary 25.
[12] Global Platform for Sustainable Cities, Project Summary 5.

> **Box 3.1 Tourism revenues to protect the environment in Zanzibar**
>
> The Revolutionary Government of Zanzibar issued a concession to develop ecofriendly bungalows and a visitors' center on a 5.9-acre island, including a marine park and a forest reserve. The revenues generated from ecotourism cover operational expenses, park management, and environmental education. The investor has a thirty-three-year lease and a ten-year management contract and had to work with seven government departments and gain the support of area fishermen and local communities before the project was approved.[13]

provide additional commercial services to passengers/residents and create a new revenue stream to fund the bus terminal.

Other benefits, such as environmental, social, and historical, can be leveraged through such commercial structures by creating commonalities and confluences of interests. Serious investors are keenly interested in the welfare of the local community, the sustainability of natural resources, local transport infrastructure, solid waste management, and so on. These are critical to the long-term viability of an investment. Innovative funding provides the opportunity to identify government needs in advance and agree between investor and government on the most important issues, such as how to allocate responsibilities and how to work together to meet different stakeholder needs (see Box 3.1).

3.2 IMPLEMENTING CVC SYSTEMATICALLY

A more comprehensive approach to identifying the needs of users and beneficiaries within a community can deliver integrated solutions. Viable CVC opportunities should be tested with national or municipal programs by

- reviewing pipelines of proposed transactions during the planning process to identify high-potential CVC opportunities;
- reviewing specific transactions that are at early stages of preparation to identify viable CVC opportunities; and
- supporting the inclusion of CVC assessments into feasibility studies for projects that are under development.

Feedback from the process of applying the CVC framework can be built into the framework to adopt lessons learned and continually improve the program.

Governments should consider possible innovative funding opportunities during early planning processes to make sure that planning does not unnecessarily limit, or fail to identify and capture, funding opportunities.

---

[13] Global Platform for Sustainable Cities, Project Summary 37.

3.2 Implementing CVC Systematically

Feasibility studies should be generated for every infrastructure project. A fundamental question to be raised in such studies is the opportunity for innovative funding sources. This involves a set of assessments to ensure that the funding opportunity is viable and should be included in the infrastructure project.

When assessing innovative funding opportunities, a number of practical features need to be considered on a preliminary basis during the planning stage and then in more detail during the feasibility study; for example:

- The difficulty of government coordination will impact the feasibility of a funding opportunity. Planning should therefore consider the complexity of the relevant levels of government involved in implementing such funding, including different central and local government stakeholders and which government stakeholders need to be involved in the discussion, planning, and funding.
- Opportunities and appropriate mechanisms for CVC should be identified, asking in particular:
  o Who directly benefits from the project?
  o Within the community, who are the users and direct beneficiaries of noncore commercial services?
  o What revenue streams can be created from noncore commercial services?
  o How much would these commercial revenue streams likely generate?
- A preliminary assessment should be made of the cost of structuring a funding opportunity, the cost of implementing the opportunity, and the revenue likely to be generated. This net revenue assessment, even if preliminary, will help to guide the planning process.
- Coordination should be improved in order to help the government create a more integrated service delivery for the project.
- Key players for delivering improved services and the additional value they could create should be identified:
  o Which party can best manage the provision of noncore commercial services?
  o Who can best deliver the improved services?
  o What is a reasonable share or innovative funding for government?
- The existing legal/regulatory enabling framework for the contemplated CVC mechanisms will need to be reviewed to assess which CVC mechanisms are legally viable, any restrictions applicable to CVC mechanisms and associated costs.
- The appropriate CVC mechanism is selected considering the viability and implementation readiness of the contracting authority:
  o Does the contracting authority have the capacity to implement the selected CVC concepts? If not, what resources does it need to develop and implement the CVC concepts identified?
  o Has the CVC concept been tested?
  o How can governments effectively share in the risks and rewards of commercial revenues streams?

- Can the project be structured to manage risks, effectively capture commercial revenues, and deliver intended project outcomes? What is the best implementation pathway for delivering value and generating additional government revenue streams from the commercial concept?
  ○ What are the risks involved?
  ○ What is the appropriate commercial structure to set contractual obligations and manage the risks identified?
  ○ How can value created be measured and verified?
  ○ How can revenues that are captured be committed to funding infrastructure to build confidence that benefits for target communities will be sustainable?

3.3 CVC IN DIFFERENT SECTORS

The nature of CVC available from different infrastructure projects also reflects the project sector. This section explores a few sectors and the nature of CVC that can be mobilized in those sectors.

3.3.1 Transport

The transportation sector can be characterized by two critical constraints: demand forecasting and land. Demand for transportation infrastructure is influenced by competing modes of transportation, demographic shifts, economic conditions, the cost of the facilities to end-users, convenience, individual preference, speed, and a number of other, often interrelated, factors that make accurate demand forecasting difficult at best. The need for access to large amounts of land and space to build transportation facilities makes them expensive, long-term, and politically sensitive undertakings. Nevertheless, the amount of land and space required for transportation projects and the number of people served by or associated with such projects make them particularly attractive for CVC.

Public reaction to new transport facilities can be heated – an example is the difficulty encountered in expanding London's Heathrow airport; no one wants a railway line or new road running through their back yard. For many projects, in particular rail, the high cost of land and construction cannot be met by the level of politically acceptable tariffs. They require specific and significant additional revenues, including government support.[14]

Transportation projects, including airports, roads, railways, ports, buses, metro, tunnels, and bridges, have traditionally been financed by a combination

---

[14] Public-Private Partnership Legal Resource Center, The World Bank Group, https://ppp.worldbank.org/public-private-partnership/; "Allocating Risks in Public-Private Partnership Contracts – Transport Sector," Global Infrastructure Hub, a G20 Initiative, https://ppp-risk.gihub.org/risk_category/transport/; "Legal Issues on Public-Private Partnerships for Transport," The World Bank Group, https://ppp.worldbank.org/public-private-partnership/sector/transportation.

3.3 CVC in Different Sectors

of private and public funding. The early days of railways in the United States involved private companies building railway networks with land provided by the public sector. Bridges have seen a similar combination of public and private involvement, benefiting from a toll from those wishing to use the bridge. Airports and roads, however, have historically been financed using public funds; it is only over the last thirty to forty years that private sector involvement has become common in these areas.

Governments are increasingly looking to the private sector for input in the development of new transportation schemes and the privatization of those already existing. This trend has developed largely as a result of the tremendous expense the public sector has incurred in subsidizing transportation operations and the less than admirable efficiency of certain publicly funded operations. The cost concern in the public sector is multiplied by the need to increase capacity in the near future. Developing economies have a particular need for increased capacity in their transportation services, yet the costs of such increases are prohibitive.

The movement of people through mass transit provides an opportunity to deliver commercial services to those users, improving their transport experience and earning additional revenues for the project.[15] Where the government sees passengers, the investor sees customers. By providing commercial services to users, the project not only mobilizes new sources of revenues but also improves the user experience, by allowing users to meet their retail and other needs during their commute.

The government may want to consider what services may also be provided in transit hubs to further improve convenience for passengers. This "transit-oriented development" (see Chapter 4) will be relevant for a number of projects, including bus and truck terminals, LRT systems, and bus rapid transit projects. The opportunity for transit-oriented development is exemplified by the Hong Kong Mass Transit Railway Corporation (MTRC), where residential and commercial properties are built above and around the railway stations and depots, improving the convenience for passengers and increasing revenues for the MTRC as well as the Hong Kong government (see Box 3.13).[16]

The need for expansion of airport facilities, particularly in the Asia-Pacific region, has led to the increased use of project financing for this sector. Airports benefit from a relatively stable minimum business baseload and a diversity of revenue sources, such as air traffic fees, car parking, concessions, and property rentals. They also generally have a strong monopoly position, limiting competition.[17]

---

[15] For further discussion of transit-oriented development, see Serge Salat and Gerald Olivier, *Transforming the Urban Space through Transit-Oriented Development: The 3V Approach* (World Bank, 2017), www.worldbank.org/en/topic/transport/publication/transforming-the-urban-space-through-transit-oriented-development-the-3v-approach.

[16] Global Platform for Sustainable Cities, Project Summary 2.

[17] Andy Ricover and Jeffrey Delmon, *A Decision-Makers Guide to Public Private Partnerships in Airports* (Routledge, 2020).

Transport projects often involve a multiplicity of commercial arrangements, across rail, ports, airports, and roads. Terminal facilities, fueling facilities, cargo warehouses and handling, catering, parking, hotels, commercial businesses, and a variety of other support and associated services can be provided by the operator, or a series of different operators, to mobilize more revenues for the project. Each of these functions must be coordinated for the entire facility to work efficiently. Given the diversity of activities, the project company may need to enlist the assistance of different operators experienced in such areas.

The contracting authority and the shareholders will also need to allow the project company sufficient flexibility in the businesses it can undertake. In most other sectors, the contracting authority and the lenders generally limit the nature of the business that can be performed by the project company and on the site. However, in the case of transport projects, they may be best served by broadening the nature of the businesses that can be operated in order to improve revenue flow and investment in infrastructure on the site as well as the experience of passengers.

3.3.2 Power

Electricity is a public good, with specific impact on environment and quality of life, and therefore pricing has political, social, health, and environmental implications. The power sector is generally heavily regulated. The construction of new generation capacity is an extremely expensive undertaking, and can meet with specific resistance in built-up areas. While the need for electricity is generally understood, many communities prefer to adopt a "not in my backyard" (NIMBY) approach. This, combined with government efforts to keep electricity prices down against high cost of new investment, fuel, and operation, can have disastrous consequences for the power sector.

The power sector is characterized by unique constraints in the delivery of electricity to public, commercial, and residential consumers.[18] Electricity is relatively easy to transmit over long distances but very hard to store, so it must be generated constantly and responsively to meet demand in its daily and seasonal variations. The ease of transmission makes it possible to create competitive markets, at least around generation and distribution. Competition in transmission can be more difficult given the practical and price implications of duplicated transmission networks. However, common carriage arrangements are feasible and increasingly successfully implemented.

The power sector has been one of the greatest beneficiaries of private investment, particularly successful in providing new generating capacity. Generation facilities are large and very expensive and therefore fit well into the project

---

[18] For a good general review of the power sector, in particular its regulation, see Sally Hunt, *Making Competition Work in Electricity* (John Wiley & Sons, 2002).

3.3 CVC in Different Sectors

financing structure. They usually involve the construction of completely new assets, which will be separate and isolated assets over which security can be provided to the lenders and whose revenue stream is easily identifiable. Less common are transmission and distribution projects within the power sector. Transmission generally fits best with an availability payment model, where the project company is paid for making the transmission facility available.

The generation of electricity is often an additional revenue stream that can be mobilized for other types of infrastructure investment. For example, many projects can install solar panels to attract revenues from electricity generated or by offsetting electricity costs. Solid waste project can generate electricity by incineration of solid waste or use of captured methane gas. Energy efficiency is a good way to reduce costs. Innovative revenue streams for power projects can also potentially attract emissions reduction credits (see Section 3.4).

Power projects may generate other offtake. For example, a hydroelectric project may also provide a reservoir for raw water that can be used for irrigation or treated and used as potable water. Many water-poor coastal countries use desalination to make up for their water deficit. Desalination uses large amounts of electricity, so combined power generation and desalination plants, also known as independent water and power producers, are popular mixed offtake plants.

Multiple offtake requires consideration of issues of resource management, operation effectiveness, and revenue flows where the various offtakes are compensated differently. Two common examples of power projects with multiple offtakes are combined heat and power (CHP) and cogeneration plants.

A CHP plant provides for the sale of the heat generated while producing power. The project company may therefore want to enter into a second offtake agreement in order to allocate the market risk for the sale of the heat produced. This demand risk may be more difficult to allocate over the concession period, since the buildings near to the site, which are most likely to purchase such heat, may change ownership and function repeatedly during the period of the concession.

A similar regime will be needed for cogeneration plants, which involve two offtake purchasers, one purchasing the electricity generated and the other purchasing steam bled off from the steam turbine during certain hours of operation.[19] The steam purchaser will need to satisfy the requirements of its facility, usually a refinery or other industrial plant. There is, therefore, a tension between the needs of the steam purchaser, the consistent supply of steam for the plant, and the power purchaser, since bleeding off steam decreases electricity output. Also, the steam purchaser may not have the technical experience of the power purchaser to run the power plant in the case of default by the operator. Cogeneration plants require careful management of these competing

---

[19] Graham Vinter, "Legal Issues Involved in Co-Generation Projects," in *Project Finance Yearbook 1995/96*, (Hornbrook, 1996), pp. 15, 32.

interests, including setting out schedules for priority of offtake (i.e., which of the purchasers has priority when ordering output).

3.3.3 Water and Wastewater

As focus turns to the standards and scope of existing water and sanitation services, private sector investment stands out as one of the vehicles available for improving these services.[20] It must be patently clear that private involvement in water provides water to more people, better quality of service, and connections to those who need the services the most. This has been evidenced in many cases, but designers of water projects must remain focused on the incentives and dynamics that encourage such performance by the private sector.[21]

One of the most dynamic and promising areas for PPP is the use of private sector innovation and capacity to improve efficiency. Public sector water companies are often run in an extremely inefficient manner. They are not accustomed to incentives to increase efficiency and are generally loath to reduce headcount or cut costs where these might be politically unpopular. An efficient private water company may employ three or four personnel per 1,000 connections. Many public water companies employ twenty-five employees or more per 1,000 connections. The private sector may also be able to implement new technology and thereby reduce total costs.

However, a reduction of material and labor costs can be extremely delicate given the potential political backlash. Mass redundancy immediately following the implementation of PPP generally results in public uprisings. Cancelling contracts with local suppliers, in particular in favor of foreign suppliers, can have similar results. The politicians approving the investment proposal will be very sensitive to these issues.[22]

Treatment costs can be reduced where large volumes of water are being treated but are not reaching consumers. Reducing unaccounted-for water, in particular leakage and illegal connections, makes more water available to meet

---

[20] Maude Barlow, *Blue Gold: The Global Water Crisis and the Commodification of the World's Water Supply* (International Forum on Globalization, 1999).

[21] Philippe Marin, *Public-Private Partnerships for Urban Water Utilities – A Review of Experiences in Developing Countries*, Trends and Policy Option No 6, PPIAF (World Bank, 2009); Luis A. Andrés, Jordan Schwartz, and J. Luis Guasch, *Uncovering the Drivers of Utility Performance, Lessons from Latin America and the Caribbean on the Role of the Private Sector, Regulation, and Governance in the Power, Water, and Telecommunication Sectors* (World Bank, 2013); Katharina Gassner, Alexander Popov, and Nataliya Pushak, *An Empirical Assessment of Private Sector Participation in Electricity and Water Distribution in Developing and Transition Countries* (World Bank, 2007); Katharina Gassner, Alexander Popov, and Nataliya Pushak, *Does Private Sector Participation Improve Performance in Electricity and Water Distribution?* Trend and Policy Option No 6. PPIAF (World Bank, 2009).

[22] This may seem a painfully obvious statement, but it is fascinating how often it is ignored by private investors and government entities alike when designing a water PPP.

3.3 CVC in Different Sectors

demand, and therefore decreases treatment costs. Identifying and repairing leakage require upfront investments whose benefits will be hard for consumers and politicians (those paying for the work) to see. Therefore, water and sanitation projects can be designed to use significantly less power and use less raw water (freeing up revenues for capital investment). Water reservoirs can be used to generate electricity or provide irrigation to agricultural areas. Treated wastewater can be used for industrial purposes.

Leakage reduction arrangements can reward the project company for the amount of water saved by them, which affords the public utility higher revenues as it has more water to sell and defers the cost of new treatment capacity. Caution should be exercised in the creation of incentives to reduce leakage. In one contract, the project company was paid a fee per leak eliminated. Of course, it is easier to eliminate small leaks, especially at meters and household connections, but these leaks have a limited impact on the system capacity. The project company was well paid, but the utility received less than anticipated aggregate benefit.

Certain effluent, including treated wastewater, sludge, used chemicals, ash, or other substances, will result from the treatment processes used by the project company. The contracting authority may wish to stipulate which types of effluent are acceptable, the permitted levels of such matter, and how the project company may dispose of it. A testing procedure will generally be implemented to ensure that effluent disposed of meets the standards required by law, by license, or by the contracting authority. It can be used for different functions such as construction core, compost for agriculture, or energy generation through methane capture or refuse derived fuel.

Land in areas newly served by water and sanitation services can increase significantly in value, creating an opportunity for land value capture, development rights, or other commercial revenues linked to land value increases.

3.3.4 Solid Waste Management

Rapidly improving technologies and a deeper understanding of the use or reuse of solid waste have created increasingly larger roles for the private sector in solid waste management. Solid waste projects tend to focus on treatment, for example, the construction and management of sanitary landfills, incineration facilities, recycling centers, or waste-to-energy facilities. These projects might include collection from transfer stations, where local waste collection is aggregated in a few locations and the project collects waste from those locations and brings it to the treatment facility, using large trucks to reduce the cost of transportation and facilitate treatment.[23]

---

[23] See also Jeffrey Delmon, *Public Private Partnerships in Infrastructure: An Essential Guide for Policy Makers*, 2nd ed. (Cambridge University Press, 2017); "Legal Issues on Municipal Solid Waste PPPs," The World Bank Group, https://ppp.worldbank.org/public-private-partnership/

People generally do not like to pay for trash collection, in particular to the levels required to pay for proper management and treatment. The contracting authority may need to start engaging with the community to communicate the need for charging for collection long before the project is launched.

Solid waste management projects can have multiple revenue sources: the collection fee paid by households, waste collection tax, associated revenues (e.g., power generation and recycling fees), and governmental budget allocations. The fees and taxes charged by the municipality for collection are usually an important part of this revenue stream, and one of the most difficult to achieve to the levels required.

Using waste to generate electricity can be a useful additional revenue stream for solid waste management projects. In the city of Poznán, Poland, the local government entered into a PPP for the design, construction, financing, management, and maintenance of a waste-to-energy production plant. About 30 percent of the city's domestic electricity is generated by this new facility.[24] In China, the city of Wenzhou generated approximately 400,000 tons in household waste each year, with a growth rate of 8–10 percent annually. A PPP developed a waste-to-energy plant able to treat 320 tons of municipal solid waste (MSW) per day and generate up to twenty-five million kilowatt-hours of electricity annually.[25] Waste-to-energy plants are often not financially feasible if they are selling electricity to the electricity grid alone and require a significant "tipping fee" per ton of waste delivered to the treatment facility.

Solid waste management projects should use technology appropriate to the local community, affordable for the community, or that reflects local demand for the services.[26] For instance, where waste to energy is contemplated, the efficiency of generation of electricity from waste depends not only on the quantum of waste generated and collected per day but also on the waste mix, in particular the quantum of organic content in the waste and the calorific value of waste. The contracting authority should first undertake a detailed assessment of waste generated from various parts of the city to understand the composition of waste and the potential of generating electricity from the waste.

---

sector/solid-waste; *Private Sector Participation in Municipal Solid Waste Management: Guidance Pack*, 5 Vols. (Swiss Centre for Development Cooperation in Technology and Management. 2000), https://ppp.worldbank.org/public-private-partnership/library/private-sector-participation-municipal-solid-waste-management-guidance-pack-5-volumes; Solid Waste Management Toolkits. Ministry of Finance of India, https://ppp.worldbank.org/public-private-partnership/library/draft-concession-agreement-municipal-solid-waste-management-delhi; Allocating Risks in Public-Private Partnership Contracts – Solid Waste Collection, Disposal, Landfill and Recycling.

[24] World Bank Municipal PPP Framework, Project Summary 19, https://ppp.worldbank.org/public-private-partnership/municipal-and-subnational/municipal-public-private-partnership-framework.

[25] World Bank Municipal PPP Framework, Project Summary 20, https://ppp.worldbank.org/public-private-partnership/municipal-and-subnational/municipal-public-private-partnership-framework.

[26] "Handshake – Issue 12, Waste PPPs," International Finance Corporation, 2014.

3.3 CVC in Different Sectors

In many developing countries, informal waste pickers are key players in solid waste, gathering, sorting, trading, and, in some cases, recycling, either individually or grouped in microenterprises. Waste pickers represent some of the most vulnerable low-income communities, whose interests need to be considered in any waste project.[27]

Where the project company is responsible for collecting waste from a transfer station or waste is delivered to the treatment facility, the contracting authority will typically have to guarantee a minimum quantity of waste that would be available to the project company every day. The treatment facility is designed to cater to this minimum guaranteed waste. If the contracting authority delivers less waste, then the contracting authority may have to compensate the project company accordingly. Therefore, a detailed and robust study of how much waste a city is actually generating, and more importantly collecting, on a daily basis is important before bidding out solid waste management projects.

If the project includes a treatment facility as well as a sanitary landfill, then the contracting authority should specify the maximum percentage or quantity of waste that can be transferred to the sanitary landfill, creating an incentive to maximize treatment efficiency and ensuring that the sanitary landfill lasts longer.

3.3.5 Urban Redevelopment

Most large urban redevelopment projects offer opportunities for CVC. Urban redevelopment can take many shapes,[28] including street space optimization, heritage conservation,[29] public facilities renovation,[30] and neighborhood rehabilitation,[31] involving a wide array of expertise, long-term planning,

---

[27] Some actors for successful informal sector integration in solid waste management systems can be found in "Role of Informal Sector in Solid Waste Management and Enabling Conditions for its Integration," World Bank, 2011.

[28] "Public Private Partnership in Urban Regeneration. A Guide to Opportunities and Practice," City of Liverpool, UK, 2006, https://urbact.eu/sites/default/files/p4a-_final_english_060906.pdf; "Handshake Issue #4: Cities & PPPs," International Finance Corporation, 2012, https://library.pppknowledgelab.org/documents/1947?ref_site=klPublic-Private Partnership in Housing and Urban Development; "Public-Private Partnerships in Housing and Urban Development," United Nations Habitat, 2011, https://unhabitat.org/books/public-private-partnership-in-housing-and-urban-development/; PPP Knowledge Lab – Urban Revitalization, The World Bank Group, https://pppknowledgelab.org/sectors/urban-revitalization.

[29] See Susan Macdonald and Caroline Cheong, *The Role of Public-Private Partnerships and the Third Sector in Conserving Heritage Buildings, Sites, and Historic Urban Areas* (Getty Conservation Institute, 2014).

[30] See public library and fire station at Washington, DC (United States), market at Mandaluyong City (the Philippines), and the completely renovated arena at Bogota. World Bank Municipal PPP Framework, Project Summaries 48, 25, and 31 respectively, https://ppp.worldbank.org/public-private-partnership/municipal-and-subnational/municipal-public-private-partnership-framework.

[31] Regent Park in Toronto, Canada, World Bank Municipal PPP Framework, Project Summary 55, https://ppp.worldbank.org/public-private-partnership/municipal-and-subnational/municipal-public-private-partnership-framework.

community engagement, maintenance, and operation risks. Cities deploy a combination of internal resources (including revenues and municipal land), external funding sources (including intergovernmental transfers, grants, and, in the case of sovereign cities, borrowing), policy and regulatory tools, and strategic partnerships with the private sector, among other resources.[32] The complexity and creativity of urban regeneration makes it difficult to establish standard bidding documents, revenue models, or model commercial structures. Partnering with the private sector is a key tool available to municipalities to achieve sustainable redevelopment.[33]

Private investment in urban redevelopment can range from a master developer for an entire new city – such as a satellite city like the Canary Wharf development in London – to the development of a discrete portion of an urban center. Significant tracts of land for these purposes can be difficult to acquire significant urban redevelopment often follows disaster, urban blight, or some other circumstance that has made a large tract of land available. Urban redevelopment is extremely difficult to define or delimit but offers extensive opportunities to deliver, through mixed-use facilities and diversification of revenues to fund, much-needed redevelopment.

In Washington, DC, two outdated public facilities, a library and a fire station, were refurbished by providing prime development rights (see Box 3.6).[34] Washington, DC also redeveloped an area over a major highway to develop new residential and retail space and to bring life to that part of the city.[35]

As cities grow and shipping transport increases and modernizes, ports are being moved out of city centers to areas more appropriate for industrial development. The historic city center port can be redeveloped to provide passenger terminal facilities (for both private craft and ferry/cruise liner traffic) surrounded by commercial space, for example, hotels, restaurants, pedestrian space, and residential space. This has been done successfully in a number of cities, including Rotterdam, the Netherlands; Sydney, Australia; Buenos Aires, Argentina; Baltimore, United States; and Cape Town, South Africa; to name but a few.[36]

Other urban services provide opportunities for commercial revenue generation. For example, public markets create an opportunity for low-income vendors

---

[32] Rana Amirtahmasebi, Mariana Orloff, Sameh Wahba, and Andrew Altman, *Regenerating Urban Land: A Practitioner's Guide to Leveraging Private Investment* (World Bank, 2016), DOI: 10.1596/978-1-4648-0473-1.

[33] Ibid.

[34] World Bank Municipal PPP Framework, Project Summary 48, https://ppp.worldbank.org/public-private-partnership/municipal-and-subnational/municipal-public-private-partnership-framework.

[35] World Bank Municipal PPP Framework, Project Summary 50, https://ppp.worldbank.org/public-private-partnership/municipal-and-subnational/municipal-public-private-partnership-framework.

[36] http://en.wikipedia.org/wiki/Category:Redeveloped_ports_and_waterfronts; http://capeinfo.com/useful-links/history/115-waterfront-development.html.

3.3 CVC in Different Sectors

to have access to retail space. But these same public markets can be used to make space available for middle- and high-income vendors and thereby mobilize more customers for low-income vendors and more revenues for the project.

Strong political support, community engagement, and proper planning are critical success factors for private investment in urban redevelopment. It is often the private sector that has more adequate human and technical resources to drive project development to achieve planning goals.[37] Designing a structure that allocates risks between the contracting authority and the project company in the most effective manner requires a thorough understanding of the redevelopment, the local community, and the likely economic and financial outcomes of the redevelopment.

Municipalities are often optimistic about the value that can be unlocked from real estate opportunities that emerge from such redevelopment projects. These projects may offer an enticing prospect but with so many challenges and uncertainties that private sector involvement in early stages may be unattractive or uneconomic. Building momentum with initial public redevelopment projects can attract investors for future-linked/adjacent projects.[38] At the project development stage, it is important to get realistic and maybe even worst-case scenarios of the unlocked real estate value from such redevelopment projects.

3.3.6 Government Offices

Governments need to invest in administrative and other office space to deliver an effective public service. But property management is often not a strength of government staff. Private investment can be a more effective mechanism to develop office facilities with latest technology and good maintenance over time.[39] Private investment can also help consolidate government offices in one location to provide more access to facilities and to other government departments, saving time and delivering better/coordinated services. The project will use a carefully crafted performance regime to ensure that the project company delivers the government offices to the right standard.

One potential model for government office space that uses the commercial strengths of private investment involves the development of a mixed-use facility, comprising government offices, private offices, commercial space, and possibly residential space. This allows government staff to work in a dynamic mixed-use space. The revenues from commercial and other activities reduce or eliminate the cost of the government offices to the contracting authority.

---

[37] "Handshake Issue #4: Cities & PPPs."
[38] Darja Reuschke, *Public-Private Partnerships in Urban Development in the United States* (University of California, 2001).
[39] Public-Private Partnership Legal Resource Center, The World Bank Group, https://ppp.worldbank.org/public-private-partnership/ppp-sector/sub-national-and-municipal-ppps/sub-national-and-municipal-ppps.

Where conditions are right (e.g., the land value is high, the site is large, and the market is buoyant), the contracting authority may also receive a revenue share from such a project.

Many governments do not want to share their office space with other users, for security or other reasons. In such cases, the project company can build and maintain government office space against availability payments from the contracting authority. Or the project may involve both government offices and commercial/residential facilities but accessed and managed separately, allowing the project company to earn revenues from the commercial space to offset the amount of revenue mobilized through government availability payments.

Guadalajara, Mexico, was struggling with outdated facilities spread around the city and was in a constant state of disrepair. The Tlajomulco Administrative Center PPP project delivered an administrative building for more than 630 public servants and with a capacity to serve more than 2,000 daily visitors. The project company also constructed a multiple-use gymnasium and outdoor sports facilities and renovated seven kilometers of main roads around the center (see Box 3.8).[40]

Proper use of space to maximize the benefits of an administrative offices project may include 24/7 public access to commercial and ancillary services, such as parks and recreation areas. A separate entrance for the government offices may be needed for security purposes, but access may be desirable where these ancillary services include things that benefit government staff such as grocery shopping, copy and printing services, photography labs (e.g., for personal identification documents), cafés, and restaurants.

3.3.7 Public/Low-Cost Housing

Private developers deliver low-cost housing where they can earn a reasonable profit.[41] Housing policies,[42] government support/incentives, and building codes/planning regulation can help create the right incentives for private developers to do more. The contracting authority can also make affordable housing commercially attractive for private developers, including through PPPs.[43]

---

[40] World Bank Municipal PPP Framework, Project Summary 30, https://ppp.worldbank.org/public-private-partnership/municipal-and-subnational/municipal-public-private-partnership-framework.
[41] Kate Owens, "Constructing Housing PPPs to Build Trust," *World Bank Group's Infrastructure and Public-Private Partnership Blog*, 2016.
[42] India passed a Housing Policy and Affordable Housing Plan in 2015 aiming to deliver between 50,000 and 100,000 affordable houses.
[43] Municipal Rental Housing – Toolkit for the Development of a Municipal Policy, South African Local Government Association and International Cooperation Agency of the Association of Netherlands Municipalities, 2012, www.cmra.org.za/sites/default/files/Toolkit%20for%20Rental%20Housing%20Policy%20%28Third%20Edition%29.pdf; "Public-Private Partnership in Housing and Urban Development"; PPP Knowledge Lab – Urban Revitalization.

3.3 CVC in Different Sectors

Affordable housing can be achieved by the contracting authority providing land and allowing the project company to develop mixed-use facilities, including high-, middle-, and low-income housing as well as retail facilities. Mixed-use facilities also create a better living experience for the low-income tenants who will prefer to be closer to economic and social opportunities, such as jobs, schools, and health care, that are available through or near such mixed-use facilities. These services increase social inclusion within the neighborhood among low-, middle-, and high-income residents; provide more revenue for the project; and create economic opportunities for residents of the low-income housing.

Affordable housing projects are capital intensive. Unless other revenues are available, the project may demand significant financial support from the contracting authority. Sometimes this financial support can be accessed through national subsidies or tax incentives designed to promote affordable housing; the project will need to be designed to access those funds. In Turin, Italy, two abandoned buildings were turned into temporary social housing projects with commercial services and affordable hotel rooms (see Box 3.7).[44]

Where affordable housing is provided through a mixed-use development, there is a risk that the project company will focus efforts and investment on the more profitable activities in the development, with less attention paid to affordable housing. Incentives should be created (and enforced) to ensure that the affordable housing is provided to the agreed specifications, quality, and liveability.

Municipalities may want to play a role in determining the specific beneficiaries or groups of beneficiaries of the contracting authority supporting low-cost housing. In such cases, the contracting authority can either require the project company to construct the low-cost houses and hand them over to the contracting authority for allocation or outline the criteria for allocation of the low-cost housing and require the project company to implement them.

At the project development stage, the contracting authority will need to decide how to allocate low-cost housing, for example, leased or sold, with the contracting authority subsidizing either the capital cost or the interest on the housing loan. Payment for maintenance of common areas needs to be designed early, for example, should the occupants of low-cost housing pay for maintenance of the common areas or is it cross-subsidized from other project revenues. If funding for maintenance is limited, the contracting authority may want the specification of the maintenance to prioritize affordability.

3.3.8 Historic and Cultural Sites

Historic and cultural sites are a key asset for government and investors alike. Innovative funding can bring private investments to refurbish and

---

[44] World Bank Municipal PPP Framework, Project Summary 56, https://ppp.worldbank.org/public-private-partnership/municipal-and-subnational/municipal-public-private-partnership-framework.

maintain historic and cultural assets and in the process create an investment opportunity. An example would be projects for the development of historic palaces in Rajasthan, India. Faced with various historic properties falling to ruins due to lack of investment and maintenance, the government turned to investors to commercialize the properties. These historic properties were leased to private investors through a competitive process that allowed them to redevelop the properties for commercial purposes, in many cases resorts and hotels. The investors have clear obligations to develop the properties in a timely manner, maintain their historic properties, and provide access to the public.

Similarly, in Jaipur, India, an eighteenth-century pleasure palace called Jal Mahal was to be redeveloped through a PPP, part private commercial development and part public space (see Box 3.23).[45]

3.3.9 Hospitality and Tourism

One sector where commercial and public services converge is tourism. In some countries, the land, licensing and regulatory system does not protect tourism investments sufficiently. Where the enterprise culture and business climate are weak, contractual arrangement can create a more conducive and enforceable arrangement than would the legal/regulatory system of the country alone. For example, in some developing countries, the tourism sector is the target of rent seeking at different levels of national and local governments. Investors find themselves faced with serial requests for payment and delays linked to permits, license, and other bureaucratic processes, whether or not official, without transparency or clarity. If well designed, a contractual regime can reduce or eliminate such rent seeking and reduce the risk premium investors would normally charge. To attract investment, and to ensure that tourism investment benefits local communities, protects natural resources, and fits with government strategy, PPPs can help create a clear agreement and partnership between the public and private sector with incentives in-built to protect investors, enable local staff and skill development, benefit local communities, and protect natural resources (see Box 3.1).

In Istanbul, Turkey, the historic Akaretler Row Houses structure, originally built as housing for palace workers in the nineteenth century, was in desperate need of restoration. The municipality awarded a PPP to a private developer to build offices, retail spaces, a luxury hotel, the Atatürk Museum, residential units, and parking spaces above and around the site (see Box 3.24). Strict regulations for the preservation of historical buildings made this redevelopment particularly complicated. A PPP arrangement was used

---

[45] World Bank Municipal PPP Framework, Project Summary 35, https://ppp.worldbank.org/public-private-partnership/municipal-and-subnational/municipal-public-private-partnership-framework.

3.3 CVC in Different Sectors

to coordinate different government stakeholders and enable the investors to redevelop the site.[46]

In 2001, SANParks signed a concession with an investor to outsource the management of sites in the Kruger National Park game reserve including support to the local community. (see Box 3.25).[47] The Jozini Tiger Lodge, in South Africa, is a partnership between the community, the government, and a private investor, the latter being responsible for the day-to-day management of the lodge. The government funded the initial working capital to ensure 80 percent of local staff. The community made land available. Thus, mobilization of community partnerships is key to rural tourism (see Box 3.21).[48]

3.3.10 Health

Health projects can provide interesting opportunities for CVC, but as always care needs to be taken to ensure that public services remain the core focus of the project. Many hospitals require government funding, yet facilities providing the hospital and its patients with high-value services, such as private specialist consultant clinics, imaging facilities, and laboratories, arise around those hospitals.

Private investment is often used to deliver specialist services, such as cancer clinics, imaging services, and dialysis centers. The National Kidney and Transplant Institute in the Philippines specializes in the treatment of renal diseases. In 2003, it entered into a Hemodialysis Center PPP, to furnish the hospital with state-of-the-art machines for patients suffering from end-stage renal diseases, serving more than 120 outpatients a day.[49] The government of Andhra Pradesh entered into a PPP in 2010 to establish and operate dialysis centers in eleven tertiary care state-run hospitals for a period of seven years.[50]

Private investment in the health sector has several advantages,[51] including more timely completion, delivery to cost, technological innovation, and service

---

[46] World Bank Municipal PPP Framework, Project Summary 34, https://ppp.worldbank.org/public-private-partnership/municipal-and-subnational/municipal-public-private-partnership-framework.
[47] World Bank Municipal PPP Framework, Project Summary 38, https://ppp.worldbank.org/public-private-partnership/municipal-and-subnational/municipal-public-private-partnership-framework.
[48] World Bank Municipal PPP Framework, Project Summary 39, https://ppp.worldbank.org/public-private-partnership/municipal-and-subnational/municipal-public-private-partnership-framework.
[49] Ibid.
[50] World Bank Municipal PPP Framework, Project Summaries 65 and 66, https://ppp.worldbank.org/public-private-partnership/municipal-and-subnational/municipal-public-private-partnership-framework.
[51] See also World Bank, *Public-Private Partnerships Legal Resource Center* (World Bank, 2017), https://ppp.worldbank.org/public-private-partnership/; *PPPs in Healthcare: Models, Lessons*

improvement, but there are also some significant challenges, including labor resistance, need for better monitoring and contract management, rapid technological change, and the need to introduce flexibility into the contract to accommodate change.[52] Developing countries also struggle with a lack of experienced health care specialists; no amount of investment in building or technology can replace the services of health care experts.

Health projects can be divided into two broad categories: facility-based and clinical.[53] Facility-based projects involve the project company providing construction, maintenance, and operation of a hospital or clinic but not the delivery of clinical services. The United Kingdom had vastly underinvested in its National Health Service (NHS) hospitals, many of which were built in the Victorian era (during the late 1800s). Beginning in the 1990s, through the private finance initiative (PFI) the United Kingdom built approximately hundred new NHS hospital buildings in twelve years. Since 2003, more than fifty hospital PPPs valued at over CAD 18 billion have been developed in Canada.[54] This model is also common in Australia and Italy. In clinical projects, the project company delivers all services, including the supply of infrastructure and clinical services. This model has been adopted in, for example, Australia, Spain, Portugal, India, and Lesotho.

Health service projects should include a thorough baseline study to capture specific performance and outcomes of the project. Clinical services are difficult to define on a performance basis; for example, if the contract requires the project company to keep fatalities below a certain level, the project company may be incentivized not to treat more complex patients. The incentive framework for a PPP providing both facilities and clinical services will need to establish the right balance and urgency of service delivery. An incentive scheme that compensates well for cleaning and maintenance may find itself with a beautiful and clean facility, but few patients treated. Where compensation is paid for patients that get better quickly (e.g., shorter stays in the hospital), the contracting authority may find that the hospital has a tendency to treat only the easiest and least complicated cases.

The split between clinical services and facilities can be challenging. Many countries use private investment to deliver facilities (the hospital building, utilities, heating, air conditioning, maybe even laundry) under simple performance-based obligations. In such projects, the interface between facilities

---

and Trends for the Future (PricewaterhouseCoopers, 2018), www.pwc.com/gx/en/industries/healthcare/publications/trends-for-the-future.html; PPP Knowledge Lab – Health, The World Bank Group, https://pppknowledgelab.org/sectors/health.

[52] A major issue in hospital PPPs is the need to constantly update medical equipment to reflect advances.

[53] UNECE, WHO, and ADB, "Discussion Paper: A Preliminary Reflection on the Best Practice in PPP in Healthcare Sector: A Review of Different PPP Case Studies and Experiences," PPPs in Health, Manila Conference, 2012.

[54] Ibid.

3.3 CVC in Different Sectors

management and clinical services (the medical services provided – doctors, nurses, and specialist technicians) can be challenging; the clinical staff will have a certain way they want the facilities managed, but a PPP establishes a mechanism for management for a long period, say, twenty to thirty years. The services should be flexible enough to allow the clinical staff to get the support they need.

The regulator for the health sector will need to adjust to the presence and context of the project to ensure that the sector remains cohesive, within the constraints created by the agreement. The regulator should be involved in project design and should develop the capacity needed to regulate both the public sector and the private investor.

3.3.11 Education

Educational facilities are often provided by national government, but municipalities may be responsible for primary or even secondary school facilities, while teachers will generally be regulated and possibly provided by the national government. Private investment has been used to develop various educational facilities and services.[55]

The education sector lends itself less directly to commercial activities, though investment in new school facilities or refurbishing school facilities will improve land values around the school. There is some opportunity for services to be offered to students and their parents outside of school hours (tutoring, hospitality, retail services, etc.).

A number of different approaches and creative commercial engagements have been developed to support the education sector through private investment. For the sake of discussion, these might be organized into the following:

- *Infrastructure Delivery.*[56] The project company builds, maintains, and operates an educational facility such as a public school, university building, or hostel. Payments under the contract are contingent upon the project company delivering services to an agreed performance standard.[57]

---

[55] PPP Knowledge Lab – Education Sector, The World Bank Group, https://pppknowledgelab.org/sectors/education; PPP Projects in the Education Sector. Hogan Lovells Lee & Lee; https://library.pppknowledgelab.org/documents/2479?ref_site=kl.

[56] For example, in Toronto, Canada, the Toronto District School Board suffered from a shortage of funds and limited land availability and the NTCI, a public high school founded in 1912, was an aging facility with a strategic location in midtown Toronto with direct access to public transit and vibrant retail main street. After a PPP for the school redevelopment, a four-story secondary school building was delivered to accommodate 1,200 students and it includes science, art, music, and drama classrooms, a 600-seat theater, library, and a triple gymnasium. World Bank Municipal PPP Framework, Project Summary 61, https://ppp.worldbank.org/public-private-partnership/municipal-and-subnational/municipal-public-private-partnership-framework.

[57] Norman LaRocque, "Public-Private Partnerships in Basic Education: An International Review," CfBT Education Trust, May 2008.

- *Management Services*: The project company manages one or more facilities. The schools remain publicly owned and all nonmanagerial personnel continue to be public sector employees.[58]
- *Service Delivery*: The project company delivers facilities and educates students, possibly a mix of private and public students. It may charge fees from private students, and the contracting authority purchases education services for public students.

Private arrangements can be used to make educational philanthropic support more sustainable and better coordinated with government activities. Examples abound globally.[59]

In 1993, the James F. Oyster Bilingual Elementary School was in danger of closure due to a crumbling and inadequate building and lack of public capital. A private partner redeveloped the school on half the site, and built a new apartment building on the other half (see Box 3.5).[60]

Educational facilities can mobilize commercial revenues; for example, the project company could utilize school infrastructure such as classrooms, the computer lab, the gymnasium, or the library to deliver other services such as training programs for adults after school hours on a for-profit basis. The contracting authority needs to work out its objectives for the PPP and create incentives accordingly.[61] Left to its own, the project company will prioritize the most profitable services.

3.4 A CVC MENU

The following provides a series of examples of commercial activities often associated with infrastructure investment. This is not an exhaustive list but is meant as descriptive to encourage the reader to think outside of the box when planning and developing infrastructure projects and to inspire new ideas and different approaches. Like any menu, it is designed to mix and match concepts and approaches to address the specific needs of a project, a sector, a country, or a context; experience from one will need to be extrapolated to others. Planners and contracting authorities should review this menu when contemplating a project, when performing prefeasibility studies, and as

---

[58] World Bank, "Understanding PPPs in Education," in Harry Anthony Patrinos, Philippe Barerra Osorio, and Jiuliana Guaceta (eds.), *The Role and Impact of Public Private Partnerships in Education* (World Bank, 2009).
[59] LaRocque, "PPPs in Basic Education."
[60] National Council for Public-Private Partnerships, James F. Oyster Bilingual Elementary School, Washington, DC, United States, www.ncppp.org/resources/case-studies/real-estate-and-economic-development/james-f-oyster-bilingual-elementary-school; World Bank Municipal PPP Framework, Project Summary 58, https://ppp.worldbank.org/public-private-partnership/municipal-and-subnational/municipal-public-private-partnership-framework.
[61] LaRocque, "PPPs in Basic Education."

3.4 A CVC Menu

part of feasibility studies to ensure that projects mobilize the right amount of innovative sources of funding.

3.4.1 Advertising and Marketing

The space in and around an infrastructure project can be used for advertising, to draw attention from consumers and increase consumption of their products or services. Global spending on advertising in 2022 was estimated at USD 808 billion.[62] Advertising space is typically used to promote a specific good or service, but there are a wide range of uses. Advertising revenues will be higher for places and spaces in prime locations (See Box 3.2).

Planners and designers should consider advertising on networks of public infrastructure such as stations, road safety structures, overpasses, public parks, and buildings. Concession rights can be granted to the private sector in return for concession fees or integrated into infrastructure projects in exchange for revenue share or reduced government payment obligations. Bus and light rail terminals often take advantage of foot traffic through advertising; an example is the Moncloa Transportation Exchanger, Madrid, Spain,[63] where urban (metro and buses) and interurban (highways and railways) transportation modes intersect to facilitate connectivity.[64]

Infrastructure projects may involve large surface areas with significant foot traffic, such as pumping stations, electricity substations, bus stops, streetlights, and smart poles. In Nairobi, Kenya, a street lighting project mobilized revenues from advertising installed on each streetlight. The project company was given strict size and other parameters to avoid abuse of the advertising space allotted. The revenues generated were sufficient to cover installation of the streetlights and maintenance, with the contracting authority providing electricity (see Box 3.3).[65]

3.4.2 Naming Rights

Naming rights is a form of advertising whereby a corporation, person, or other entity purchases the right to name a facility, object, location, program,

---

[62] www.statista.com/statistics/236943/global-advertising-spending/.
[63] www.thegpsc.org/sites/gpsc/files/1._moncloa_transportation_exchanger_madrid_spain.pdf.
[64] World Bank Municipal PPP Framework, Project Summary 1, https://ppp.worldbank.org/public-private-partnership/municipal-and-subnational/municipal-public-private-partnership-framework; Other examples include the Amritsar Intercity Bus Terminal, Punjab, India, www.thegpsc.org/sites/gpsc/files/7._amritsar_intercity_bus_terminal_punjab_india.pdf, and advertising in Singapore MRT Stations by Stellar Ace, Singapore, all using advertising as a key revenue source.
[65] Other similar projects include the smart poles and streetlights project, Bhopal, Madhya Pradesh, India, www.thegpsc.org/sites/gpsc/files/36._smart_poles_and_streetlights_bhopal_madhya_pradesh_india.pdf, and the urban transport services project, Peja, Kosovo, www.thegpsc.org/sites/gpsc/files/9._urban_transport_services_peja_kosovo.pdf.

> **Box 3.2 Urban transport services, Peja, Kosovo (2012)**
>
> A private partner undertook exclusive responsibility for providing bus transportation services and designing, constructing, and maintaining bus stops, recouping its investment by selling advertising space near bus stops and on buses, in addition to collecting fares from passengers.[66]

> **Box 3.3 Smart poles and streetlights, Bhopal, Madhya Pradesh, India (2017)**
>
> This project included an estimated USD 6.9 million in expenditures for the installation and operation of 400 smart poles (functioning as, inter alia, energy-efficient and remotely controllable LED streetlights, surveillance cameras, environmental sensors, Wi-Fi hotspot providers, and electric vehicle charging points) and 20,000 energy-efficient LED streetlights. Funding streams for the project included a share of the realized energy cost savings, sale of pole-mounted advertisements, and laying 180 kilometers of fiber-optic cable beneath the poles that can be leased to telecoms operators and internet service providers. Revenues would be shared by the public and private partners to the PPP.[67]

[66] Vesa Dinarama, *Analysis on Public-Private Partnership Kosovo* (Balkan Monitoring Public Finances, 2017), http://wings-of-hope.ba/wp-content/uploads/2016/12/D3.4.4.3.-Analysis-on-Public-Private-Partnerships-Kosovo.pdf; Ljerka G. Bregant and Dalia Dubovske, *Comparative Analysis of Lessons Learned from Recent Development in the Implementation of PPP Program in the Western Balkan Region* (ReSPA, 2015), www.respaweb.eu/download/doc/ReSPA+PPP+Working+Paper.pdf/303a4782ecd38f039d270ac39dba69ee.pdf.

[67] "Smart Roads (Smart Poles and Street Lights) on PPP Basis – Bhopal," Smartnet, Ministry of Housing and Urban Affairs. n.d., https://smartnet.niua.org/sites/default/files/resources/3_0.pdf; Danish Khan, "Ericsson, Bharti Infratel Bag Smart City Deal for Bhopal City, to Deploy 400 Smart Poles with WiFi Service," *The Economic Times*, April 1, 2017, https://telecom.economictimes.indiatimes.com/news/ericsson-bharti-infratel-bag-smart-city-deal-for-bhopal-city-to-deploy-400-smart-poles-with-wifi-service/58161194; "Bhopal Smart City Development Corporation Limited," ITU, Bhopal Smart City. n.d., www.itu.int/en/ITU-D/Regional-Presence/AsiaPacific/SiteAssets/Pages/Events/2018/CoESmartcityoct2018/IOT_SmartCity/BSCDCL%20 1-Nov-18.pdf; Shreya Roy Chowdhury, "As Bhopal Is Recast as a Smart City, Its Poor Have a Question: Where's the Room for Us?" *Scroll*, January 28, 2019, https://scroll.in/article/910434/as-bhopal-is-recast-as-a-smart-city-poor-residents-worry-if-they-will-have-a-place-in-it; "Smart Pole and Intelligent Street Light Project," Smart Bhopal, 2019, https://smartbhopal.city/smart-pole-and-intelligent-street-light-project; Bhopal Smart City Development, "Request for Proposal of Intelligent Street Pole: Selection of Bidder for Implementing Smart City Pan City Projects in Bhopal under PPP on BOOT Model," Bhopal Smart City Co. Ltd., Madhya Pradesh, 2016, http://smartcities.gov.in/upload/tender/582d4607ab71fbhopalSmartCity_Part1.pdf; Zhuolun Chen et al., "Bhopal: District Energy in Cities Initiative," District Energy in Cities Initiative in India workshop, November 2, 2017, www.districtenergyinitiative.org/sites/default/files/Bhopal%20Rapid%20Assessment%20Report%20Version%201.0.pdf.

3.4 A CVC Menu

> **Box 3.4 Campin Coliseum (Movistar Arena), Bogota, Colombia (2015)**
>
> A private partner agreed to undertake the structural renovation, technological updating, and operation and maintenance of a forty-year-old multipurpose event facility. Sale of the naming rights to the arena, which were purchased by Telefonica Movistar, a telecommunications company, was included among the principal revenue streams by which the concessionaire would recoup its investment.[68]

or event, typically for a defined period.[69] Longer terms are more common for high-profile venues such as professional sports facilities. The sponsor may attach its name at the end (or, sometimes, beginning) of a generic, usually traditional, name (e.g., Mall of America Field at Hubert H. Humphrey Metrodome), or the sponsor replaces the original name of the property (e.g., Ricoh Coliseum at Exhibition Place, Toronto, Canada,[70] Campin Coliseum [Movistar Arena], Bogota, Colombia,[71] and Metro Dubai Naming Rights, Dubai, United Arab Emirates).

Naming rights fees are of course potentially higher for city icons in prime locations (see Box 3.4). Auctions of such rights will bring the highest valuation. Any project that might involve an iconic asset should consider monetizing naming rights. Naming stadiums in North America for professional sports teams can attract significant fees, in the neighborhood of USD 1–4 million per annum.[72] One of the most significant naming rights deals is Scotiabank Arena, home of the National Hockey League's Toronto Maple Leafs and the National Basketball Association's Toronto Raptors. On August 29, 2017, Canada's Bank of Nova Scotia agreed to a twenty-year, CAD 800-million sponsorship deal.[73]

3.4.3 Residential Space

Many infrastructure projects offer space and opportunity for residential property development and the revenues it mobilizes (see Box 3.5).[74] Where

---

[68] Total transfiguration of Colombia venue, Coliseum News, November 4, 2021, www.coliseum-online.com/total-transfiguration-of-colombia-venue/.
[69] www.managingip.com/article/2a5cyvdl53v4r4d8t3ytc/naming-rights-a-two-way-synergy.
[70] www.thegpsc.org/sites/gpsc/files/project_summaries_part_2_0_0.pdf.
[71] www.thegpsc.org/sites/gpsc/files/module_15.pdf.
[72] For a more extensive list of stadium naming deals, see www.espn.com/sportsbusiness/s/stadiumnames.html.
[73] "MLSE Agrees to Record Arena Rights Deal with Scotiabank," August 29, 2017.
[74] A few useful examples include: Bus Terminal-cum-Commercial Complex, Mohali, India, www.thegpsc.org/sites/gpsc/files/6._bus_terminal-cum-commercial_complex_mohali_india.pdf; Automated Multi-level Car Park, Connaught Place, New Delhi, India, www.thegpsc.org/

> **Box 3.5 James F. Oyster Bilingual Elementary School, Washington, DC, United States**
>
> In 1993, the James F. Oyster Bilingual Elementary School was in danger of closure due to a crumbling and inadequate building and lack of public capital. Led by concerned parents and 21st Century School Fund, a nonprofit, a PPP was formed between District of Columbia Public Schools, the District of Columbia, and a national real estate development firm. They divided the school property in half to make room for a new school and a new residential development. The District of Columbia issued a thirty-five-year, USD 11 million tax-exempt bond for the construction costs, to be repaid entirely with the revenue generated by the private apartment building. The private partner redeveloped the school on half the site, built a new 211-unit apartment building on the other half, and agreed to pay USD 804,000 a year for thirty-five years to repay the bond. The design and construction of the school included a proper level of oversight by the School Board and community involvement to ensure it was built to standards. The school facilities included a computer lab, library, gym, and classrooms designed to accommodate the school's bilingual program and office space.[75]

residential space is developed, there is often opportunity to include low-cost housing. Mixed-use property developments include residential space from different cost bases, retail, office, and other types of development. Residential space can be developed by, for example, the contracting authority providing land and allowing the project company to develop mixed-use facilities, including high-, middle-, and low-income housing as well as retail facilities. Mixed-use facilities also create a better living experience for the low-income tenants who will prefer to be closer to economic and social opportunities, such as jobs, schools, and health care, that are available through or near such mixed-use facilities.

sites/gpsc/files/44._automated_multi-level_car_park_connaught_place_new_delhi_india.pdf; Düsseldorf Museum, Kunstpalast, Germany, www.tandfonline.com/doi/pdf/10.1080/0393630.2020.1758498; Akaretler Row Houses, Istanbul, Turkey, www.thegpsc.org/sites/gpsc/files/project_summaries_part_2_0_0.pdf; Fire Station Refurbishment, Chapel Hill, North Carolina, United States, www.daviskane.com/p-s-chapel-hill-fire-station-no-2-replacement; Mixed Use Development, Virginia Beach, Virginia, United States, www.thegpsc.org/sites/gpsc/files/module_15.pdf; Regent Park Affordable Housing Project, Toronto, Canada, https://metcalffoundation.com/wp-content/uploads/2022/02/Regent-Park-2022-ONLINE-metcalf.pdf; James F. Oyster Bilingual Elementary School, Washington, DC, United States, www.thegpsc.org/sites/gpsc/files/project_summaries_part_2_0_0.pdf; The North Toronto Collegiate Institute, Toronto, Canada, https://documents.pub/document/north-toronto-collegiate-institute-redevelopment-ntci.html?page=1.

[75] National Council for Public-Private Partnerships, James F. Oyster Bilingual Elementary School; World Bank Municipal PPP Framework, Project Summary 58.

3.4 A CVC Menu

> **Box 3.6 Public spaces in Washington, DC**
>
> In Washington, DC, two outdated public facilities, a library and a fire station, were refurbished with latest technology and improved capacity in addition to providing approximately 150 multifamily residential condominiums, 9,600 square feet for retail space, and 52 residential rental units affordable to households earning at or below 60 percent of the area median income. By providing prime development rights above the library and fire station, the contracting authority was able to provide refurbished public facilities and affordable housing.[76]

> **Box 3.7 Social housing in Italy**
>
> In Turin, Italy, two abandoned buildings were turned into temporary social housing projects to provide housing to support disadvantaged population groups, that is, families waiting for public housing, low-income young couples, postal workers, students, and immigrants. The building consisted of 182 flats, equipped with 470 beds with kitchen, and ancillary services such as restaurant, laundry, grocery store, medical clinic, employment office, after-school activity, and car-/bike-sharing system. Aside from the flats, which are rentable for twelve months maximum, the building is also equipped with fifty-eight affordable hotel rooms.[77]

In many countries, government can use zoning and permitting to encourage mixed-use investments and the advantages it can bring to economic and social development. But for many (in particular for developing countries) enforcing zoning and other rules can be challenging. By setting space aside and allowing the infrastructure developer to use some of the space in, around, or above the project to develop residential space, an important source of funding can be mobilized (see Box 3.6).

As mentioned above, where affordable housing is provided through a mixed-use development, the project company may focus on the more profitable activities, and ignore affordable housing (see Box 3.7). Affordable housing is capital intensive and tends to attract limited revenues. The greater the proportion of affordable housing, the more additional revenues will be needed. Unless other revenues are available, the project may demand significant financial support from the contracting authority. Sometimes this financial support can be accessed through national subsidies or tax incentives designed to promote affordable housing. The project will need to be designed to access those

---

[76] World Bank Municipal PPP Framework, Project Summary 48.
[77] World Bank Municipal PPP Framework, Project Summary 56.

> **Box 3.8 Government offices in Mexico**
>
> Guadalajara, Mexico, was struggling with outdated facilities spread around the city and was in a constant state of disrepair. The Tlajomulco Administrative Center PPP project delivered an administrative building for more than 630 public servants and with a capacity to serve more than 2,000 daily visitors. The project company also constructed a multiple-use gymnasium and outdoor sports facilities and renovated seven kilometers of main roads around the center.[78]

funds. If there are no such funds, or if the affordable housing is not funded, there is a greater risk that during development the affordable portion of the housing will be reduced or even abandoned.

3.4.4 Government Office Space

As discussed in more detail above in Section 3.3.6, development of office space (commercial or government) as part of an infrastructure project can provide an important source of revenue, in particular where the project site is located in a high property value area with good transport links.

One potential model for government office space involves the development of a mixed-use facility, comprising government offices, private offices, commercial space, and possibly residential space; this allows government staff to work in a dynamic, mixed-use space (see Box 3.8).

Proper use of space to maximize the benefits of administrative offices project can include access to commercial and ancillary services, such as parks and recreation areas. A separate entrance for the government offices may be needed for security purposes, but access may be desirable where these ancillary services include things that benefit government staff such as grocery shopping, copy and printing services, photography labs (e.g., for personal identification documents), cafes, restaurants.

Public buildings need to be multifunctional to address changes in usage over time. Infrastructure development is long term, and therefore any associated public office development must be able to adjust to changes in use and needs of government staff; this may include reduction of costs where the level of occupancy is reduced or where the office is left empty for a time.

3.4.5 Retail Space

Infrastructure projects may be located in an urban center or may by nature attract customers and foot traffic. These projects can attract additional revenues

---

[78] World Bank Municipal PPP Framework, Project Summary 30.

3.4 A CVC Menu

> **Box 3.9 Mandaluyong City market, Manila, the Philippines (1994)**
>
> The main market in Mandaluyong City was destroyed by a fire in 1991. Due to lack of funds, serious traffic congestion, and sanitation problems, the city decided to rebuild the public market through PPP. It competitively awarded a forty-year concession to build, operate, and manage Mandaluyong City's primary market, after which the property would be handed back to the local government. A seven-story commercial center, named "The Marketplace," was designed to include a public market, street-front stores, a parking garage, commercial shops, department stores, a bowling alley, and a movie theater. In addition, the private developer constructed a box culvert from the main road to the San Juan River. This box culvert has helped address the problem of frequent flooding in the area. Revenues derived from the commercial complex were sufficient to recoup its capital and operating costs, including the cost of the new box culvert.[79]

through retail services, provided in, above, under, or around the infrastructure facility. The nature of retail space should be designed to deliver services to infrastructure users, foot traffic, and the local community (see Box 3.9). For example, where the infrastructure involves a hospital, retail space might be designed for health services, like imaging services, clinical services, specialist consultant offices, and pharmacy.[80]

Where the facility is located in a dense urban area, building up or digging down may provide opportunities for commercial revenues. Washington, DC, redeveloped an area, building over a major highway to develop new residential and retail space and to bring life to that part of the city. The platform supports

---

[79] World Bank Municipal PPP Framework, Project Summary 25, https://ppp.worldbank.org/public-private-partnership/municipal-and-subnational/municipal-public-private-partnership-framework; *Examples of Successful Public- Private Partnerships (Vol. 15)*, Special Unit for South-South Cooperation, United Nations Development Program. 2008, http://tcdc2.undp.org/GSSDAcademy/SIE/Docs/Vol15/6Philippines.pdf; Art Smith, "PPP Contract Models and Enabling Environment," Masterclass Presentation, Geneva, July 7, 2014, www.unece.org/fileadmin/DAM/ceci/documents/2014/PPP_Materclass/Day1_Art_Smith.pdf; "The Mandaluyong Market, Philippines," ESCAP, 2008, www.unescap.org/ttdw/ppp/ppp_primer/96_the_mandaluyong_market_philippines.html; "Summary of Mandaluyong City Market Rebuilding on a BOT Basis (UNDP)," PPP LRC, World Bank Group, 2016, https://ppp.worldbank.org/public-private-partnership/library/summary-mandaluyong-city-market-rebuilding-bot-basis-undp; "Mandaluyong City, Philippines: Case Study (Public Buildings)," Esc Pau, n.d., www.esc-pau.fr/ppp/documents/featured_projects/philippines_mandaluyong_city.pdf.

[80] See, for example, Majadahonda's Puerta de Hierro Hospital, Madrid, Spain, www.thegpsc.org/sites/gpsc/files/project_summaries_part_2_0_0.pdf.

> **Box 3.10 City bus terminal, Sheberghan, Afghanistan (2013)**
>
> To fund the construction of a new bus terminal in Sheberghan, the private partner in the PPP agreed to construct sixteen municipality-owned shops adjacent to the terminal and lease them from the municipality at no cost for five years. This period was deemed sufficient for the private partner to recover its capital investment plus a reasonable return by subleasing the premises, which included a restaurant, modern toilets, a canopy, and other retail stores. After the initial five-year period, the private developer agreed to make lease payments to the municipality, which the municipality planned to use for reconstruction projects throughout the city.[81]

a seven-acre (204,386 square meter) mixed-use development space for four office buildings, one residential structure with retail facilities at the ground floor, parking facilities with four underground levels and a capacity of 1,146 vehicles, and green space.[82]

Strong political support, community engagement, and proper planning are critical success factors for commercial and retail development. It is often the private sector that has more adequate human and technical resources to drive project development to achieve planning goals (see Box 3.10).[83] Designing a structure that allocates risks between the contracting authority and the project company in the most effective manner requires a thorough understanding of the redevelopment, the local community, and the likely economic and financial outcomes of the redevelopment (see Box 3.11).

Redevelopment projects may offer an enticing prospect but with so many challenges and uncertainties that private sector involvement in early stages may be unattractive or uneconomic. Building momentum with initial public redevelopment projects can attract investors for future-linked/adjacent projects (see Box 3.12).[84]

Governments are often overly optimistic about the value that can be unlocked from real estate opportunities that emerge from such redevelopment projects (see Box 3.14). At the project development stage, it is important to get realistic as well as worst-case scenarios of the unlocked real estate value from such redevelopment projects, to make sure government does not get caught up in unrealistic expectations (see Box 3.15).

---

[81] USAID, "Sheberghan Bus Terminal Includes Two Public-Private Partnerships," ICMA, n.d., https://icma.org/documents/sheberghan-bus-terminal-includes-two-public-private-partnerships; "Modern Bus Station to Be Established in Sheberghan," Wadsam, 2013, https://wadsam.com/afghan-business-news/modern-bus-station-to-be-established-in-sheberghan-343/.
[82] World Bank Municipal PPP Framework, Project Summary 50.
[83] "Handshake Issue #4: Cities & PPPs."
[84] Reuschke, *Public-Private Partnerships in Urban Development in the United States.*

Box 3.11 Commercial and landside operations of I Gusti Ngurah Rai International Airport, Bali, Indonesia (2012)

Bali's airport, the second busiest in Indonesia, had been historically dependent on aeronautical activities, such as passenger service charges and aircraft landing and take-off fees. To increase revenues from nonaeronautical (i.e., landside) commercial operations, the airport operator decided to pursue a PPP with a multinational private company with expertise in the field to prepare, develop, operate, and manage the landside commercial facilities at the airport. The resulting management contract was established on a base fee and an incentive fee-based remuneration structure. After conducting a series of successful tenders for commercial activities at the airport, nonaeronautical revenues increased fifteen times, reflecting an increase from USD 444,000 to USD 6.8 million, and the airport's customer satisfaction score increased from 2.89 to 4.9 (on a scale of 5).[85]

Box 3.12 Modern bus terminal and municipal market, Danli, Honduras (2016)

An unsolicited PPP proposal to improve and expand the Danli bus terminal and municipal market was designed to include 418 commercial stalls, warehouse space, meeting rooms, bus parking, waiting rooms, and ticket stalls at an estimated investment cost of USD 4 million. The project was funded by selling the improved bus terminal spaces to small and medium carriers, as well as by selling commercial stalls to transporters, current tenants, small and medium enterprises, and/or the municipality, both at a price preset by the municipality and included in the PPP agreement.[86]

---

[85] "GVK's Bali International Airport Awards Duty Free and Retail Contracts," Airport World, 2019, www.airport-world.com/news/general-news/2632-gvk-s-bali-international-airport-awards-duty-free-and-retail-contracts.html; "Indonesia," GVK, n.d., www.gvk.com/ourbusiness/airports/iiaindonesia.aspx; "India's GVK Plans Indonesia's First Privately-Built Airport," Global Construction Review, 2016, www.globalconstructionreview.com/7indias-gvk-plans-indo7nesias-fir7st-priva7tely/; Martha Eva Rahayu, "PT Angkasa Pura I: Pendapatan Non-aeronautical Melonjak Hingga Ratusan Kali," SWA, 2015, https://swa.co.id/swa/trends/management/pt-angkasa-pura-pendapatan-non-aeronautical-melonjak-hingga-ratusan-kali; PTI, "GVK Calls Tenders for Services Contracts at Bali Airport," The Economic Times, May 29, 2013, https://economictimes.indiatimes.com/news/international/gvk-calls-tenders-for-services-contracts-at-bali-airport/articleshow/20332322.cms; Angkasa Pura, "Selesaikan Proyek Bandara I Gusti Ngurah Rai, Angkasa Pura Airports Gandeng Umkm Dan Pengusaha Lokal," Information, 2014, https://ap1.co.id/en/information/news/detail/selesaikan-proyek-bandara-i-gusti-ngurah-rai--angkasa-pura-airports-gandeng--umkm-dan-pengusaha-lokal; IBNS, "GVK Hands Over Bali Airport Project Contracts," Sify News, May 13, 2013, www.sify.com/news/gvk-hands-over-bali-airport-project-contracts-news-default-nfnxpoeecbfsi.html.

[86] Vatsala Shrangi, "Delhi's Hi-Tech Ghost Parking Lots," DNA News, January 21, 2017, www.dnaindia.com/india/report-delhi-s-hi-tech-ghost-parking-lots-2294616; "DLF & NDMC

Commercial and property development opportunities at terminal stations can be particularly important. In Hong Kong Special Administrative Region (SAR), China, the mass rapid transit system not only pays for itself through commercial revenues but it also provides a revenue stream for the Hong Kong government (see Box 3.13).[87]

Box 3.13 Hong Kong Mass Transit Railway Corporation, Hong Kong SAR, China (1995)

When planning a new railway line, the publicly owned Mass Transit Railway Corporation in the densely populated city of Hong Kong prepares a master plan to assess the potential for property developments along the railway line. It then purchases the development rights from the public administration at a price that takes no account of any rises in value expected to result from the transport project. The corporation then publicly tenders these rights to private developers, with an additional land premium that includes the projected added value from the planned railway expansion. Generating profits from both the transit system and its real estate business has allowed the corporation to be highly profitable and operate without public subsidies.[88]

Box 3.14 Amritsar Intercity Bus Terminal, Punjab, India (2004)

A PPP was awarded to rehabilitate and expand the Amritsar bus terminal, permitting the private concessionaire to derive revenues from several ancillary sources, in addition to tariffs paid by buses for using the facility. In the event, the buses chose to stop outside of the terminal to avoid paying tariffs. The PPP was renegotiated to provide additional revenue streams from commercial leases for retail shops, sale of advertising space, and parking fees.[89]

Launch 'Capitol Point', Multi-Level Car Park at C.P," Parking Network, 2012, www.parking-net.com/parking-news/dlf-ndmc-launch-capitol-point-multi-level-car-park-at-c-p; "Urban Infrastructure," DSC Limited, n.d., www.dsclimited.com/dev/index.php?modepage=57&m=8&c=18; "Connaught Place in Delhi Gets Its First Automatic Multi-level Parking Complex," *India Today*, 2012, www.indiatoday.in/india/north/story/connaught-place-delhi-first-automatic-multi-level-parking-complex-105505-2012-06-13; "At Rs. 10 Per Hour, Connaught Place Gets Its First Multi-level Parking Lot," *Hindustan Times*, June 13, 2012, www.hindustantimes.com/delhi-news/at-rs-10-per-hour-connaught-place-gets-its-first-multi-level-parking-lot/story-sXqIMhPjCOyWizvhKgTh6M.html; NDMC, "New Delhi's Municipal Council's Smart Parking RFP," NDMC, 2016, http://smartcities.gov.in/upload/tender/58a149148b320RFP-SMART-PARKING.pdf.

[87] World Bank Municipal PPP Framework, Project Summary 2, https://ppp.worldbank.org/public-private-partnership/municipal-and-subnational/municipal-public-private-partnership-framework.

[88] Mathieu Verougstraete and Han Zeng. *Land Value Capture Mechanism: The Case of the Hong Kong MTR* (ESCAP, 2014), https://repository.unescap.org/handle/20.500.12870/3895.

[89] Coalianza, "Proyecto 'Terminal de buses y plaza comercial municipal, Danlí – El Paraíso'," n.d., http://app.sisocs.org/index.php?r=ciudadano/FichaTecnica&control=Contratacion&id=13.

3.4 *A CVC Menu*

> **Box 3.15 Bus terminal-cum-commercial complex, Mohali, India (2012)**
>
> Public authorities wanted to pursue a PPP for the design, construction, operation, and transfer of a new bus terminal to meet Mohali's growing transportation demands. As the terminal facility alone, however, was not viewed as commercially desirable enough to attract investors, the project design incorporated the development of adjacent commercial facilities to increase its financial viability. The project design, considered to be the first-of-its-kind "busopolis" in India, included three main facilities: a bus terminal with passenger amenities and retail space, a hotel, and a commercial office tower. Hotel operations and the sale, long-term lease, or rental of commercial developments for retail and office space were expected to provide substantial additional revenue for the concessionaire.[90]

3.4.6 Parking

Rapid growth has its challenges, including the proliferation of vehicles and urban congestion. Parking in major urban centers is often a key challenge for municipalities looking to reduce congestion and free up space at street level.[91]

Public parking offers a number of commercial opportunities from parking fees and from development rights within and above the parking facility (see Box 3.16). Parking has the added advantage of not needing natural light. Underground space is ideal for parking and is often not thoroughly exploited when land is developed, in particular for public facilities. Parking fees can be fixed or variable depending on the amount of time spent in the facility. The mechanisms to collect parking fees can vary from self-payment kiosks or in-person assisted payment to basic parking meters. Parking garages can utilized for public use and to support residential units at the same time (see Box 3.17).

A parking garage was built in the center of Dar es Salaam, Tanzania, with office space and a commercial shopping center built above and around the

---

[90] SBI Capital Markets, "PPP in Urban Transport Infra," *Infrastructure Today*, January 2011, www.candcinfrastructure.com/images/PPP%20in%20Urban%20Transport%20Infra.pdf; Government of India Department of Economic Affairs, Database of Infrastructure Projects in India, www.pppinindia.gov.in/infrastructureindia/web/guest/home; Harmaneep Singh, "Mohali Terminal Chairman Booked for Duping Buyers," *Times of India*, February 27, 2019, https://timesofindia.indiatimes.com/city/chandigarh/mohali-terminal-chairman-booked-for-duping-buyers/articleshow/68195418.cms; "Mohali ISBT: Dream Project of Former Deputy CM Proved a Failure," *Rozana Spokesman*, October 23, 2017, www.rozanaspokesman.com/news/punjab/mohali-isbt-dream-project-of-former-deputy-cm-proved-a-failure.html.

[91] Public-Private Partnership Legal Resource Center, The World Bank Group, https://ppp.worldbank.org/public-private-partnership/municipal-parking; Bureau of Transportation, "Portland Parking Analysis and Toolkit for Mixed-Use Centres and Corridors Parking Management Toolkit," City of Portland, 2016, www.portlandoregon.gov/transportation/article/567030.

> **Box 3.16 Automated multilevel car park, Connaught Place, New Delhi, India (2012)**
>
> A private partner was awarded a thirty-year concession to design, finance, construct, and operate an automated multilevel car park to reduce congestion at one of the city's busiest public markets, Connaught Place. The estimated USD 17.1 million project cost and USD 31,325 in annual lease payments payable by the concessionaire to the municipality were funded by leasing commercial units and office space built into the car park's first two floors, in addition to parking fees.[92]

> **Box 3.17 Parking in Chicago**
>
> In 2008, Chicago agreed to lease the city's parking meters through a seventy-five-year concession agreement for the operation of the city's 36,000 parking meters to a consortium led by Morgan Stanley Infrastructure Partners. Although the city received USD 1.15 billion upfront, with sixty-one years remaining, the company (Chicago Parking Meters LLC) has not only recouped its entire investment but has also collected an additional USD 502.5 million. It is estimated that the city's drivers will pay the consortium at least USD 11.6 billion to park at meters over the life of the contract, revenue that the city would otherwise have received.[93]

parking structure. The commercial facilities earned important revenue for the project and allowed the operator to charge only modest parking fees, which helped the contracting authority to reduce congestion.[94]

A PPP parking project in Peru's capital city, Lima, reduced traffic congestion in a highly commercial area by providing parking spaces under an existing public park. The three-story underground facility provides more than 9,000 square meters for 353 vehicle spaces and about 5,200 square meters for commercial areas. Revenues from the project also fund the refurbishment and maintenance of the public park (see Box 3.18).[95]

---

[92] "Acuerdo de Concejo N 057-2018," "Acuerdo de Concejo N 004-2016," Acuerdo de Concejo N 018-2015, "Iniciativas Privadas," Municipalidad de San Borja, n.d., http://website.msb.gob.pe/index.php/component/search/?searchword=ecopark&ordering=&searchphrase=all.
[93] See more in https://ppp.worldbank.org/public-private-partnership/library/chicago-metered-parking-system-concession-of-2008.
[94] World Bank Municipal PPP Framework, https://ppp.worldbank.org/public-private-partnership/municipal-and-subnational/municipal-public-private-partnership-framework.
[95] World Bank Municipal PPP Framework, Project Summary 27, https://ppp.worldbank.org/public-private-partnership/municipal-and-subnational/municipal-public-private-partnership-framework.

3.4 A CVC Menu

> **Box 3.18 Underground parking and commercial services center, San Borja, Peru (2018)**
>
> A private partner agreed to design, finance, build, operate, maintain, and transfer a facility comprising 14,320 square meters of underground space in a commercial center of the city, helping alleviate the area's significant deficit in public parking. Given the space constraints the parking center would be located below a public park and the completed facility was designed to include space for commercial enterprises, such as banks and pharmacies (5,180 square meters), in addition to 353 parking spaces (9,160 square meters). The inclusion of the commercial spaces would help create additional revenue streams, while also making the project more attractive to end-users, who could benefit from the conveniently located services.[96]

In Virginia Beach, United States, a PPP project turned a little-used 244-vehicle capacity parking lot into 147 residential apartments, a unique indoor skydiving facility, and a public parking garage with 377 spots. The residential building provides parking to its tenants in the public parking garage.[97]

Integral planning, proper land/space management, and community engagement are key elements for successful public parking projects (see Box 3.19).[98] Public parking facilities reduce congestion by moving vehicles out of on-street parking and into the parking facility. This will work only to the extent that vehicles are incentivized to use the parking facility. If the rates charged in the public parking garage are too high, or if the municipality does not enforce parking restrictions on the street, the parking project will not achieve its goals and may not be financially viable (see Box 3.20).

The provision of commercial activities in and around a parking garage can create additional congestion and increase the number of parking spaces needed.

---

[96] Underground Parking and Commercial Services Centre, San Borja, Peru; Parking Area under Rivera Navarrete Avenue, San Isidro, Peru.

[97] World Bank Municipal PPP Framework, Project Summary 53, https://ppp.worldbank.org/public-private-partnership/municipal-and-subnational/municipal-public-private-partnership-framework.

[98] Examples of parking projects include Underground Parking and Commercial Services Centre, San Borja, Peru, www.thegpsc.org/sites/gpsc/files/45._underground_parking_and_commercial_services_center_san_borja_peru.pdf; Parking Area under Rivera Navarrete Avenue, San Isidro, Peru, www.thegpsc.org/sites/gpsc/files/46._parking_area_under_rivera_navarrete_avenue_san_isidro_peru.pdf; Pike Place Market, Seattle, United States, www.thegpsc.org/sites/gpsc/files/39._pike_place_market_seattle_united_states.pdf; Automated Multi-level Car Park, Connaught Place, New Delhi, India, www.thegpsc.org/content/automated-multi-level-car-park-connaught-place-new-delhi-india; Queen Elizabeth II Medical Centre Car Parking Project, Western Australia, Australia, www.wa.gov.au/system/files/2020-01/qeii-medical-centre-car-parking-project-project-summary.pdf; Multi-level Car Park, Thimphu City, Bhutan, www.thegpsc.org/sites/gpsc/files/48._multi-level_car_park_thimphu_city_bhutan.pdf.

> **Box 3.19 Parking area under Rivera Navarrete Avenue, San Isidro, Peru (2016)**
>
> A PPP was established to design, finance, build, operate, and maintain a three-story underground parking area in the financial center of Peru, which was struggling with a severe deficit in public parking and high levels of congestion. Due to space constraints, the project would be built below four blocks of the main thoroughfare in the financial center, with funding for the USD 25 million in investment costs derived principally from parking fees collected over the thirty-year concession term.[99]

> **Box 3.20 Multilevel car park, Thimphu City, Bhutan (2014)**
>
> A PPP was competitively awarded to a consortium that undertook to design, develop, finance, operate, and maintain two multilevel car parks located at either end of the city's main road. The two facilities were required to contain at least 550 parking spaces, while commercial facilities would be allowed to occupy 20 percent of the total project area. In addition, the consortium would be responsible for refurbishing, operating, and maintaining about 1,000 existing, off- and on-street public parking spaces in the city center. The private partner was responsible for financing the full cost of the project, as well as paying the city an annual concession fee of USD 230,000. It would earn revenue to recoup its investment entirely from commercial rental income and parking fees.[100]

Therefore, a project design including associated commercial activities needs to achieve a balance between financial feasibility and the incremental number of cars that can fit in the facility.

---

[99] "To the Neighbors of San Isidro and Public Opinion in General," Municipalidad de San Isidro, n.d., http://msi.gob.pe/portal/.

[100] "Public-Private Partnership Stories – Bhutan: Thimphu Parking," International Finance Corporation, The World Bank Group, 2015, www.ifc.org/wps/wcm/connect/5e9b7c12-9e17-47ef-9b53-9b23b9f7919a/PPPStories_Bhutan_ThimphuParking.pdf?MOD=AJPERES&CVID=lHovEoo; Pema Seldon, "Thimpu Thromde to Give Parking Space with One Hand but Takes with Another," *The Bhutanese*, July 21, 2018, https://thebhutanese.bt/thimphu-thromde-to-give-parking-space-with-one-hand-but-takes-with-another/; Karma Cheki, "Multi-level Car Parking to Be Completed by the End of This Year," *Kuensel*, August 15, 2018. www.kuenselonline.com/multi-level-car-parking-to-be-completed-by-the-end-of-this-year/; Phurpa Lhamo, "MKCP at Norzin Lam to Open this Month," *Kuensel*, January 8, 2019. www.kuenselonline.com/mlcp-at-norzin-lam-to-open-this-month/.

3.4 A CVC Menu

3.4.7 Hospitality and Tourism

Hotels, restaurants, cafes, catering, and other hospitality and tourism facilities can bring significant revenues for infrastructure. These commercial activities are particularly profitable when located near or associated with locations or facilities that attract crowds. This can provide a particular opportunity for infrastructure projects that may not themselves generate significant revenues but do attract visitors; for example, nature conservancy and historic, cultural, and sporting facilities provide key economic and social benefits for government but tend to be a heavy fiscal commitment. By developing these facilities in tandem with associated commercial services, the public infrastructure will be developed in a more sustainable and less fiscally costly manner, and visitors will benefit from well-coordinated commercial services, designed to fit well with the infrastructure (see Box 3.21).[101]

Community engagement is of critical importance in these types of projects. Local communities are similarly interested in maintaining local natural resources or key cultural facilities and can be a key partner for any project to help ensure its success and to resolve any conflict with the community that

---

Box 3.21 Jozini Tiger Lodge, South Africa, 2010

Located in the Jozini Municipality, in Northern KwaZulu Natal, the Jozini Tiger Lodge is a partnership between the community and a private sector investor (the Three Cities Hotel), which is responsible for the day-to-day management of the lodge. The community made land available. The National Empowerment Fund (NEF) provided initial working capital of ZAR 28 million as community contribution to the project, on the condition that a large number of employees of the lodge must be locals. The private investors provided the rest of the capital needed for the project. Before the project, the community suffered from poor access to basic infrastructure, unemployment, and poor access to social development. The lodge currently employs a total of seventy-nine staff, of which 80 percent are from the Jozini community. A number of lessons can be learned from this project – in particular, mobilization of community partnerships is key to rural tourism success, and land ownership and security of tenure (licenses and permits) can improve investor appetite.[102]

---

[101] A few examples include Elbphilharmonie, Hamburg, Germany, www.thegpsc.org/sites/gpsc/files/project_summaries_part_2_0_0.pdf; Mixed Use Development, Virginia Beach, Virginia, United States, www.thegpsc.org/sites/gpsc/files/module_15.pdf; Sustainable Housing Project, Turin, Italy, www.thegpsc.org/sites/gpsc/files/project_summaries_part_2_0_0.pdf.

[102] "Tourism Development: Why Local Government Matters," Local Government Tourism Conference Report, National Department of Tourism, Republic of South Africa, 2013.

> **Box 3.22 Protecting nature – Marine sanctuary and forest reserve, Chumbe Island, Tanzania (1994)**
>
> Chumbe Island (a fifty-five-acre island) is a successful self-sustaining marine park and forest reserve, covered by a coral rag forest and bordered by a fringing coral reef, which is home to over 420 fish species and 200 stone coral species. The marine and forest sanctuary is a partnership between a private company, Chumbe Island Coral Park Ltd. (CICP), and the Revolutionary Government of Zanzibar, further to an unsolicited proposal to use revenues generated from ecotourism to cover operational expenses, manage the park, and support environmental education. CICP has a thirty-three-year lease on 5.9 acres of land on the island and a ten-year management and operation contract. The initial capital investment of USD 1.2 million was two-thirds financed privately by the project initiator and one-thirds by academic, environmental, and conservation groups. CICP had to work with seven different government departments before the project was approved and worked hard to gain the support of area fishermen and other local communities.[103]

might arise. The project design and communication to the public need to ensure that the tourism, sports, or cultural attraction is not perceived to have been sold to the private partner (see Box 3.22). It should be as easily accessible to the public and remain as much a part of the community as before.

Providing space to the community for sport and culture facilities can help afford a better life quality, attract more tourism, and create new revenue sources (see Box 3.23).[104] For example, convention centers are often developed next to hotels and shopping centers, where those attending conventions can spend their money. In Bogota, Colombia, a private developer renovated an old coliseum that was being underutilized, mobilizing commercial revenues from hospitality and tourism services as well as providing access to a revitalized cultural facility; today the new venue is one of the most modern arenas in Latin America.[105]

---

[103] Chumbe Island, Tanzania, Coral Park Case Study (Environment) November 2012 article from the United Nations Office for South-South Cooperation, www.esc-pau.fr/ppp/documents/featured_projects/tanzania.pdf; "Chumbe Island, Tanzania, Coral Park," ESC Pau, n.d., www.esc-pau.fr/ppp/documents/featured_projects/tanzania.pdf; World Bank Municipal PPP Framework, Project Summary 35.

[104] See also Delmon, *Public Private Partnerships in Infrastructure*; Public-Private Partnership Legal Resource Center, The World Bank Group; E. R. Akhmetshina, O. A. Ignatjeva, and I. M. Ablaev, "Tendencies and Prospects of Public-Private Partnership Development in the Field of Physical Culture and Sport," *European Research Studies Journal* 20, no. 24 (2017): 422–430, https://core.ac.uk/download/pdf/155235631.pdf.

[105] World Bank Municipal PPP Framework, Project Summary 31, https://ppp.worldbank.org/public-private-partnership/municipal-and-subnational/municipal-public-private-partnership-framework.

3.4 A CVC Menu

> **Box 3.23 Jal Mahal Palace, Jaipur, India**
>
> Jal Mahal is an eighteenth-century pleasure palace located in the middle of a 300-acre lake surrounded by the Nahargarh hills, in the Jaipur–Amer tourist corridor. About 800,000 tourists visit Jaipur every year, including 175,000 foreign nationals.
>
> The lake was an ecological disaster, with the dumping of untreated sewage from the city and general poor upkeep. After several failed attempts at restoration through other means, the government of Rajasthan awarded a nine-nine-year lease for the 100 acres of land encompassing the site. Part of the site was allocated for private commercial development according to agreed parameters to generate revenues to fund the restoration and maintenance of the public space. Most of the lake restoration program has been completed with all requisite environmental approvals.[106]

An art museum in Düsseldorf, Germany, was revitalized through a PPP for its reconstruction, operation, and maintenance, allowing the developer to deliver commercial as well as cultural services.[107]

Historic sites can generate commercial revenues which in turn can mobilize private investments to refurbish and maintain historic and cultural assets (see Box 3.24). An example would be PPP projects for the development of historic palaces in Rajasthan, India, that were falling to ruins due to lack of investment and maintenance. These historic properties were leased to private investors through a competitive process that allowed them to redevelop the properties for commercial purposes, in many cases resorts and hotels. The investors have clear obligations to develop the properties on time, maintain their historic properties, and provide access to the public.[108] In Turkey, the historic Akaretler Row Houses sat dilapidated for years as different government entities tried to coordinate to refurbish the facility but was redeveloped through a PPP providing the local community with jobs and new business opportunities (see Box 3.24).[109]

Ideally, commercial activities should be designed to further bolster the attractiveness of the underlying infrastructure project (see Box 3.25). For example, in commercial activities in nature reserves or safari parks, the project company is incentivized to maintain the natural surroundings as they are directly linked to the profits the project company will make from the commercial

---

[106] www.ilfsindia.com.
[107] World Bank Municipal PPP Framework, Project Summary 33, https://ppp.worldbank.org/public-private-partnership/municipal-and-subnational/municipal-public-private-partnership-framework.
[108] World Bank Municipal PPP Framework, Project Summary 35.
[109] www.thegpsc.org/sites/gpsc/files/project_summaries_part_2_0_0.pdf.

Box 3.24 How level is your playing field?

Akaretler Row Houses, in Istanbul, Turkey, were originally built as housing for palace workers in the nineteenth century. They represent one of the best examples of 1870s civil architecture. Strict regulations for the preservation of historical buildings and extensive procedures for obtaining permits hindered their restoration for many years. To overcome these regulatory and bureaucratic constraints, the General Directorate of Preservation of Cultural and Historical Heritage and the General Directorate of the Turkish Foundation approved a PPP arrangement. In addition to redeveloping the site, the private partner helped to market the area and assumed the management of surrounding public spaces (including a local park). The restoration of 60,000 square meters was completed in 2008, including a luxury hotel with 134 rooms, shops, offices, cafés and restaurants, the Atatürk Museum, and a car park. It has contributed to the creation of new jobs in the area and a rising number of tourists.[110]

Box 3.25 Ecotourism concession in Kruger National Park, South Africa (2001)

In 2001, SANParks signed a ten-year concession with a consortium to outsource the management of eleven restaurants, two shops, and three picnic sites in the Kruger National Park game reserve against a monthly concession fee of approximately 13 percent of its turnover being paid back to the park manager. The national parks manager elected to pursue a PPP to reduce the parks system's dependence on state grants, transfer risks to the private sector, and allow the parks to focus on their core function of wildlife conservation. The concession has resulted in a significant increase in SANParks' profit, an upgrading of restaurants and shops, an improvement in service and quality, the development of skills, and the creation of an incentives program for staff. The concession has not been without its challenges, including staff resistance, due to new conditions of service (improved performance and strict control of stock).[111]

---

[110] "Akaretler Row Houses," Bilgili Holding, n.d., www.bilgiliholding.com/en/projects/mixed-use/akaretler-row-houses.html; Joe Huxley, *Value Capture Finance: Making Urban Development Pay Its Way* (ULI, 2009), http://1jh8wu3evfw z3jruef1p1wj2-wpengine.netdna-ssl.com/wp-content/uploads/sites/127/ULI-Documents/Value-Capture-Finance-Report1.pdf; Guido Licciardi and Rana Amirtahmasebi, *The Economics of Uniqueness* (World Bank, 2012).

[111] Peter Farlam, *Working Together, Assessing Public–Private Partnerships in Africa* (The South African Institute of International Affairs, 2005), www.oecd.org/investment/investmentfordevelopment/34867724.pdf; SAN Parks, "Commercialization & Public-Private Partnerships: A Critical Role for Research," Presentation, Pretoria, 2012, www.sanparks.org/assets/docs/

3.4 A CVC Menu

facilities – if the natural beauty of the area is lost, the tourists will stop coming. Similarly, a hotel next to a convention center will have fewer vacancies if the convention center is used more often.

3.4.8 Vehicle, Logistics, and Other Sector Services

Commercial services may be closely related to the services provided by the infrastructure. For example, infrastructure investments often provide facilities to manage and coordinate transportation modes, such as buses, taxis, and trucks.[112] These facilities help reduce congestion, centralize services for the community, and provide services for passengers, for example, shelter while waiting for transport and a centralized access point. Revenues collected from buses, taxis, and trucks in these terminals are generally limited, often not enough to cover operating costs. Charging high fees for transport operators to use the terminal can create perverse incentives, causing fewer transport operators to use the facility, increasing congestion, and depriving the contracting authority of other benefits to be obtained from the terminal.

A confluence of passengers provides the opportunity to deliver commercial services to those passengers (as discussed earlier) but also provides opportunities for commercial services to the transport entities, the bus, truck, and taxi companies, such as petrol stations, maintenance/repair facilities, vehicle parts, truck/bus parking, lodging, and cafeteria. The development of the modern bus terminal and municipal market in Danli, Honduras, provides a good example of coordinated transport infrastructure and commercial transport service delivery, with the associated reduction in the level of fiscal liability further to the improved commercial viability of the project.[113]

---

parks_kruger/conservation/scientific/noticeboard/science_network_meeting_2012/6-1-varghese.pdf; "Public-Private Partnerships in National Parks to Boost Tourism," Brand South Africa, 2017, https://brandsouthafrica.com/66942/public-private-partnerships-national-parks-boost-tourism/.

[112] "Legal Issues on Public-Private Partnerships for Transport";"The Urban Bus Toolkit," PPIAF, 2007, https://ppp.worldbank.org/public-private-partnership/library/ppiaf-urban-bus-toolkit-2007; "Railway Reform: Toolkit for Improving Rail Sector Performance," PPIAF, 2017, http://documents.worldbank.org/curated/en/529921469672181559/Railway-reform-Toolkit-for-improving-rail-sector-performance; "Toolkit for Public-Private Partnerships in Roads and Highways," PPIAF, 2009, https://ppiaf.org/sites/ppiaf.org/files/documents/toolkits/highwaystoolkit/index.html; "Toolkit for Public-Private Partnerships in Urban Bus Transport – Maharashtra India," Asian Development Bank and Government of India, 2011, https://ppp.worldbank.org/public-private-partnership/library/toolkit-public-private-partnerships-urban-bus-transport-maharashtra-india. This includes case studies and detailed term sheets for different PPP options; "Bus Rapid Transport: Toolkit for Feasibility Studies," Asian Development Bank, 2008, https://ppp.worldbank.org/public-private-partnership/library/bus-rapid-transport-toolkit-feasibility-studies (for medium-size cities in India).

[113] www.thegpsc.org/sites/gpsc/files/5._modern_bus_terminal_and_municipal_market_danli_honduras.pdf.

> **Box 3.26 Hangzhou Bay Bridge, China (2001)**
>
> A PPP was awarded for the financing, construction, operation, maintenance, and transfer of a trans-sea bridge connecting two municipalities. While the primary revenue source for the project was expected to be toll fees, additional income was expected to be generated from hotels, restaurants, gas stations, and a viewing tower located on a platform in the middle of the bridge. Feasibility studies projected a 12.58 percent return on the USD 1.42 billion in investment costs over the thirty-year concession term, though actual returns fell short of these projections, largely due to the construction of a competing facility nearby.[114]

Bus/truck terminal projects require robust consultation processes to understand the context of bus and truck companies, their clients and passengers, their business models, the local community, and the services that can or should be provided in these terminals (see Box 3.26). This consultation process ensures that design, service offerings, and construction methodologies are appropriate, minimize disruption, and avoid resistance from and conflict with key stakeholders.

Infrastructure services may also include those closely associated with the infrastructure; for example, in transport projects the goods transported need to be received, processed, and delivered, making opportunity for cargo handling, warehousing, chillers, dry port facilities, and so on (see Box 3.27). These services can generate important revenues that can be captured by the infrastructure project.

3.4.9 Development Rights

Infrastructure can be considered in a holistic manner, mandating a developer to deliver a larger investment program including commercial, economic, and social assets. Industrial zones can be developed on this basis, with common facilities to improve efficiency and reduce energy and other resource requirements. Revenues from the commercial space then cross-subsidize infrastructure

---

[114] www.thegpsc.org/sites/gpsc/files/16._hangzhou_bay_bridge_china.pdf; Queena Likun Wang, "Case Study on P3 Failures in China: Taking Hangzhou Bay Bridge as an Example," McMaster University, 2016, www.eng.mcmaster.ca/sites/default/files/uploads/case_study_on_p3_failures_in_china_report-likun_wang.pdf; Paul Urio, *Public-Private Partnerships: Success and Failure Factors for In-Transition Countries* (University Press of America, Inc., 2010); Yongjian Ke, Shou Qing Wang, and Albert Chang. "Public- Private Partnerships in China's Infrastructure Development: Lessons Learnt," Paper presented at Changing Roles: New Roles, New Challenges, CIB International Conference, Noordwijk, January 2019.

3.4 A CVC Menu

> **Box 3.27 Slaughterhouse redevelopment, Cagayan de Oro City, Philippines (2004)**
>
> The city's sole slaughterhouse was inadequate to meet the growing demands of the livestock industry, which is at the heart of the local economy. To address this, a PPP was competitively awarded in the form of a twenty-five-year build, operate, and transfer contract with a total investment value of USD 3 million. The project entailed converting the old slaughterhouse into a 2.45-hectare modern abattoir complex containing, inter alia, a slaughterhouse for small and large animals, as well as supporting facilities, such as water treatment, a livestock auction market, a deep well water source, and meat delivery vans. Under the PPP agreement, the private operator pays the city a monthly facility usage fee in exchange for the right to operate the expanded facility. The revenue to pay this fee and recover the private partner's investment is derived from the fees collected from the varied users of the expanded multipurpose facility.[115]

investments (see Box 3.28). The developer can capture value through land or property rentals, betterment fees, impact fees, and other mechanisms designed to capture the value added of the developer and the magnitude of the development (where symbiotic investments into different parts of the development create in aggregate a more significant investment opportunity). Lease payment and/or upfront fees tend to be higher for serviced plots of land and prime locations, making space under master developers more valuable and better value for money.[116]

---

[115] Republic of the Philippines, "Redevelopment of the CDO City Slaughterhouse PPP Project," Public-Private Partnership Center, 2017, https://ppp.gov.ph/press_releases/redevelopment-of-the-cdo-city-slaughterhouse-project/; G. E. Potutan, W. H. Schnitzler, J. M. Arnado, L. G. Janubas, and R. J. Holmer, *Urban Agriculture in Cagayan De Oro: A Favorable Response of City Government and NGOs* (DSE, 2000), www.ruaf.org/sites/default/files/Cagayan_1_1.PDF; ADB. *Philippines: Public-Private Partnerships by Local Government Units* (ADB, 2016); www.thegpsc.org/sites/gpsc/files/41._slaughterhouse_redevelopment_cagayan_de_oro_city_philippines.pdf; www.adb.org/sites/default/files/publication/213606/philippines-ppp-lgus.pdf.

[116] Examples of infrastructure supported by development rights include Hong Kong Mass Transit Railway Corporation, Hong Kong SAR, China, www.thegpsc.org/content/hong-kong-mass-transit-railway-corporation-hong-kong-sar-china; Durban Point Waterfront Development Project, eThekwini, South Africa, https://ppp.worldbank.org/public-private-partnership/sites/ppp.worldbank.org/files/2020-02/World%20Bank_Municipal%20PPP_Project%20Summaries%20Part%202%20%287Sept%29_Content.pdf; Redevelopment of Library and Fire Station, Washington, DC, United States, https://sra.gov.in/dashboard; Slum Rehabilitation Scheme, Maharashtra, India, www.thegpsc.org/sites/gpsc/files/project_summaries_part_2_0_0.pdf; Hudson Yards Air Rights Monetization, New York, United States, www.gihub.org/innovative-funding-and-financing/case-studies/hudson-yards-air-rights-monetisation/; Financing Transportation Infrastructure through Sale of Land and Development Rights,

> **Box 3.28 Using development rights to acquire land for infrastructure projects in dense urban areas, Porto Alegre, Rio Grande do Sul, Brazil (2004)**
>
> The municipality planned to build a new transit artery connecting twenty neighborhoods across the city, including dedicated lanes for the bus rapid transit service, but the required land was mostly privately owned and public funding for land acquisition was limited. To address this, the municipality acquired 13.2 hectares of necessary land by compensating owners with development rights elsewhere in the city. Depending on the estimate, transferring development rights reduced land acquisition costs by between 50 percent and 65 percent overall compared to traditional acquisition methods. Ultimately, the municipality was able to complete the project, including the envisioned bus rapid transit system, at a reduced cost compared to benchmarks and forecasts due to innovative use of development rights. In addition, reaching mutual agreements with residents on transferable development rights, rather than expropriating property outright, reduced the number of lawsuits and other bureaucratic obstacles to construction.[117]

An example of a large master development might be a tourism development project, where government sets aside a large plot of land and provides a concession to a master developer. Under the master concession the master developer is required to provide common infrastructure (e.g., electricity, water, solid waste management, sewerage, roads, port/jetty, airfield). The master concessionaire then leases plots to hotels, restaurants, residential property developments, harbor services, parking, and so on. A master concession can deliver large-scale investments more quickly and efficiently, reducing costs and helping small and medium commercial investments blossom in and around the large/anchor investors. The master concessionaire will often be selected at least partially on its ability to bring large/anchor investors to such a development (see Box 3.29). Common infrastructure can be more efficient, have less climate impact, and deliver services to local communities. The government will want to be clear with the master concessionaire on its expectations as to the nature and quality of these common services to avoid misunderstandings and conflict later.

Copenhagen, Denmark, www.dlapiperrealworld.com/export/sites/real-world/guides/downloads/Denmark-Investment-Guide.pdf; Using Development Rights to Acquire Land for Infrastructure Projects in Dense Urban Areas, Rio Grande do Sul, Brazil, https://documents.worldbank.org/en/publication/documents-reports/documentdetail/725111468227648160/brazil-bage-rio-grande-do-sul-integrated-municipal-development-program.

[117] Global Infrastructure Hub, "Using Development Rights to Acquire Land for Infrastructure Projects in Dense Urban Areas, Porto Alegre, Rio Grande do Sul, Brazil," Case Studies, 2014, www.gihub.org/innovative-funding-and-financing/case-studies/using-development-rights-to-acquire-land-for-infrastructure-projects-in-deep-dives-dense-urban-areas/.

3.4 A CVC Menu

> **Box 3.29 Slum rehabilitation scheme, Maharashtra, India (1995)**
> A PPP scheme invited private developers to invest in slum rehabilitation projects in return for extra floor square index, which meant that any extra units constructed on the project site could be sold at market price, with the private developer retaining the full proceeds of these sales. This was designed to allow the private developers to cross-subsidize new affordable units with the sale of surplus units at market rates. In addition, the scheme operated on the basis of transferable development rights (TDR), which would allow developers to transfer a portion of the surplus development rights provided under the rehabilitation scheme to any other sites in the city, which were many times more profitable than the sites in need of rehabilitation. However, the PPP did not realize all the projected results, in part due to the collapse of the Mumbai real estate market in the 2000s, which created an unstable market for the TDR – which was supposed to be one of the primary sources of revenue for the private developers.[118]

Monetizing development rights is most effective when it is part of a larger master plan that addresses developmental and commercial needs. This will help purchasers of development rights appreciate the key economic growth drivers and coordinated planning surrounding the infrastructure investment (see Box 3.30). Investors will also need to understand government commitment to these master plans and whether it will pursue rigorously the associated infrastructure investments and development projects to achieve the impact and potential of the masterplan. It can be challenging for government to demonstrate its commitment; policy statements help, as do regulations and decrees, but these commitments are often easily unwound by future governments. Laws or other more significant legal commitments can be more sustainable. A significant investment by government in funding for the master development will be an important indicator, as is extensive engagement with local communities. Where local residents, businesses, and industries are consulted and supportive of the development, the master plan is more likely to survive political and economic change.

[118] Rohit Jagdale, "An Overview of Slum Rehabilitation Schemes in Mumbai, India," Repositories, 2014, https://repositories.lib.utexas.edu/bitstream/handle/2152/26620/JAGDALE-MASTERSREPORT-2014.pdf?sequence=1&isAllowed=y; Shrabana Mukherjee and Omkar Raut, "Assessment of Slum Rehabilitation Scheme: A Case Study of Pune, Maharashtra," *Journal of Applied Management – Jidnyasa* 9, no. 1 (2017): 54–66, https://doi.org/10.22214/ijraset.2019.5554; David E. Spicer and Howard Husock, "Financing Slum Rehabilitation in Mumbai: A Non-profit Caught in the Middle," Kennedy School of Government, 2003, www.careinstitute.org/wp-content/uploads/2011/03/03-Financing-Slum-Rehabilitation-in-Mumbai-A-Non-Profit-Caught-in-the-Middle-Case-Study.pdf; "Opinion: India's Failure to Address Its Urban Slum Problem," *Live Mint*, October 23, 2018, www.livemint.com/Opinion/AhwjNLTtMS8GK7i1RBqnSI/Opinion--Indias-failure-to-address-its-urban-slum-problem.html.

> **Box 3.30 Croydon Council Urban Regeneration Vehicle**
>
> The Croydon Council Urban Regeneration Vehicle is a twenty-eight-year joint venture with the aim of regenerating a portfolio of key sites across the London Borough of Croydon in the United Kingdom. The project involves the investment of land by Croydon Council, with John Laing investing equity and providing development expertise. The partnership includes 2.2 hectares, 1,250 homes, and 2 forty-story towers to house 650 residential units (private and affordable).[119]

3.4.10 Infrastructure Sharing

Governments can be proactive in identifying opportunities to use the land acquired or rights of way obtained for an infrastructure project to provide access to other infrastructure, for example, through the construction of a common utility tunnel alongside a railway line, power transmission lines, or water pipes.[120] Utility providers can pay for access to these tunnels upfront to help defray the cost of construction or periodically to provide an additional revenue stream for the infrastructure project (see Box 3.31). Infrastructure sharing can include telecoms, power and water transmission, central heating and cooling delivery, sewerage, solid waste management, and power generation (e.g., rooftop solar), among others (see Box 3.32).

Rooftop solar projects generally involve the contracting authority paying fees for energy or efficiencies delivered. The project company will need to be confident that the contracting authority will pay fees when due. In some cases, this may require a guaranty, escrow arrangement, or other credit enhancement.

Rooftop solar can be an interesting opportunity for the contracting authority to take more control of its power needs, in particular where the cost of power to be purchased from rooftop solar is cheaper than power purchased from the

---

[119] Capital Strategy 2010–2030, Croydon Observatory, www.londoncouncils.gov.uk/node/5024; https://ppp.worldbank.org/public-private-partnership/sites/ppp.worldbank.org/files/2020-02/World%20Bank_Municipal%20PPP_Project%20Summaries%20Part%202%20%287Sept%29_Content.pdf.

[120] Some example of case studies include: Moncloa Transportation Exchanger, Madrid, Spain, www.thegpsc.org/sites/gpsc/files/1._moncloa_transportation_exchanger_madrid_spain.pdf; Integral Treatment of Wastewater and Bio-solids, Municipality of Saltillo, Mexico, www.mdpi.com/2071-1050/11/8/2217/pdf; Industrial Water Supply, Surat Municipal Corporation, India, www.thegpsc.org/sites/gpsc/files/26._industrial_water_supply_surat_municipal_corporation_india.pdf; IT Network Integration, Barcelona, Spain, www.thegpsc.org/sites/gpsc/files/31._it_network_integration_barcelona_spain.pdf; www.iese.edu/wp-content/uploads/2019/03/ST-0445-E.pdf; Smart Poles and Streetlights, Bhopal, Madhya Pradesh, India, www.thegpsc.org/sites/gpsc/files/36._smart_poles_and_streetlights_bhopal_madhya_pradesh_india.pdf; Solar Leasing to Reduce Port Emissions, Singapore, www.gihub.org/innovative-funding-and-financing/case-studies/solar-leasing-to-reduce-port-emissions/.

3.4 A CVC Menu

> ### Box 3.31 Rooftop solar program, Gujarat, Gandhinagar, India (2012)
>
> Two private developers were selected through a tariff-based competitive bidding process for installing photovoltaic panels on government buildings and private residences in Gandhinagar, and each were allocated the development of 2.5 megawatts of rooftop solar power. The private developers agreed to design, finance, install, operate, and maintain the required solar energy infrastructure for twenty-five years, recovering their capital investment and operating costs by selling the power generated by the solar installations to an offtaker for distribution to end-users. The municipality agreed to provide sufficient space on government buildings to accommodate 80 percent of the required installations, accounting for four megawatts of generation, while the project developers needed to secure additional space on private residences to produce the remaining one megawatt.[121]

> ### Box 3.32 Durban Point Waterfront development project, eThekwini, South Africa (2018)
>
> The Durban Point Waterfront lies at the entrance to Durban Harbor, which is among the busiest ports in Africa. However, the waterfront was largely abandoned and only used by a relatively small community of people. To optimize the use of this space, the municipality entered a joint venture with a private consortium to undertake a USD 2.5 billion redevelopment of this underutilized space. The planned mixed-use development would be conducted in three stages over ten years, spanning six distinct precincts. To date, the municipality has invested about USD 8 million to upgrade infrastructure on the project site and has sold land valued at about USD 13 million to private developers, which has helped facilitate about USD 71 million in privately financed construction.[122]

---

[121] World Bank Municipal PPP Framework, Project Summary 41, https://ppp.worldbank.org/public-private-partnership/municipal-and-subnational/municipal-public-private-partnership-framework.

[122] "Special Zone 91 – Point Waterfront," eThekwini Municipality, n.d., www.durban.gov.za/City_Services/development_planning_management/Land_Use_Management/Town_Planning_Regulations/Special_Zones/Pages/Point_Waterfront.aspx; "Background Report on the Durban Point Development with Emphasis on the Proposed Small Craft Harbour," Pravinamar, 2007, www.pravinamar.com/reports/downloads/small_craft_harbour/BRDPDC.pdf; Tozi Mthethwa, "Beachfront Promenade Extension to Support Point Waterfront Development," eThekwini Municipality, 2018, www.durban.gov.za/Resource_Centre/Press_Releases/Pages/Beachfront-Promenade-Extension-to-Support-Point-Waterfront-Development.aspx; "A Transformational Waterfront Urban Development," UEM Sunrise Introduction, n.d., https://uemsunrise.com/property/region/durban-point; "Home Page," Durban Point Waterfront Company, 2019, www.durbanpoint.co.za/.

> **Box 3.33 Energy-efficient street lighting, Bhubaneswar, Odisha, India (2013)**
>
> A PPP was awarded to finance and install energy-efficient street lighting, as well as operate and maintain the city's street lighting system by way of a remote-control center covering 20,000 streetlights in Bhubaneswar. With the installation of the energy-efficient lighting system, the municipality was expected to realize annual savings of around USD 100,000. The private company would be entitled to a regular monthly fee from the municipality, defined as 90 percent of its energy cost savings, plus a flat operation and maintenance fee for each light pole.[123]

grid. In some cases, the lower price of solar is achieved through government subsidies for the use of renewable energy. The contracting authority will need to consider the risk that these subsidies might be withdrawn by the government.

3.4.11 Cost Reductions

When developing infrastructure, there may be an opportunity to attract revenues by reducing costs, for example, by replacing local street lighting with LED to reduce energy costs. Street lighting can be an energy-intensive and expensive service for the contracting authority to provide. Latest technology in lightbulbs and energy management provide even more of an opportunity for private investment in street lighting. The savings can be shared between the two partners according to agreed percentages. For example, in Nashik, Maharashtra, India, a PPP contract provides for different sharing percentages depending on the year of the contract.[124]

Street lighting investment can result in the total cost of street lighting increasing because (a) a larger number of streetlights are installed and (b) more streetlights are operational (see Box 3.33). This means that while energy cost per streetlight is lower, total energy usage may be higher. Project analysis should

---

[123] "Public-Private Partnership Stories, India: Bhubaneswar Street Lighting," The World Bank Group, 2013, https://ppp.worldbank.org/public-private-partnership/sites/ppp.worldbank.org/files/documents/PPP_Stories_India_Bhubaneswar_Street_Lighting_EN_2013.pdf; "Odisha Public Street Lighting," Private Infrastructure Development Group, n.d., www.pidg.org/project/odisha-public-street-lighting/; Jeffrey Delmon, "Municipal PPP," Presentation on Municipal PPPs, Washington, DC, n.d., https://slideplayer.com/slide/4895501/; "Bhubaneswar Street Lighting Goes Smart – Now Can Be Controlled via Control Room Computer," *Bhubaneswar Buzz*, July 21, 2015, www.bhubaneswarbuzz.com/updates/infrastructure/bhubaneswar-street-lighting-goes-smart-now-can-be-controlled-via-control-room-computer.

[124] World Bank Municipal PPP Framework, Project Summary 42, https://ppp.worldbank.org/public-private-partnership/municipal-and-subnational/municipal-public-private-partnership-framework.

3.4 *A CVC Menu* 77

> **Box 3.34 Street lighting project, Nasik, Maharashtra, India (2004)**
>
> A private company was appointed to deliver the first Energy Saving Company (ESCO) project to be implemented in Maharashtra state on a shared-savings basis, which entailed upgrading existing street lighting facilities. Under an Energy Services Agreement, and following a build, operate, and transfer project structure, the private company agreed to design, manufacture, supply, erect, commission, and maintain 486 streetlight controllers at various lighting stations, covering about 19,000 streetlights, at an estimated cost of USD 290,200. The company guarantees a minimum of 25 percent in energy savings to the municipality from these installations. To recoup its investment in installing the controllers, cover its operation and maintenance costs, and obtain a reasonable return on investment, the company is entitled to a fixed and predetermined share of the municipality's energy cost savings for a period of five years, at the conclusion of which the ownership and control of the installations would transfer to the municipality. The value of the savings achieved totaled USD 232,170 per year and the average energy cost savings per year was 31 percent, with peak savings for some subsections reaching as high as 44 percent. This was reported to be the first energy savings company project in India to be implemented under the concept of sharing basis and has since served as a model for other municipalities in the country.[125]

incorporate the social and economic benefits of better street lighting rather than only the financial saving in energy costs (see Box 3.34).[126]

The financial rewards of switching to electric vehicles (EVs) can be substantial, even considering the upfront 70–80 percent cost premium compared with fossil-fueled vehicles. EVs are less expensive to run and maintain than two-wheeled scooters and diesel buses. Lower maintenance costs alone can amount to a significant saving over the life of the EV. An assessment of the cost of fuel

---

[125] "Compendium on Public Private Partnership in Urban Infrastructure," Smart Cities Mission, Ministry of Urban Development, Government of India, n.d., http://smartcities.gov.in/upload/uploadfiles/files/Compendium_of_PPP_CasesMoUDs.pdf; "Public Private Partnership in Street Lighting in Nashik, Maharashtra," Centre for Innovations in Public Systems, n.d., www.cips.org.in/documents/DownloadPDF/downloadpdf.php?id=232&category=Urban+Governance.

[126] Other examples, include Smart Poles and Streetlights, Bhopal, Madhya Pradesh, India, www.thegpsc.org/sites/gpsc/files/36._smart_poles_and_streetlights_bhopal_madhya_pradesh_india.pdf; Street Lighting Project, Nasik, Maharashtra, India, www.thegpsc.org/sites/gpsc/files/project_summaries_part_2_0_0.pdf; Energy-Efficient Street Lighting, Bhubaneswar, Odisha, India, https://ppp.worldbank.org/public-private-partnership/library/ppp-stories-india-bhubaneswar-street-lighting; SOFIAC – Energy Efficiency Turnkey Solutions, Canada, https://sofiac.ca/en/; Sembcorp Tengeh Floating Solar Farm, Singapore; SolarNova Rooftop Solar Program, Singapore, and EV Charging Infrastructure, India.

versus electricity may be complicated by subsidy and tax regimes provided by many low- and middle-income countries (LMICs) for gasoline and electricity.

3.4.12 Additional Offtake from the Facility

In some cases, infrastructure is able to generate additional offtake; for example, a solid waste management plant can also generate compost, recyclable materials, refuse derived fuel, waste to energy, and biofuel and can capture methane (see Box 3.37).[127] Wastewater treatment produces sludge, which can be used for different purposes, including building materials, compost, animal feed, treated water for industrial processes (or even human consumption) and biofuel (see Box 3.35).[128] These additional offtakes may require modification of designs, land allocation, capital, and specialist knowledge from the operator and should therefore be contemplated early in the planning stage and developed in the feasibility study to ensure the best value is obtained from these additional revenues (see Box 3.36).

Box 3.35   Integral treatment of wastewater and biosolids, Municipality of Saltillo, Mexico (2006)

This PPP involved a twenty-year concession for the design, construction, operation, and maintenance of a wastewater treatment plant, funded primarily by periodic payments from the public partner. In 2016, however, the wastewater treatment plant began operating a system for electric and thermic energy cogeneration, which would allow the plant to stop emitting greenhouse gasses (GHGs) and produce the energy needed to run the plant. Furthermore, the plant would begin selling treated water (between one and six liters per second) to three companies.[129]

---

[127] "Bridging the Gap in Solid Waste Management Governance Requirements for Results," World Bank, 2021, https://openknowledge.worldbank.org/bitstream/handle/10986/35703/Bridging-the-Gap-in-Solid-Waste-Management-Governance-Requirements-for-Results.pdf?sequence=6&isAllowed=y; "What a Waste 2.0: A Global Snapshot of Solid Waste Management to 2050," World Bank, 2018, https://datatopics.worldbank.org/what-a-waste/trends_in_solid_waste_management.html.
[128] For further discussion of innovative uses for sludge, some of which may be commercially viable, see www.conserve-energy-future.com/types-uses-methods-sludge.php#:~:text=After%20the%20treatment%20process%2C%20the,powdered%20industrial%20fuel%20and%20electricity; https://ec.europa.eu/environment/archives/waste/sludge/pdf/workshoppart4.pdf; "From Waste to Resource: Shifting Paradigms for Smarter Wastewater Interventions in Latin America and the Caribbean," World Bank, 2020, https://openknowledge.worldbank.org/handle/10986/33436.
[129] MuniAPP, "Asociacion Publico- Privada Entre la Empresa Ideal Saneamiento de Saltillo S.A. de C. V. y el Municipio de Saltillo Coahuila," CCA, 2013, www.cca.org.mx/ps/funcionarios/muniapp/descargas/Documentos_de_apoyo/informaciontematica/

3.4 *A CVC Menu* 79

Box 3.36 Wastewater treatment plant, Udaipur, India (2014)

This unsolicited PPP designed, built, owned, and operated Udaipur's first wastewater treatment plant, to be transferred to the public partner at the conclusion of a twenty-five-year concession. The project was implemented by a zinc mining company to find additional water resources that would reduce its dependence on costly freshwater extraction. The private partner was responsible for fully financing the investment cost of the new treatment plant (estimated at USD 27 million), land acquisition, and construction of the plant and the seventy-eight-kilometer pipeline linking the plant with the industrial complex. The local government financed the pipeline connecting the city's sewerage system with the plant. The treated effluent, amounting to 20,000 cubic meters per day, is used by the company for its mining and smelting operations. However, the company's operations require only 9,500 cubic meters of treated effluent per day, so the excess is used in horticulture or released back into the river. In addition, the plant produces treated manure, amounting to 120 tons per year, which is sold to local farmers. Sales of the treated manure are expected to generate annual revenue of around USD 156,000.[130]

Box 3.37 Bioenergy plant, Nuevo Leon, Mexico (2001)

To reduce the methane gas emissions from a local landfill and leverage the biogas for productive use, the government aimed to construct a biogas plant for converting this byproduct into electrical power. A PPP was competitively awarded, with the primary objective of operating and managing the bioenergy plant adjacent to the landfill (which had been designed and built by a different company). The plant would sell any surplus energy to

---

capp/Saneamiento_Integral_Aguas.pdf; Jussaira R. Paz and Priscilla Delgadilo Diaz, "Asociaciones Publico Privadas (APP's)," Contraloria del Poder Legislativo, 2017, www.contraloriadelpoderlegislativo.gob.mx/pdf/Cursos/A_P_P.pdf; "Arranca Cogeneracion de Energua Electrica y Termica en Planta Tratadora," El Diario, 2016, www.eldiariodecoahuila.com.mx/locales/2016/8/3/arranca-cogeneracion-energia-electrica-termica-planta-tratadora-594631.html; Jose Reyes, "Finalmente sera util la planta tratadora de Saltillo, venderan el agua a empresas de Ramos Arizpe," *Vanguardia*, February 21, 2019, https://vanguardia.com.mx/articulo/finalmente-sera-util-la-planta-tratadora-de-saltillo-venderan-el-agua-a-empresas-de-ramos-arizpe.

[130] "Innovative Public-Private Partnership to Improve Water Quality and Availability, Udaipur, India," Water Scarcity Solutions, 2016, www.waterscarcitysolutions.org/wp-content/uploads/2016/02/A-Innovative-public-private-partnership.pdf; "Sewage Treatment Plant – Hindustan Zinc Limited," India Sanitation Coalition, n.d., www.indiasanitationcoalition.org/resources/Case-Study-Hindustan-Zinc.pdf; "CSR Project by Hindustan Zinc Ltd," CSR Box, n.d., https://csrbox.org/India_CSR_Project_Hindustan-Zinc-Ltd-Sewage-Treatment-Plant-Rajasthan_7398.

seven municipalities and three government agencies. The plant currently supplies almost 60 percent of the energy needed to power the Monterrey Metropolitan Area's public street lighting, public buildings, and drinking water pump, as well as 80 percent of Monterrey's transportation system energy requirements, in addition to covering all its own energy needs.[131]

3.4.13 Beneficiary Contributions, Prepurchase of Services, and Congestion Pricing

Beneficiary contributions, in particular large-scale future beneficiaries of any infrastructure investment, can take many forms. Future beneficiaries wanting to encourage investment may be willing to contribute funds to offset capital costs (see Box 3.38). Such contributions may not be financially or fiscally efficient, and therefore the beneficiary may be willing to provide patient equity contributions, not looking for immediate or any equity return but using the equity contribution as a loss-making tax deduction or otherwise fiscally responsible investment.

The beneficiary may also be willing to prepurchase capacity for the project. For example, in Burundi, in order to anchor an investment in extending the fiber-optic backbone into less affluent and less commercially attractive areas of the country, the government chose to prepurchase capacity on the extended backbone for connectivity of universities, hospitals, and schools (see Box 3.39). The government purchased services, making it easier to justify financial support for the project and also receive value for the funds contributed.[132] The Hong Kong government provided access to land to the Mass Transit Railway Corporation to avoid the fiscal liabilities that would have resulted from a partially publicly funded transport system.[133]

Urban congestion zone charges provide a method for reducing congestion, improving environmental impact, reducing accidents, and creating an additional revenue stream for transit projects in the zone. Congestion pricing in Stockholm has reduced ambient air pollution between 5 percent and 15 percent. This was associated with a significant decrease in acute asthma attacks among children. Seattle has developed a series of community health indicators as part of its congestion pricing plan. For example, the city will monitor changes in pollution and publicize the share of revenues spent on bicycle and pedestrian improvements in vulnerable communities. New York City

---

[131] Fabián Pino Pérez "Caso Monterrey, Nuevo León, México, Adquisición de Energía Renovable," CCA, 2013, www.cca.org.mx/ps/funcionarios/muniapp/descargas/Documentos_de_apoyo/informaciontematica/capp/APP_Bioelectrica.pdf.
[132] www.africaoutlookmag.com/company-profiles/899-burundi-backbone-systems.
[133] www.thegpsc.org/content/hong-kong-mass-transit-railway-corporation-hong-kong-sar-china.

3.4 A CVC Menu

> **Box 3.38 The adopt-a-light project: Report on best practice (Habitat Business Award, 2009)**
>
> A PPP was established between the City Council of Nairobi and Adopt a Light Ltd. with the council providing the legal and political framework, providing advisory support, and paying the electricity bills. The private partner provided materials such as poles, lanterns, high masts, advertising boards, and vehicles; operated an equipped workshop; paid for labor; provided managerial and administrative services; paid for rented office and storage space; developed marketing materials and paid for promotion; and met part of the cost of the electricity consumed for slum and street lighting. The private company also provided start-up capital and commercial loans from commercial banks. The initiative obtains funds from corporate entities, organizations, and individuals who sponsor the installation of light poles or high masts and benefit from having their advertisement hosted on the adopted light pole or mast for a determined period (based on the value of the sponsorship). The project also gets organizations to sponsor the installation of infrastructure, particularly in slums, not necessarily for advertising but as a social service to the community. Funds generated from the renewal of pole/mast adoptions and from sites that are more attractive to advertisers are used to subsidize expansion to other areas.
>
> The initiative has installed 3,000 streetlights along 50 streets covering an estimated 150 kilometers of roads used by millions of motorists and pedestrians daily. It has erected 33 high mast lights in several slums serving over 150,000 households or an approximate population of 500,000 persons. A study conducted by an independent research organization, Steadman Group, in 2006 found that the slum lighting initiative has
>
> - improved security in the slums;
> - enabled business people to extend opening hours and hence improve sales;
> - enabled residents to do certain tasks such as cooking outside at night, thus reducing their expenditure on house lighting;
> - improved social life, with residents able to host visitors for longer hours in the evenings; and
> - improved access to toilets at night, thereby enhancing hygiene and safety.

has estimated congestion pricing will bring over USD 100 million of health cost savings annually. London uses revenue from its congestion pricing program to improve bus service, which serves a disproportionately high number of low-income individuals. London added 300 new buses and bus ridership increased 18 percent in the first year of the program. In Singapore, money

> **Box 3.39 Leveraging property tax to finance transit infrastructure, Vancouver, Canada**
>
> The South Coast British Columbia Transportation Authority (TransLink) is Metro Vancouver's regional transportation authority. TransLink is responsible for planning, financing, and managing the regional transportation system to move people and goods. As part of this mandate, it launched the construction and operation of the Surrey–Newton–Guildford LRT Line and the Millennium Line Broadway LRT Extension, modernization of the Expo-Millennium Line, upgrades to the SkyTrain and Millennium lines, and project development for the Surrey–Langley LRT Line. Funding is being mobilized from all levels of government – federal, provincial, and regional – as well as from the local community through increases in transit fares in 2020 and 2021, an increase in property taxes beginning in 2019, estimated at USD 5.50 per average household, the collection of new commercial revenues (retail, filming, fiber optics) around SkyTrain infrastructure, and a 3 percentage point increase in the parking tax beginning in 2019.[134]

raised from congestion pricing goes into a general fund, which invests in both transit improvements and affordable housing close to transit.[135]

3.5 EMISSIONS REDUCTION CREDITS/OFFSETS

Emission reduction credits (ERCs) provide an intriguing, complex, and growing opportunity to generate revenues for infrastructure. Corporates and governments around the world are making commitments to achieve net-zero emissions (reducing the amount of GHGs produced and increasing the amount of GHGs absorbed by human activity, such that the net sum of GHGs produced is zero) by specific dates. In addition to reducing own emissions and those of associated businesses, suppliers, and service providers, corporates and governments also seek to outsource some of these emissions reductions by purchasing ERCs (sometimes called offsets or carbon credits).

It is possible to generate ERCs by investments/activities that mitigate the amount of GHG emissions (e.g., replacing diesel buses with electric buses using renewable energy) or increasing absorption of GHGs (e.g., by planting more trees or preserving forests that would otherwise be cut down). Infrastructure investments can be designed to mitigate emissions and thereby generate ERCs.

---

[134] www.gihub.org/innovative-funding-and-financing/case-studies/leveraging-property-tax-to-finance-transit-infrastructure/; Translink, Phase Two of the 10-Year Vision 2018–2027 Investment Plan, tenyearvision.translink.ca.
[135] www.sfcta.org/sites/default/files/2020-02/Congestion%20Pricing%20Case%20Studies%20 200213%20-%20London.pdf.

3.5 Emissions Reduction Credits/Offsets

An ERC represents a standard unit to measure emission reductions equivalent to one metric ton of carbon dioxide (tCO$_2$e). An ERC can be sold either in a compliance market or in the voluntary market.[136]

- Compliance carbon markets (CCMs) are regulated systems under national, regional, or provincial authorities that impose restrictions on emissions by companies (and possibly individuals) in that jurisdiction and may allow trading of ERCs to meet those restrictions through an emission trading system (ETS). An ERC is a creature of the relevant CCM. A CCM will have a regulatory body that defines and verifies ERCs, in particular measurement, reporting, and verification (MRV) methodologies and audit processes during the preparation and implementation of the project, to provide certainty to the purchaser that the relevant ERC exists and meets the requirements of the CCM.
- Nonstate actors such as corporations, institutions, and individuals that wish to offset their emissions by purchasing ERCs (e.g., to meet corporate net-zero commitments) but do not need those ERCs to meet any legal obligation can purchase ERCs on the voluntary carbon market (VCM). The VCM is not regulated legally but is monitored closely by nongovernmental organizations, consumers, and shareholders. Since the VCM has no regulatory body, a VCM ERC requires a certification standard, MRV, established and overseen by an authorization entity that is trusted by the eventual purchaser of the ERCs. A few of the prominent global authorization entities include Gold Standard, Verra, and PlanVivo. MRV is equally important to VCM ERCs during the preparation and implementation of the project, in particular in the face of criticism and heightened scrutiny due to incidents of "green washing" (making claims of emission reductions that were exaggerated or otherwise inaccurate).

The rules behind the generation, regulation, and trading of ERCs are complex, diverse, and evolving and are likely to remain fluid for some time. This dynamic market can be difficult for developing countries to follow, especially when they undertake low-carbon projects and policies as part of their nationally determined contribution (NDC) implementation. It can also be difficult for more risk-sensitive investors (e.g., commercial debt financers), given the lack of historical price points and established regulators outside of a few developed markets such as the European Union, the United Kingdom, and California.

The Taskforce on Scaling Voluntary Carbon Markets (TSVCM) estimates that the demand for ERCs in the VCM could increase fifteen times or more by 2030 and up to hundred times by 2050,[137] with an overall ERC market of

---

[136] For more on global ERC markets and how developing countries can prepare to engage effectively with these markets, see https://ppp.worldbank.org/public-private-partnership/Emission_Reduction_Program.

[137] The TSVCM (an initiative led by the Institute of International Finance) is a private sector-led initiative to scale voluntary carbon markets and includes over 250 member institutions (representing buyers and sellers of carbon credits, standard setters, the financial sector, market infrastructure providers, civil society, international organizations, and academics), www.iif.com/tsvcm.

more than USD 50 billion by 2030.[138] The evolution of the VCM includes specific sectors seeking to adopt VCM – for example, the Carbon Offsetting and Reduction Scheme for International Aviation – for international airline travel and the similar efforts for the international maritime sector, and various efforts to improve the integrity and quality of the VCM – for example, the TSVCM, the Voluntary Carbon Markets Integrity Initiative,[139] and the Integrity Council for Voluntary Carbon Markets.[140]

The global market for ERCs will be further boosted by the Paris Agreement (2015),[141] as well as its Article 6, which allows the trading of ERCs to meet NDCs.[142] An ERC sold under Article 6, which counts against the purchasing country's NDCs and not the selling country's, is said to include a "corresponding adjustment" (the Paris Agreement uses the very elegant term "Internationally Traded Mitigation Outcome"). Corresponding adjustments are an accounting system, helping to avoid double-counting, and will require a letter of authorization from the host country. While the Paris Agreement rules afford some discretion, a country's efforts to measure, report, and verify progress toward its targets must nevertheless follow international standards set out by the Intergovernmental Panel on Climate Change and United Nations Framework Convention on Climate Change.

Figure 3.1 illustrates the complexity of the ERC markets and the difficult trade-offs facing governments and investors around the world.

In the face of this evolving market, efforts should be made to ensure that ERCs generated are of high quality – that is, they satisfy the requirements of those CCMs most likely to pay high values for ERCs in the medium to long term, they meet the highest standards of the VCM, they benefit from a robust and reliable MRV system, and they generate cobenefits where possible (e.g., they also benefit the community, women, biodiversity, water resource management, etc.). This additional investment of time and effort is key as it will increase the likelihood that the project once completed still meets the requirements of the global ERC markets (as those markets will continue to evolve and enhance applicable requirements during project implementation before ERCs are generated) and will reinforce the eventual value of the ERCs generated and the ability to trade them across CCMs and the VCM. Investments in high-quality ERCs will make the host country more attractive to developed CCMs as they open up to import ERCs and will generate significant returns for the developer and the government alike.

---

[138] Christopher Blaufelder, Cindy Levy, Peter Mannion, and Dickon Pinner, "A blueprint for scaling voluntary carbon markets," McKinsey, January 2021.

[139] A global taskforce of private and public sectors participants aiming to provide guidance and monitor the integrity of voluntary markets, https://vcmintegrity.org.

[140] A multistakeholder process devising Core Carbon Principles to identify and assess high-integrity carbon credits, https://icvcm.org/.

[141] https://unfccc.int/process-and-meetings/the-paris-agreement/the-paris-agreement.

[142] NDCs are commitments made by different countries under the Paris Agreement to reduce emissions.

3.5 Emissions Reduction Credits/Offsets

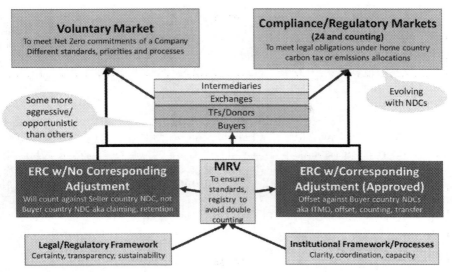

FIGURE 3.1 Global ERC markets
Source: Author

Box 3.40 Okhla solid waste management, India

A compost plant in India was shut down in 2000 due to insufficient revenue from the sale of compost. To rehabilitate the plant, in 2007, the Municipality of Delhi entered into a twenty-five-year PPP, with a capex of around USD 1.5 million. The municipality provided the land. The organic compost is rich in organic carbon content and increases the soil fertility and farm productivity. Field trials demonstrated that yields obtained using the organic compost were 25 percent to 30 percent higher than the yield obtained using chemical fertilizers. The rehabilitated composting plant began operations in 2008 and produces 14,600 tons/year of compost. Around 1,600 tons of CH_4 (34,000 ton CO_2eq) emissions are avoided on average per year, and it is estimated that 234,231 tons CO_2eq was achieved within the seven-year renewable crediting period.

The project is designed to supplement revenues from compost sales with the sale of certified ERCs to countries that agreed to purchase them under the United Nations Framework Convention on Climate Change. The private operator also agreed to share 25 percent of the ERC earnings with the municipality for the first five years. With the sale of ERCs, and a 75:25 debt–equity ratio, the project's projected internal rate of return of 7 percent increased to 14.5 percent. The final project boasted a payback period of six to seven years and a posttax internal rate of return of 14.48 percent. Due

> to concerns over the volatility of the carbon market, the private operator also produced refuse derived fuel, which is an alternative fuel to coal produced from the combustible components of solid waste (e.g., plastics and other biodegradable waste), and sold to the cement industry.[143]

Infrastructure projects should consider early on whether they might generate ERCs, what it would cost to enable the project to generate those ERCs, and what revenues such ERCs are likely to generate (see Box 3.40). This should be a systematic part of the planning process and feasibility study to ensure the project mobilizes all available innovative revenues and achieves important climate goals.

3.6 LESSONS LEARNED IN IMPLEMENTING INNOVATIVE FUNDING

Governments are able to capture a diverse range of revenues from a wide variety of beneficiaries in places and spaces created by infrastructure investments. In planning CVC, governments are encouraged to consider the following key lessons learned from the case studies presented:[144]

- Noncore services should address the wider needs of end-users and the surrounding community. By addressing their needs, provision of noncore services is backed by demand, and stakeholder support can be more easily obtained.
- A dedicated team needs to be set up to focus on CVC, separate from the team focusing on delivering core services, to manage noncore commercial activities. The dedicated team would have a clear mandate for delivering and growing noncore services and would have access to necessary technical expertise either in-house or by engaging consultants.
- Focus should be on quality delivery of core services. Noncore services should not be allowed to distract from core services. The provision of core services is the primary reason for investing in the public infrastructure. Noncore services are meant to complement core services and improve end-user experience.
- A clear flow of monies should be set up that captures a portion of commercial revenues for funding core services. A clear rationale for generating additional revenues through CVC mechanisms is to improve funding for the delivery of core services. A CVC mechanism is successful only if a

---

[143] Solomie Gebrezgabher, Sampath N. Kumar, Pushkar S. Vishwanath, and Miriam Otoo, "Municipal Solid Waste Composting with Carbon Credits for Profit," 2018, www.iwmi.cgiar.org/Publications/Books/PDF/resource_recovery_from_waste-391-399.pdf.

[144] For more on innovative funding see generally, https://ppp.worldbank.org/public-private-partnership/Innovative_Revenues_for_Infrastructure.

3.6 Lessons Learned in Implementing Innovative Funding

reasonable share of revenues is directed back to funding the upfront capital investment and subsequent asset maintenance.
- The complexity of the commercial structure should be matched with the capability of the government entity; there should be no overstretch or overcomplication.

Delivering CVC raises a number of challenges. This section maps out a few key lessons learned when mobilizing new sources of capital.

3.6.1 Think Outside the Box

The commercial world is heavily driven by precedent, what others have done in similar projects, in the same country or region. We take comfort in what has been done before, what is proven. But this approach also limits creativity. Be open-minded. Learn from other sectors and regions. There are creative approaches being used around the globe. A few of these are described in this book.

3.6.2 Don't Try to Be Too Clever

When structuring commercial revenues, it is often tempting to overengineer. The commercial complexity of the chosen structure should reflect the capability of the government entity meant to implement that structure. A structure that exceed the ability of the government entity to implement is more likely to fail. The marginal increases in efficiency or additional revenues may not be worth the risk of failure.

3.6.3 Community Engagement

Consultation is key. Bring in local businesses as partners to create local economic opportunities that also mobilize additional capital. Commercial activities often draw from the community, either seeking customers/users from the community or leveraging the location and resources of the community to sell goods and services. Early engagement with the community can help identify opportunities for commercial revenues and associated challenges, based on geography, local development, and local facilities. A happy community can help protect a project from government interference or other events.

3.6.4 Maintain Focus on Service Delivery

The focus on commercial revenues must never take the focus off the public facility. For example, a public market looking for high-value commercial space might be tempted to reduce the space made available for low-cost vendor space. A low-cost housing project looking to mobilize commercial revenues through mixed-use space might be tempted to reduce the number of low-cost units developed. In some cases, this loss of focus results from overly ambitious government staff and in some cases it results from investors whose primary line of business is commercial profitability.

As an example, airport developments provide ample opportunities for commercial revenues, from duty free shopping to car parking to property development. The consortium that makes up the airport developer will include firms with experience in airport operation, commercial service delivery, and possibly property development. If the partners focused on commercial services have too much influence in the consortium, the focus of the project might prioritize those commercial activities to the detriment of airport operations.

A diversion of focus of the investment onto noncore functions can make the project vulnerable to regulatory challenge (where infrastructure services do not meet regulatory or contractual requirements) and to political challenge (where the investment is perceived by the public or by the government as focused primarily on profit and not on public service). This can reduce the sustainability of the project increasing the likelihood of future governments challenging the project or of regulatory intervention that cuts short the life of the investment. It may be apt to specify the maximum space that can be used for commercial activities, in an effort to meet the objectives of financial feasibility as well as terminal operating efficiency. A robust regime of results indicators and verification focused on public services can also help focus efforts. In general:

- Service parameters must be clearly and objectively defined. For example,
  o within how many minutes should a user be able to access services;
  o how long should someone take to find a parking spot or exit the parking; and
  o what frequency and standard should be applied to maintenance and cleaning, for example, minimum luminosity levels, energy conservation, schedule for repainting, and the quality of maintenance of the toilets.
- Support infrastructure is typically underdesigned for most public infrastructure, leading to heavy congestion and resulting in a drop in levels of services. The project design needs to follow master planning guidelines to ensure that the support infrastructure is designed to reflect the projected reality of the facility.
- Engagement with community and main stakeholders throughout the project cycle is particularly critical.[145] The local community can provide critical information about project design and implementation parameters. Consulting vendors during project development is crucial due to their knowledge of the market and customers.

[145] World Bank Municipal PPP Framework, Module 18, https://ppp.worldbank.org/public-private-partnership/municipal-and-subnational/municipal-public-private-partnership-framework.

3.6 Lessons Learned in Implementing Innovative Funding

Increasing commercial activities may also increase demand on public services. For example, a parking garage with office space developed above it will need to provide additional parking to address the needs of the tenants of the office space. A bus terminal offering additional commercial services might need to be designed for a larger foot traffic, as passengers remain in the terminal longer than normal to benefit from the commercial services and other customers come to the terminal who are not otherwise bus passengers. The Moncloa Transportation Exchanger in Madrid, Spain, an integrated multimodal transportation terminal equipped with commercial and office areas, was expanded and improved in 2009 to cater for the increasing number of passengers. As a result, it was able to cater for 110,000 passengers in 2011, up from only 44,000 in 1995.[146]

---

[146] World Bank Municipal PPP Framework, Project Summary 1.

4

Programmatic Value Capture
Transit-Oriented Development

Innovative funding can be delivered across a sector, area, municipality, or economy. While this programmatic approach can require more coordination and effort to deliver, it will generally be significantly more attractive to investors, achieve greater impact, and mobilize more additional funding. Examples of programmatic value capture include master developers to deliver tourism, economic/industrial zones, ports, airport cities, low-carbon cities, smart cities, and so on.

One of these programmatic approaches is transit-oriented development (TOD), which coordinates transport, area, and land use planning to make transport modes sustainable, convenient, and desirable by concentrating urban development around transit stations and using this concentration to improve economic impact, leverage commercial opportunities, and create jobs. TOD can help (a) encourage efficient use of public transport and infrastructure, (b) reduce costs related to congestion, (c) increase local economic and commercial activity using the transit station as a center of gravity to attract consumers, (d) revitalize local economies, (e) increase property values, and (f) increase physical activity of residents as a result of increased proximity to commercial centers, green spaces, and schools.

Typically, the private sector is well equipped to harness potential programmatic commercial opportunities arising from communities converging around public infrastructure; these could be transport hubs, education hubs, healthcare hubs, and so on. Governments often consider these commercial opportunities to be noncore activities that should be left to the free market. By planning for places and spaces that create commercial opportunity and tapping private sector expertise in the planning of infrastructure services to meet the diverse needs of communities, governments are in a stronger position to capture a fair share of the commercial value created and to provide more and better funding for infrastructure and to provide more infrastructure than they would be able to provide when relying only on user fees and government contributions.

Programmatic Value Capture

Public transit areas create an opportunity for mixed-use developments because high footfall and well-connected places create a good environment for a community to converge, interact, and thrive. TOD brings together elements of land use and transport planning, urban design, urban regeneration, real estate development, financing, land value capture, and infrastructure implementation to achieve more sustainable urban development (see Box 4.1).[1] It creates robust ridership and commercial opportunities by turning stations into destinations and promotes a symbiotic relationship between dense and compact urban form and public transport use. This comprehensive approach allows governments to participate in commercial activities within the TOD and earn revenue to reinvest in improving or maintaining public transport services. Governments can proactively address wider needs in the community by developing TOD around mass transit facilities (for reference, numerous World Bank publications have supported socioeconomic benefits of TOD for communities).[2]

Transit-oriented cities are more competitive than other cities, as a result of agglomeration effects; TOD neighborhoods in the United States have seen land values increased by nearly two to one and people living near TOD stations spend only 37 percent of their income on transport plus housing, as compared with 51 percent for other people.[3]

Box 4.1 Fruitvale, Oakland, California

In 1995, the Unity Council (a local nonprofit), Bay Area Rapid Transit (BART), and the City Council launched a plan for development around the transit station, including affordable housing and senior citizen friendly housing, as well as retail facilities and higher-income housing whose revenues will help fund the affordable housing units. About forty-seven apartments were constructed out of which ten were affordable units while another sixty-eight affordable units were constructed specially for seniors. The community space, including a health clinic, library, Head Start program, and senior center, is almost three times the retail space in the area.

Finding tenants for the commercial space took a long time, due to lack of foot traffic. The buildings of the shops had high construction standards, which increased the rents, but the high-income shops didn't fit with the

---

[1] World Bank, *Transit-Oriented Development Implementation Resources and Tools*, 2nd ed. (World Bank, 2021).
[2] https://documents1.worldbank.org/curated/en/261041545071842767/pdf/Transit-Oriented-Development-Implementation-Resources-and-Tools-Second-Edition.pdf; https://documents1.worldbank.org/curated/en/818701555088451429/pdf/Volume-3-Benchmarking-Transit-Oriented-Development.pdf; Serge Salat and Gerald Olivier, *Transforming the Urban Space through Transit-Oriented Development: The 3V Approach* (World Bank, 2017).
[3] Salat and Olivier, *Transforming the Urban Space through Transit-Oriented Development*.

residents' tastes. Fruitvale is an origin point rather than a destination; people generally shop at destinations, which hindered shop sales.

The funding of this USD 100 million project came from twenty different mechanisms; prepaid leases, tax increment financing, grants from different foundations, and community development block grant funds helped finance the development.[4]

Box 4.2 Center Commons, Portland, Oregon

This 4.9-acre residential and retail development has senior housing, affordable family housing, a day-care facility, and pedestrian accessibility to the nearby transit station. The Portland Development Commission bought the land and engaged a master developer that made affordable housing the priority and constructed more affordable units than required. Developers and residents were provided with property tax abatement, loans, tax credits, revenue bonds, and ten-year transit-oriented property tax abatement. The neighbors to the property were also involved in decision-making, and as a result, a range of housing types, income levels, rental/owner ratio reflecting the neighborhood and creation of commercial space was achieved in addition to the preservation of several large oak trees.[5]

TOD leverages transit opportunities to encourage people to move from personal private transport to public transit, reducing local congestion and increasing foot traffic around local commerce (see Box 4.2). An important part of the population most attracted to this TOD opportunity would benefit from access to affordable housing. Reaching out to this part of the population will also help mitigate the tendency for the opportunities created by TOD to result in excessive gentrification, which in turn can limit the scope of investment and attract criticism of misuse of public funds. For these reasons, government may want to consider strong intervention in the provision of affordable housing near the transit stations.[6]

In the United Kingdom, TOD in the 1880s included master plans for worker housing, with urban amenities like parks to mimic the rural hinterland. These regulations restricted the number of factories near residential units. These master plans were facilitated by the single ownership of large companies.[7]

---

[4] Rutul Joshi, Yogi Joseph, Kavina Patel, and Vishal Darji, "Transit-Oriented Development: Lessons from International Experiences," Working Paper 38, Centre for Urban Equity (CUE), CEPT University, Ahmedabad, 2017.
[5] Ibid.
[6] Ibid.
[7] Ibid.

> **Box 4.3 Edmonton, Alberta**
>
> Century Park is a growing condo community in southern Edmonton at the south end of Edmonton's light rail transit (LRT); it includes low- to high-rise condos, recreational services, shops, restaurants, and a fitness center. Edmonton has had a transit-proximate development for some time in the northeastern suburbs at Clareview, which includes a large park and ride and low-rise apartments among big box stores and associated power center parking. It is also looking into some new TODs in various parts of the city. In the northeast, there are plans to redevelop underutilized land at two sites around the existing LRT, Fort Road and Stadium station. In the west, there are plans to have some medium density condos in the Glenora neighborhood along a future LRT route as well as a TOD in the southeast in the Strathearn neighborhood along the same future LRT on existing low-rise apartments.[8]

TOD typically includes a central transit stop (such as a train station or a light rail or bus stop) surrounded by a high-density mixed-use area, with low-density areas spreading out from this center. TOD is also typically designed to be more walkable than other built-up areas, by using smaller block sizes and reducing the land area dedicated to automobiles. This creates a more liveable, densely populated area, providing access to transportation other than private vehicles, allowing more access to services, retail and other private business; and improved access to jobs.

Creating vibrant, inclusive, and sustainable communities involves much more than increasing density or designing a TOD strategy; it also requires social and economic engagement. In order to promote community diversity, the following factors are said to be most influential: (a) land use, (b) affordable housing, (c) diverse jobs and retail opportunities, (d) social infrastructure like schools, hospitals, and gardens, (e) improved access and movement, (f) open spaces, recreation, and improved public realm, and (g) community facilities.[9]

Land value is generally closely associated with place value, which reflects the liveability of an urban space, for example, access to jobs, shopping, services, and walkability (see Box 4.3). Perceptions of place value can change rapidly and can be significantly influenced by urban planning and public service investments (in particular transit).

TOD can reduce infrastructure costs and CO_2 emissions per unit of activity. In Los Angeles, TOD has reduced multiple types of emissions, including

---

[8] Ibid; Rohit Sharma and Peter Newman, "Land Value Capture Tools: Integrating Transit and Land Use through Finance to Enable Economic Value Creation," *Modern Economy* 11, no. 4 (2020): 938–964.
[9] Ibid.

greenhouse gasses, respiratory irritants, and smog-forming emissions, by approximately 30 percent, when compared to lower-density areas. In Dhaka, TOD has helped to reduce travel-related CO_2 emissions on a community level.[10]

Moreover, TOD demonstrates that the use of urban space for public services such as cycling paths, pedestrian areas, and parks can actually increase the value of land within that area and accentuate place value. As an example, New York City's New West Side achieved tremendous success through investment in the High Line, which resulted in USD 2 billion of private investment, 12,000 new jobs, and 29 development projects since June 2009. This allocation of urban space to value enhancing public services resulted in a significant increase in economic activity and value for the municipality.[11]

Opponents of compact- or transit-oriented development typically argue that people (in particular Americans) prefer low-density living and that any policies that encourage compact development will result in substantial utility decreases and hence large social welfare costs. Proponents of compact development argue that there are large and often unmeasured benefits of compact development or that the American preference for low-density living is a misinterpretation made possible in part by substantial local government interference in the land market.

Also, TOD provides an optimum programmatic platform for generating land value capture (LVC), commercial value capture (CVC), and other sources of funding for infrastructure. It is also a key mechanism to deliver more environmentally friendly municipal development, by reducing the use of automobiles, attracting residents back to city centers, reducing gentrification of city centers, increasing inclusivity of residential space available near transport hubs, and so on. While these are important functions of TOD, this chapter will focus primarily on the potential of TOD to attract LVC and CVC on a programmatic basis.

4.1 TOD PRINCIPLES

Transit-oriented development maximizes residential, commercial, and entertainment space within walking distance of public transport nodes. As population growth is increasingly centered in cities, building around and on top of multimodal transport stations has become a popular way to cross-finance urban transportation and public amenities in well-connected locations. TOD offers a strategic spatial planning tool to direct and regulate mobility in accordance with the government's development vision, foster a greater certainty of demand, and make it more viable for projects to mobilize investment in the design, implementation, and operation of mass transport systems and

---

[10] Joshi et al., "Transit-Oriented Development."
[11] Salat and Olivier, *Transforming the Urban Space through Transit-Oriented Development.*

4.1 TOD Principles

associated infrastructure. It is well known that TOD improves the livability of cities, but its effect on the business case for infrastructure projects is often neglected.

Well-planned cities are engines of growth. Good design supports high density and ensures people and the economy are not constrained by congestion. A TOD program needs to ensure design that is based on economic development plans, associated with relevant transit corridors the potential for connectivity and verified market demand. Limited public resources must be used efficiently to achieve coordinated interagency interventions, communicate with residents, communicate with other government agencies, and engage with private developers to share the vision and achieve its goals.[12] Rapid urbanization, intensifying congestion, and the new work dynamic in the wake of Covid-19 have created an increasingly strong drive to achieve TOD, focused on

- higher quality of life to live, work, and play in town centers with more walking, less stress, and higher property values;
- greater mobility with reduced traffic congestion, car accidents, and injuries; and
- reduced dependence on fossil fuels, reduced pollution, and improved environmental context.[13]

TOD, specifically along mass transit lines, has increased the amount of new businesses in Phoenix within one mile of a station, with businesses in the knowledge, service, and retail industries experiencing, respectively, 88 percent, 40 percent, and 24 percent more new starts than non-TOD areas.[14]

TOD uses transit zones or corridors to coordinate development to achieve these goals. Elements of TOD include

- train stations and other public transport hubs (rail, light rail, bus, etc.) with a mix of uses (office, residential, retail, civic, food and beverage, grocery, etc.) as a prominent feature of town centers and
- extensive pedestrianization and systems for bikes and scooters (priority paths, share, parking, etc.), with car parking on the periphery.[15]

TOD can boost urban transport financing. Integrated spatial and transport planning provides improved traffic flow and growth potential, and more robust traffic lowers the risk of future deviation from ridership and cashflow projections (see Box 4.4). TOD also creates opportunities for new revenue sources from the space surrounding and within the station. Commercial returns through advertising, taxation, and revenue sharing with developers of

---

[12] Ibid.
[13] "Factors Driving the Trend toward TOD," Transit Oriented Development Institute, 2021.
[14] Kevin Credit, "Transit-Oriented Economic Development: The Impact of Light Rail on New Business Starts in the Phoenix, AZ Region, USA," *Urban Studies* 55, no. 13 (2018): 2838–2862.
[15] "Factors Driving the Trend toward TOD."

> **Box 4.4 Curitiba, Brazil**
>
> One of the earliest and most successful examples of TOD is Curitiba, which was organized into transport corridors early on. Over the years, it has integrated its zoning laws and transportation planning to place high-density development adjacent to high-capacity transportation systems, particularly in its bus rapid transit corridors. Since the failure of its first city plan due to lack of funding, Curitiba has focused on working with economical forms of infrastructure, such as bus routes with routing systems, limited access, and speeds similar to subway systems. One source of innovation in Curitiba has been participatory city planning with public education, discussion, and agreement.[16]

residential and office spaces offer alternative non-fare box revenue streams as foot traffic in the transit hub increases. TOD principles also make it easier to mobilize central government and donor support to improve bankability and investability. These principles incorporate higher prudence in planning and prioritize stronger public connectivity, which will in turn mitigate demand risks, improve project economics, and reduce vulnerability to political risk.

TOD results from integrated economic, transport, and land use planning around transport hubs, where passengers can switch between lines or between transport modes. Public transit hubs include large subway stations with multiple lines, train stations, rapid transit stations, bus stations, tram stations, and airports. Some complex hubs combine several modes in a single integrated multimodal station or a complex of stations. Studies indicate that land values around urban rail stations increase from 7 percent to 17 percent for property within five hundred meters to one kilometer from the station,[17] doubling job density and increasing economic productivity by 5–10 percent.[18] This is an enormous value creation out of coordinated urban transit planning.

Locating amenities, jobs, shops, and housing around transit hubs promote public and nonmotorized transit use, softens the perceptions of density, and facilitates the emergence of vibrant communities. Singapore, for example, decided that, by 2030, 80 percent of its residents will live within a ten-minute walk from a train station and 75 percent of peak-hour trips will be made using public transport (see Box 4.5). This can be achieved only through applying TOD principles and an integrated interagency approach.[19] A successful TOD

---

[16] Joshi et al., "Transit-Oriented Development." Sharma and Newman, "Land Value Capture Tools."
[17] Ibid.
[18] Salat and Olivier, *Transforming the Urban Space through Transit-Oriented Development*; S. Salat, L. Bourdic, and M. Kamiya, *Economic Foundations for Sustainable Urbanization: A Study on Three-Pronged Approach: Planned City Extensions, Legal Framework, and Municipal Finance* (UN-HABITAT and Urban Morphology Institute and Complex Systems, 2017).
[19] Salat and Olivier, *Transforming the Urban Space through Transit-Oriented Development*.

4.1 TOD Principles   97

Box 4.5 Singapore's TOD

Singapore complements its public transit with high parking charges, electronic road pricing, and a vehicle quota scheme that limits annual vehicle registrations. All the revenue coming from motor vehicle tax goes to a consolidated fund used in various sectors, including housing and public transport. The urban structure of Singapore focuses on "new towns," with residential populations envisaged to be about 60,000 to 120,000, located around metro stops with local shopping, other commercial opportunities, community services, and diverse activities. About seven residential neighborhoods are grouped around the center with schools, community, and recreation facilities.[20]

Box 4.6 Hong Kong

Hong Kong is known for its public and private partnership using the TOD concept. The government provides land and development rights around the station to the Mass Transit Railway Corporation. The corporation develops master plans for the area, including a focus on public interests and planning for a built environment that promotes transit use, density, diversity, and design.[21] Property development brought in about HKD 5 billion in revenues, commercial activities about HKD 3 billion, and rail operation about HKD 13 billion in 2021 and has unlocked land for 600,000 public housing units.[22] The model is profitable for both the public and the private partners.

---

must juggle a number of competing priorities, like land use, jobs, housing, and commercial profits (see Box 4.6). TOD will fail unless carefully implemented.[23]

Transport and housing are traditionally the largest expenditures for households, often accounting for more than half of their income. Accordingly, the shape of the mass transit network drives urban development, and density patterns form through feedback loops within the transit network. Transit networks often follow a core-and-branch system, which helps agglomeration and the distribution of densities across the urban space and can provide higher levels of accessibility for people and businesses. Subcenters around stations at the intersection of transit networks concentrate passenger flows and deliver higher growth potential.[24]

---

[20] Ibid.
[21] Joshi et al., "Transit-Oriented Development."
[22] MTR Corporation, "Annual Report 2021," www.mtr.com.hk/archive/corporate/en/investor/10yr_stat_en.pdf.
[23] Joshi et al., "Transit-Oriented Development."
[24] Salat and Olivier, *Transforming the Urban Space through Transit-Oriented Development*.

Inclusive TOD plans for low-income and affordable housing near mass transit stations enhance access to job opportunities and reduce costs for all. The government could provide incentives in the TOD framework to help developers provide affordable housing. Regulations can ensure that a certain proportion of new units are suitable for disabled or aged residents. Design can be used to ensure easy access to open spaces and forced interactions between people belonging to different socioeconomic groups.

While TOD often prioritizes public transportation, consideration needs to be given to the automobile. Convenient parking and drop-off zones need to be planned for in all station area plans. Enough parking should be available, but not too much. Setting both minimum and maximum parking standards can help optimize transit ridership. Surface parking areas can overwhelm a station area. Structured parking consumes less land than surface parking and allows maximum development. Station areas should be designed to allow for the evolution of parking from surface lots to parking structures. Bicycles can extend the local commuting range. Ample, convenient, and secured bicycle storage locations should be provided at each station, close to the entrance of the transit station.

4.2 CHALLENGES WHEN DELIVERING TOD AND BEST PRACTICES

Transit-oriented development merges transport planning, urban planning, and economic development strategies.[25] One would hope that this is always the case, but it is not; transport teams will be overly busy trying to deliver on transport projects, while the urban planners are wrestling with intragovernmental politics and coordination issues, treasury and others are focused on economic development. TOD seeks to provide an overarching narrative (see Box 4.7). But different governments use TOD in different ways. In some countries, TOD is more about transport, coordinating between different modes of transport to help improve user experience. In others, it is about neighborhood rehabilitation, using transport links to reduce the use of motorized transport. In others, TOD is a pseudonym for CVC. Few countries get the difficult balance of all three dynamics of TOD.

This section discusses some of the key challenges to implementing TOD programs and some of the lessons learned from TOD programs around the world. This is a rich topic and well covered in the literature, and reference to some of the key resources on this topic is provided in footnotes.

---

[25] For further reference, see Sharma and Newman, "Land Value Capture Tools"; "Factors Driving the Trend toward TOD"; Hiroaki Suzuki, Jin Murakami, Yu-Hung Hong, and Beth Tamayose, *Financing Transit-Oriented Development with Land Values Adapting Land Value Capture (English)*, Urban Development Series (World Bank, 2015).

4.2 Challenges When Delivering TOD and Best Practices

Box 4.7 Denver

To coordinate the planning and implementation of the multistakeholder fifty-acre Denver Union Station Project at and around Denver Union Station project, the city established the Denver Union Station Project Authority in 2008. The project comprises an intermodal transit district (commuter rail, LRT, intercity bus, and local bus) surrounded by TOD, including a mix of residential, retail, and office space. Various schemes funded the USD 487.7 million project, including tax increment financing (TIF), special improvement districts, land sales, joint development, and federal subsidies. To use the TIF mechanism in Denver, a project site must meet the definition of blight as defined in statutes and reported by the Denver Urban Renewal Authority. The joint development may involve private developers' air rights development, ground lease to private developers, or the outright sale of land.[26]

Efforts to deliver TOD have encountered a number of constraints and challenges, including the following:[27]

- Lack of regional coordination at the city level, including silo behavior at the neighborhood or sector level, and lack of an empowered institution that is able to work across various scales, levels of government, and planning sectors;
- Lack of clear TOD policy – national, regional, or city policy and development regulations sometimes conflict, creating confusion over expectations for development;
- A slow and inconsistent development review process, with conflicts between various government policies, plans, and development standards can lead to a lengthy review process;
- Restrictive national and administrative rules and regulations including inadequate policies and deficiencies in planning instruments for creating densities that are strategically distributed and match the level of accessibility and connectivity offered by public transit. TOD is a more complex form of development that poses greater uncertainty and higher financial risks for developers. Market dynamics need to justify the risk;
- Lack of prioritized public investment to support TOD with a strategic sequence of capital improvements around transit stations. This signals to developers a disconnect between TOD developments and government expectations; hence, increased financial risks for builders and developers which can diminish market interest in TOD;

---

[26] Tetsuo Kidokoro, *Transit-Oriented Development Policies and Station Area: Development in Asian Cities* (Asian Development Bank Institute, 2019).
[27] World Bank, *Transit-Oriented Development Implementation Resources and Tools*; The City of Calgary, "Transit-Oriented Development: Implementation Strategy," 2019.

- Community opposition – trying to address community opposition to TOD projects that meet the government's long-term strategic goals is costly, Failure to engage with communities, identify concerns and address those concerns will make those projects less attractive for private investment.

To identify these and other relevant constraints, successful implementation of a TOD project requires a robust feasibility study to assess and improve the development proposition, regulations and institutional mechanisms, traffic and demand data, market testing of infrastructure services and commercial activities, and stakeholder acceptance of social and community impacts.

Governments committed to large TOD projects may wish to enact, by law or other appropriately robust and formal instrument, the creation of a special body (task force, committee, or agency) that, from inception, has strong ties to the TOD plan. This organization must be held accountable to the public and operate transparently. The organization will promote the development of planning research, design master plans and regulations, oversee implementation and continued adaption of systems, and coordinate with planning guidelines and professionals from different levels of government and the private sector. It may help if this agency exists outside of the political sphere.[28]

To summarize, successful implementation of TOD is generally supported by the following:[29]

- A TOD strategy, a multimodal, transit-oriented regional growth master plan, linking transit services, municipal services, commercial activities and affordable housing – planning policy guides capital improvements and sets expectations for builders, developers, and communities that include conducive design elements including scale, mix of uses, and public spaces to develop "places" that generate economic opportunities and make transit hubs more attractive;
- Access to land – available land and restrictions on land use should support TOD plans. Land costs and the cost of capital improvements can impact market interest;
- Capital improvements, include infrastructure, such as utilities, streetscapes and parks, that help provide a high quality of life in an active urban environment and to attract commercial investments to create jobs and economic growth;
- Market opportunities, to attract private investment, making space for private sector involvement, providing open competition for investment opportunities;
- A supportive legal and regulatory framework that reflects the needs of TOD development, including zoning regulations (mixed use, minimum density,

---

[28] World Bank, *Transit-Oriented Development Implementation Resources and Tools*.
[29] Kidokoro, *Transit-Oriented Development Policies and Station Area*; The City of Calgary, "Transit-Oriented Development Implementation Strategy."

4.2 Challenges When Delivering TOD and Best Practices

etc.), public asset and procurement rules that allow for master developer and other public-private investment programs;
- Incentives for environmental sustainability – TOD can help reduce impact on climate change by providing low-carbon mobility and environmentally sustainable design practices (e.g., storm water management, energy generation, district heating, and energy efficiency). Some of these investments will make good, commercial investments, but in other cases public support including through subsidies, may be needed to incentivize developers;
- Coordination, including through a coordination body, among local governments, transit agencies, local communities, and private developers and an institutional mechanism for public and private cooperation. The process of planning TOD in communities can provide government and developers a better understanding of what is important to residents and businesses, driving growth and change, and preparing the community to take advantage of the development.

PART II

FINANCING

5

Principles of Finance

Public budget (through taxing or borrowing) generally deliver investments in public infrastructure, possibly with a contribution from the enterprises' retained earnings (consumers). Part I of this book described innovative sources of funding for infrastructure and how developers of infrastructure should seek to maximize and diversify sources of revenues (funding) for their projects to improve financial and economic viability and sustainability of infrastructure investments. Part II will explore innovative sources of financing for infrastructure projects, including climate finance, Islamic finance, and blended finance. Even the most innovative of financing structures needs to address the basic principles of financing (both debt and equity), the fundamental risks and challenges that any decision maker will assess when considering financing infrastructure. For this reason, Part II starts with this chapter providing an overview of the fundamental principles of financing.

A project will involve financing from various sources, in some combination of equity and debt.

- *Equity contributions* – Equity refers to funds invested in the project company and comprise its share capital and other shareholder funds. It holds the lowest priority of the contributions; for example, debt contributors will have the right to project assets and revenues to meet debt service obligations before the equity contributors can obtain any return or, on termination or insolvency, any repayment, and equity shareholders cannot normally receive distributions unless the company is in profit. Equity contributions bear the highest risk and therefore potentially receive the highest returns.
- *Debt contributions* – Debt has the highest priority among the invested funds (e.g., senior debt must be serviced before most other debts are repaid).
- *Mezzanine/subordinated contributions* – Located somewhere between equity and debt, mezzanine contributions are accorded lower priority than senior debt but higher priority than equity. Examples of mezzanine contributions are subordinated loans and preference shares.

Figure 5.1 sets out three of the more common sources of financing for infrastructure projects (based on the nature of the borrower):

- *Government financing* – where the government borrows money and provides it to the project through on-lending, grants, subsidies, or guarantees of indebtedness. The government can usually borrow money at a lower interest rate but is constrained by its fiscal space (the amount it is able to borrow) and will have a number of worthy initiatives competing for scarce fiscal resources; the government is also generally less able of managing commercial risk efficiently.
- *Corporate financing* – where a company borrows money against its proven credit profile and ongoing business (debt may be secured against specific assets or revenues, or the debt may be "unsecured") and invests it in the project. Utilities and state-owned enterprises often do not have the needed debt capacity and may have a number of competing investment requirements. External investors may have sufficient debt capacity, but the size of investment required and the returns that such companies seek from their investments may result in a relatively high cost of financing and therefore can be prohibitive for the contracting authority.
- *Project financing* – where nonrecourse or limited recourse (these terms can be used interchangeably) loans are made directly to a special purpose vehicle. Lenders rely on the cash flow of the project for repayment of the debt; security for the debt is primarily limited to the project assets and revenue stream. The debt can therefore be off-balance sheet for the shareholders and possibly also for the contracting authority.

The proportion used of each source of financing and the decision as to which form of financing to adopt will depend on market availability of financing and the willingness of lenders to bear certain project risks or credit risks according to their view of how the market is developing and changing and of their own internal risk management regime.

One of the most efficient private financing arrangements for infrastructure projects is "project financing." Project financing normally takes the form of limited recourse lending to a specially created project company (or vehicle) that has the right to carry out the construction and operation of the project. Project financing achieves a better/lower weighted average cost of capital (WACC) than pure equity financing. It also promotes a transparent risk-sharing regime and creates incentives across different project parties to encourage good performance and efficient risk management.

> *Off-balance sheet* – One of the advantages of project financing is that it can provide off-balance sheet financing – that is, the debt does not appear as a liability on the balance sheet of the shareholders – and shifts some of the project risk to the lenders in exchange for which the lenders obtain a higher interest rate than for normal corporate lending. Project finance

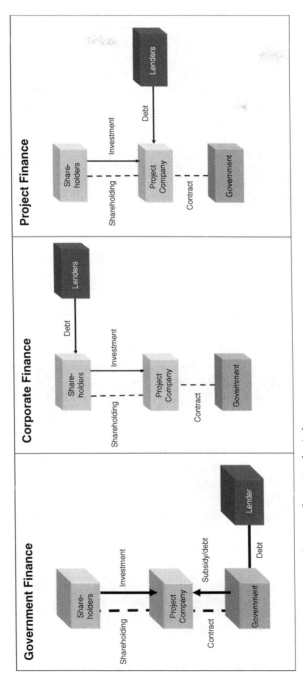

FIGURE 5.1 Sources of private financing for infrastructure

debt is held by the project company, which is a sufficiently minority subsidiary so that any project debt is not consolidated onto the balance sheet of the respective shareholders. This reduces the impact of the project on the cost of shareholders' existing debt and on their debt capacity. To a certain extent, the contracting authority can also use project finance to keep project debt and liabilities "off-balance sheet," that is, not counted as contracting authority debt and taking up less fiscal space, though rating agencies and other market actors will consider the risks associated with project finance structures.[1]

Limited recourse financing – Another advantage to the shareholders of project financing is the absence, or limitation, of recourse by the lenders to the shareholders. The project company is generally a limited liability special purpose vehicle (SPV). The shareholders in a limited liability company are at risk only for the amount of equity they invest in the SPV and any "sponsor support" that the shareholders agree to provide.

Bankability – The key principles for sustainable and commercially viable debt for lenders is known as "bankability." A "bankable" project provides lenders with confidence that the project will succeed and the lending is secured sufficiently to attract financing. This concept applies to all kinds of financing but is more important and better defined when it comes to limited recourse financing, because the lenders' recourse for repayment of debt will be limited primarily to the revenue flow from the project. This makes lenders extremely risk-averse. Before committing themselves to a project, lenders will perform an in-depth review of the viability of the project (their "due diligence"). Bankability requirements will vary based on the identity of the lenders, who will have different interests and concerns and perceptions of risk.

In an effort to explore different innovative approaches to financing infrastructure, this chapter sets out some of the key principles of borrowing, as these will apply to even the most innovative structures, including the types of financing contributions needed (Section 5.1), the nature of different financiers (Section 5.2), key project risks (Section 5.3), important investor concerns (Section 5.4), and characteristics of project finance (Section 5.5).

Chapters 6–8 will explore three different innovative financing models:

---

[1] Fiscal space indicates the debt capacity of a sovereign entity and is a function of the requirements placed on the host country by its own laws or by the rules applied by supranational or international bodies (such as the International Monetary Fund) or by market actors (such as credit rating agencies). It should be noted that keeping debt off-balance sheet does not necessarily reduce actual liabilities for the government and may merely disguise government liabilities, reducing the effectiveness of government debt monitoring mechanisms. As a policy issue, the use of off-balance sheet debt should be considered carefully and protective mechanisms should be implemented accordingly.

5.1 Sources of Financing

- Climate finance (Chapter 6) – Innovation can also be linked to the activities that are being financed. Climate finance is available where the investment to be financed, or the borrower, meet certain climate standards and have those climate credentials verified.
- Islamic finance (Chapter 7) – Where project finance looks to the nature of the borrower for its innovation, Islamic finance looks to new sources of capital that are available only for financing that has equity, rather than debt, characteristics. The form of the financing instrument is therefore critical.
- Blended finance (Chapter 8) – The source of capital may also be blended, in particular between development financiers and commercial financiers. Given the diversity of financiers, blended finance looks to leverage the strengths of the different financiers but also needs to coordinate between them. It is covered last because blended finance is relevant for each of the financing models mentioned above.

5.1 SOURCES OF FINANCING

As mentioned earlier, project finance will involve financing from various sources, in some combination of equity and debt.

5.1.1 Equity Contributions

Equity is the amount of money invested in a company that comprises its share capital and other shareholder funds (divided into many equal parts owned by the shareholders). It is the value of a company's assets, minus its liabilities. Equity holds the lowest priority of the contributions; for example, any creditors will need to be satisfied before the equity contributors can obtain any repayment on termination or insolvency. Equity investors cannot normally receive distributions unless the company is in profit (i.e., dividends for shareholders can be declared only from profits, after providing for depreciation). Equity contributions bear the highest risk and therefore potentially receive the highest returns.

5.1.2 Debt Contributions

Debt is an amount owed to another party, usually repaid on an agreed periodic basis and amount, with interest. Debt contributions have the highest priority among the invested funds (e.g., senior debt must be serviced before most other debts are repaid). Under most loans, the borrower receives a set amount of money, which they must repay in full by a certain date, which may be years in the future, or in the case of revolving debt there is no fixed date for repayment, so long as the maximum amount of debt available is not fully drawn. The terms of the loan will also stipulate the amount of interest that the borrower

> **Box 5.1 Market flex**
>
> A "market flex" clause allows an arranger to change the price, structure, or terms of the lending facilities in the face of changes in financial markets, in order to enhance the prospects of a successful syndication. This right is generally provided only to arrangers taking significant underwriting risks.

is required to pay, expressed as a percentage of the loan amount, generally a fixed or floating rate of interest. Interest compensates the lender for taking on the risk of the loan. Since lenders receive only repayment plus interest and are not normally beneficiaries of profits earned by the borrower, lenders tend to be more conservative, concerned to avoid losing money rather than focused on potential upside.

The source of debt will have an important influence on the nature of the debt provided. Debt can be obtained from many creditors, including commercial lenders, export credit agencies, bilateral or multilateral organizations, bondholders (such as institutional investors), shareholders, and sometimes the host country government. Infrastructure generally involves the construction of high-value long-life assets with stable revenues and therefore seeks long-term fixed-interest debt (see Box 5.1). This debt profile fits well with the asset profile of pension funds and other institutional investors.

5.1.2.1 Bonds

Bond financing allows the borrower to access debt directly from individuals and institutions, rather than using commercial lenders as intermediaries (though commercial lenders also buy bonds).[2] The issuer (the borrower) sells the bonds to the investors. The lead manager helps the issuer to market the bonds. A trustee holds the rights and acts on behalf of the investors, stopping any one investor from independently declaring a default. Bond financing generally provides lower borrowing costs and longer tenors (duration), if the credit position of the bond is sufficiently strong. Rating agencies may be consulted when structuring the project to maximize the credit rating for the project and the bonds to be issued. These agencies will assess the riskiness of the project and assign a credit rating to the bonds, which will signal to bond purchasers the attractiveness of the investment and the price they should pay.

The following are some of the disadvantages associated with financing through bond issues:

- "Negative carry," as bond financing is drawn all at once, upfront, and therefore interest is charged on the entire amount from day one. The borrower

---

[2] For further discussion of documenting a bond issue, see Graham Vinter and Gareth Price, *Project Finance: A Legal Guide*, 3rd ed. (Sweet & Maxwell, 2006).

5.1 Sources of Financing

will have to bear the "cost of carry," being the interest paid on the bond proceeds from the date of receipt to the date it is used to invest in capital expenditure. Bond holders will also not roll up interest during construction (there will be no grace period), requiring the project company to borrow enough to pay interest during construction where it has no revenues during this period. Banks will charge a commitment fee on amounts of bank debt not yet drawn, but this commitment fee will be substantially less than the cost of carry of bond financing.

- Less certainty in the underwriting process due to the volatility in the securities market and uncertainty unless the bonds are underwritten (which is rare). This said, though the pricing for a bond is not known until the bond is issued to the market, bond underwriters should have a good idea of actual pricing based on their premarketing work.
- Less flexibility during project implementation (e.g., to approve waivers and amendments), given the diversity of bondholders and the difficulty of getting approval for changes.
- More time and cost, due to more extensive disclosure processes and the rating process.

Bond financing has seen limited use for initial private infrastructure financing but is used more commonly for refinancing, once construction risks have been largely mitigated.

5.1.2.2 Credit Enhancement

Different types of credit enhancement can be used to increase availability and reduce the cost of debt. For example, a commercial bank, monoline insurer, or a multilateral lending agency (like the World Bank) may provide credit enhancement to bond investors, also known as an "insurance wrap."[3] The "insurer" has a superior credit rating and provides some undertaking to investors using that superior credit rating to reduce the risk for investors, thereby improving the rating for the bond and reducing the yield required, justifying the cost of the insurance wrap.

5.1.3 Mezzanine/Subordinated Contributions

Located somewhere between equity and debt, mezzanine contributions are accorded lower priority than senior debt but higher priority than equity – being subordinate to pure debt but senior to pure equity. In practice, mezzanine debt behaves more like equity than debt because the embedded risk in mezzanine debt makes lenders seek some controls over company decisions like equity. Mezzanine debt may also include call options, rights, and warrants that give the lender the right to convert debt to equity in certain cases.

---

[3] However, the collateralized debt obligations and the subprime mortgage crash of 2008 seriously reduced the availability of monoline instruments.

> **Box 5.2 Bonds using subordinated debt to credit enhance**
>
> Subordinated debt can be used to credit enhance a project in order to facilitate bond financing. One structure might involve tranched debt, a senior tranche as A Notes and a subordinated tranche as B Notes. The A Notes are issued to capital markets and the B Notes are placed with a fund that provides a "first loss" tranche of debt. For example, A Notes might represent 70 percent, with B Notes representing 15 percent and equity 15 percent. The aim would be to take the total project debt with a rating of BBB-/BBB and use the fund to enhance the risk profile of the A Notes to at least BBB+. The structure could use the principle of some real estate funds where the B Notes are the controlling creditor of the project unless the project performance falls below predefined thresholds, in which case the A Notes take control. This alleviates the need for bondholders to manage the project on a day-to-day basis unless the project is in distress.

Examples of mezzanine contributions are subordinated loans and preference shares. Subordinated loans involve a lender agreeing not to be paid until more "senior" lenders to the same borrower have been paid, whether in relation to specific project revenues or in the event of insolvency. Preference shares are equity shares but with priority over other "common" shares when it comes to distributions. Mezzanine contributors will be compensated for the added risk they take by receiving higher interest rates on loans than the senior debt contributors and/or by participating in the project profits or the capital gains achieved by project equity. Use of mezzanine contributions (which can also be characterized as quasi-equity) will allow the project company to maintain greater levels of debt-to-equity ratio in the project, although at a higher cost than senior debt (see Box 5.2). Shareholders may prefer to provide subordinated debt instead of equity to

- benefit from tax deductible interest payments;
- avoid withholding tax;
- avoid restrictions on some institutions not permitted to invest in equity;
- allow the project company to service its subordinated debt when it would not be permitted to make distributions; and
- permit shareholders to obtain some security, for example, to rank senior against trade creditors.

But, unlike equity holders, subordinated lenders

- do not share in profits;
- do not normally have voting and control rights; and
- may be subject to usury laws on the amount of interest they are allowed to charge, where equity distributions would not.

5.1 Sources of Financing

5.1.4 Securitization and Syndication

Syndication and securitization both involve packaging/repackaging of debt.

Debt syndication assembles a group of lenders to finance different portions of a loan to a single borrower. A syndicated loan is a structured product that needs to be arranged and administered effectively. This is usually done by a third party or a consulting firm since there are a number of lending parties involved.

The syndication process may be organized during the origination of debt (the negotiation of the debt position with the borrower) or may involve one of the origination banks selling a portion of its lending commitment to a syndicate of lenders to reduce its own credit exposure to the borrower.

In syndicated lending, each amount advanced by one of the syndicated banks constitutes a separate loan, with the bank's obligations and rights being several. The banks will not underwrite each other's obligations, and each bank will want to sue separately and make its own set off arrangements. The agent bank for the syndicate will verify conditions precedent, receive funds, calculate interest rates, and make demands on the borrower on behalf of the syndicate. Only certain bank actions will be subject to majority bank control, for example, acceleration (where the whole amount due under the loan becomes due and payable immediately). If one bank in the syndicate receives more money than it should, there will be a sharing clause that requires the syndicate banks to share funds received. Such sharing may create challenges in some jurisdictions, where holding funds on trust is not enforceable. Syndicate members may not be comfortable with simple rights in contract to claim repayment of monies from other syndicate members.

Syndicated lending generally involves a common terms agreement to coordinate basic terms of debt, even though each loan will be separately documented, including defining the roles to be played. Different bank roles within a syndicate include the following:

- Account bank – holds different bank accounts on behalf of the syndicate;
- Security trustee – holds security rights for the benefit of the syndicate; and
- Hedging providers – provider of, often very profitable, hedging arrangements for the borrower.

Securitization mobilizes capital against project receivables; it is the structured process whereby interests in loans and other receivables are packaged, underwritten, and sold in the form of asset-backed securities. The assets can be structured and credit enhanced to bring down the cost of borrowing. Credit rating agencies are often used to test the quality of the packaged assets, and thereby protect purchasers of the asset-backed securities, and to help set the pricing for the securities. For infrastructure projects, this can be a way to refinance project debt after the completion of construction and once the assets have demonstrated revenue generation. Some governments prefer to finance infrastructure development and construction with public resources, then use securitization to bring in private capital after the asset is built and operational. For example, Dubai hired local and international banks to raise USD 800 million by securitizing road toll receipts to fund infrastructure projects in the Gulf emirate.[4] Securitization requires a reliable revenue stream, careful structuring from experienced and well-respected advisers, and possibly credit enhancement to ensure the placement is sufficiently credit worthy to attract debt at the cost and tenor desired.

By enabling the original lenders to sell down debt to other financiers (syndication) or to repackage project assets to mobilize financing (securitization), the debt providers are removed from the origination process and in many cases from project oversight and may not pay as much attention to the quality of the underlying project, which can lead to poor risk management. This "originate and distribute" paradigm has been heavily criticized and was one of the causes blamed for the 2008 Global Financial Crisis.[5] Yet, the ability to sell down debt positions is critical to a vibrant infrastructure financing sector, as it allows more proactive lenders to invest in the capacity to originate complex lending, then pass some of those loans to other (less proactive) lenders and earn a return for their efforts.

5.1.5 Value for Money

For government borrowers, the assessment of whether debt is sustainable and economically viable is known as "value for money" (VfM), a measure of the net value that a government receives from an investment. The assessment of VfM helps the government decide whether a project should be implemented as a public–private partnership (PPP) and how much support the government should provide to that project (see Box 5.3). Assessing VfM is as much an art as a science, given the various and changing concepts of "value" that the government will want to access and apply to an investment.

Various approaches and models endeavor to quantify VfM, in particular through public sector comparators (PSCs; see Box 5.4), cost benefit analysis, and shadow models (where a financial model is developed from the bidder's perspective to test likely bidder concerns). Best practice uses such quantitative analysis as important data but looks to a qualitative analysis to respond to all relevant parameters rather than seek measurable accuracy in assessment (see Box 5.3).

In some cases, VfM is used as an ex post rationalization of a political decision to implement a project. This can jeopardize the sustainability of the project

---

[4] "Dubai Completes $800m Road Tolls Monetization," Infrastructure Investor, July 11, 2011, www.infrastructureinvestor.com/dubai-completes-800m-road-tolls-monetisation.
[5] Vincenzo Bavoso, "Financial Innovation, Structured Finance and Off Balance Sheet Financing: The Case of Securitisation," *SSRN Electronic Journal*, January 1, 2010, https://ssrn.com/abstract=1746109 or http://dx.doi.org/10.2139/ssrn.1746109.

5.2 Financiers

> **Box 5.3 Quantitative versus qualitative VfM**
>
> The UK National Audit Office emphasizes that financial appraisal and cost modelling are just one part of the overall assessment of projects and has sought to discourage appraisers from striving for disproportionate levels of accuracy. Qualitative considerations – viability, desirability, achievability – should frame the approach to quantitative assessment. The quantitative assessment should form part of the overall VfM judgment rather than be seen as a stand-alone pass/fail test. Neither the quantitative nor the qualitative assessment should be considered in isolation.[6]

> **Box 5.4 PSC**
>
> A comparison between the cost of public delivery of the project and that through PPP can provide a useful mechanism in assessing VfM. But a PSC is difficult to calculate with any accuracy. In order to assess PSC properly, full information is needed on how the project would be implemented by the public sector, including the actual cost of construction, cost of operation, cost of financing, and risk borne by the public sector (these can be difficult calculations without someone in government losing face).[7]

and the entire program. A robust VfM exercise at the time of project selection and procurement can protect a project from ex post challenges.

In order to test VfM, the government will undertake a feasibility study, usually before launching the bidding process. This will help design the project structure and bid documents and help the government understand the key issues that will need to be addressed during bidding and negotiation.

Bankability is generally assessed in two stages. First, when bidders are assessing the project to submit a bid, they will perform due diligence and assess investability. Then, once a bidder is ready to bid and has assessed investability, or once it has been selected as the preferred bidder, the prospective lenders will perform due diligence to assess bankability.[8]

5.2 FINANCIERS

Financing for infrastructure ideally involves long-tenor debt at fixed rates. This allows the high upfront cost of infrastructure to be spread out over its long life

---

[6] "A New Approach to Public Private Partnerships," Infrastructure UK, 2012.
[7] For further discussion of PSCs, www.treasury.gov.uk.
[8] For a further discussion of this topic see Jeffrey Delmon, *Public Private Partnership Projects in Infrastructure* (Cambridge University Press, 2020).

cycle (as much as thirty to fifty years) and therefore makes the infrastructure more affordable; the fixed rates help avoid sudden changes in financing costs and therefore user tariffs. Long-term financing (twelve to eighteen years tenor), either with fixed interest rates or with variable interest rates that are supported by interest rate swaps to become fixed, are generally available in the global currencies, such as US dollar, euro, yen, and pound sterling (with notable exceptions, for example, during the credit crunches in 2008/9 and 2011/12), but is more difficult to access in developing financial markets.

Long-term infrastructure investments can provide opportunities to debt capital markets, help to increase the depth and breadth of the markets, establish robust yield curves, and provide long-term placement opportunities in local markets that are often starved of such opportunities. Long-term capital for infrastructure, and their associated long-term returns, can provide a platform for reforms and market dynamism.

Accessing long-term financing for infrastructure in local currency is not so simple. Commercial banks in many countries do not have access to long-term liquidity, and they fund themselves primarily through short-term deposits. The debt capital markets may offer only short- to medium-term positions (e.g., three to five years), depriving banks of the opportunity to lay off long-term loans against long-term bond issuances. These banks will face a "liability mismatch" to the extent they lend long term (long-term loans funded with the volatility of short-term deposits).

Governments can do much to help mobilize long-term local currency debt. They regulate financial markets, setting rules for banking and capital markets, to protect different market actors and encourage activity in those markets. They also enable and provide market information, clearing functions, rating of credit risk, exchanges for different instruments, and so on. One of the key sources of long-term local currency financing is institutional investors, such as pension and insurance funds. Government reform programs can do much to protect institutional investors and thereby enable them to invest in good projects.

This section discusses different financiers of capital and how to attract such resources to infrastructure.

5.2.1 Local Commercial Banks

Local banks (public and private) may provide a very convenient source of long-term financing. While often less sophisticated than their global brethren, local banks have more access to local currency. They also tend to be less risk-averse when assessing projects in their own country, having better "on-the-ground" knowledge of factors affecting the project, taking a more "pragmatic" view of government and political risk, and having the confidence that local bureaucratic and technocratic challenges can be resolved in a satisfactory manner.

5.2.2 Global Commercial Banks

Global commercial banks are often more sophisticated, with experience in construction risk, the operation of infrastructure, and project finance, which will give them a clear competitive edge (though this capacity may be located in other offices and not in the local office). Commercial banks are desirable as long-term debt providers, given their flexibility in renegotiating loans and reacting to new or unforeseen conditions. This flexibility may not be available, for example, from bondholders.

Global banks may also have superior access to global financial markets – with deep pools of liquidity and long tenors – which are well suited to infrastructure finance. Global banks may have local activities, giving them access to local currency liquidity, but generally in limited volumes. There are exceptions, where the global bank has a strong local subsidiary or branch, but the local offices of global banks may have competing interests and are unlikely to have serious capacity on infrastructure finance located in the local offices, as they will be staffed for local operations. For these reasons, global banks tend to focus on foreign currency finance for infrastructure and are less competitive in local currency finance for infrastructure.

5.2.3 Development Financial Institutions

External development financial institutions (DFIs), including multilateral institutions like the World Bank and the International Finance Corporation (IFC) and bilateral institutions like Agence Francaise de Developpement of France, are ideally placed to support infrastructure finance and are increasingly critical to PPP in developing countries. They tend to have relatively low interest rates, long tenors, and grace periods. In addition to debt, they can also provide guarantees and insurance that may address specific financing risks faced by the project.

Where multilateral or bilateral lending agencies and export credit agencies number among the lenders, the debt package may benefit from certain insulation from political risk and preferential treatment by the host government in relation to repayment, although such lending may be more difficult to obtain due to restrictions and requirements of DFIs. Some of these DFIs also benefit from preferred creditor status, providing greater comfort to the lender group.

DFI financing tends to be in foreign currencies and can involve additional costs, related to the conditions imposed (such as procurement, safeguards, and financial management), complying with DFI practices and the time it takes to access finance.

5.2.4 Institutional and Retail Investors

Long-term liquidity may be available from institutional investors like pension and insurance funds, who may hold large volumes of long-term capital. In most countries they have difficulty finding long-term placements outside of government bonds and real estate. Long-term liquidity may also be available from retail investors, such as high wealth individuals otherwise tempted to move capital offshore, retirees looking for long-term security, and so on, in particular where other long-term investment opportunities are not available in local currency. Access to these investors is often facilitated through capital markets.

5.2.5 Debt Capital Markets

Capital markets hold depth of liquidity in addition to that available from commercial banks. Debt capital markets (through the issuance of debt securities often called "bonds") may provide access to credit at lower interest rates and longer tenors than commercial banks by providing access to retail investors and to institutional investors. However, the financing available through capital markets is often less flexible than the financial instruments available from commercial banks. For example, they are not designed to provide grace periods (where the lenders agree to defer payment of debt service during an initial period and instead to capitalize these payments) nor to provide debt in tranches (where the borrower must pay a commitment fee from financial close but pays interest only once it has drawn down the amount needed). Instead, under a bond issuance, the project company must borrow the full amount of debt needed at financial close and pay interest on that full amount until repayment (the extra interest charged for funds not yet needed is called "carry cost"). Also, the most active purchasers of debt securities (i.e., pension funds, insurance funds, and other institutional investors) do not generally have the expert staff and processes of commercial banks – designed to assess and manage risk and respond to changes and requirements of dynamic investments like infrastructure – and must hire advisors or investment banks and other intermediaries to provide such expertise.

5.2.5.1 *Global Capital Markets*
The global capital markets have access to deep and long-term capital, from sophisticated investors likely to be more interested in infrastructure investments. However, these investors are likely to have limited appetite for some country risk and for local currency placements. Even in foreign currency, these investors will be subject to certain limitations on the credit rating of the securities they purchase; in particular the prominence of pension, insurance, and other prudential funds in the global markets may limit appetite for anything less than investment grade, or even higher international credit ratings. Global capital markets are unlikely to be a significant source of local currency debt. There have been local currency bonds issued in the global markets (e.g., diaspora bonds), with some success, but usually not in large volumes. These efforts often focus on currencies from countries with large emigrant communities with close contact with their home country and desiring investments in local currency.

5.2 Financiers

5.2.5.2 Domestic Capital Markets

Local capital markets have more appetite for local currency positions and will be less sensitive to political and other country specific risk. However, for the purposes of financing infrastructure, local debt capital markets often elicit a number of challenges:

- lack of liquidity, in particular in the long term;
- short tenors and lack of a long-term yield curve; in sum, there are no comparable long-term financial instruments freely traded in the local market, so no objective basis to set a price; and
- local investors unfamiliar with the risk profile of infrastructure.

5.2.6 Equity Investors

Equity contributors in infrastructure finance transactions might include the project participants, financial investors, the host government, the contracting authority, other interested government entities, institutional investors, and bilateral or multilateral lending agencies. Investors in equity in infrastructure projects (often known as shareholders or sponsors) can provide a variety of types of financing, including ordinary and preferred equity contributions and mezzanine finance (subordinated debt sometimes known as shareholder financing).

Equity investors will want to pay in their equity investment as late as possible in the construction period, even wholly back-ended, to save costs and improve their equity return. Lenders will prefer front-ended or pro rata equity investment to maintain their cushion ratios on debt drawn down. They may want a bank or third-party payment guarantee on equity payments to be made later in the project to ensure they will be available at the time agreed.

Equity contributions earn returns from distributions by the project company, when the company earns a profit, the lending agreements allow distributions, and the board of the company approves. Generally, distributions will be paid in the currency of revenues; therefore, shareholders take foreign exchange risk to the extent their investment was made in foreign currency.

Shareholder loans are generally subordinated debt treated as quasi-equity. There are various benefits to providing debt rather than equity, including tax and priority of repayment.

Shareholders tend to be one of three project actors:

- Project participants are often shareholders, such as construction companies, operators, and suppliers. They take on a shareholding position often as much to obtain the contract for the project as to earn returns on their equity investment. They often seek to sell down their equity position as soon as possible, since equity investment is not their core business. Contractors may form a separate company to act as investor.
- Financial investors may also be shareholders. These are equity funds, banks, or other financial entities who invest solely to obtain equity returns.

The focus of these investors will be significantly different from project participant investors, which can create tension when making shareholder decisions.
- The government may also be a shareholder. The government may insist on equity shares as part of the project but may not provide additional capital in the process. Having the government (effectively the transaction counterpart) in the project company can complicate project company decision processes, in particular when deciding how to respond to disputes with the contracting authority.

5.3 KEY RISKS

A number of important risk issues will be key to the successful financing of the project. Lenders will want to see these risks allocated and managed accordingly.

5.3.1 Completion

Completion represents the end of the construction phase of the project. The construction contractor will be liable for liquidated damages for late completion; therefore, the definition of "completion" will have an important impact on the construction contractor's risk. The lenders will want to ensure that completion requires the works to be in a condition sufficient to merit release of the construction contractor from the delay liquidated damages liability. The works will therefore be subject to certain technical tests and demonstration of performance capacity before completion is achieved.

The project company will want to ensure that the criteria placed on completion can be measured objectively as set out in the construction contract and that the lenders do not have the right to refuse completion owing to their own subjective evaluation of the works. This may involve technical testing effectuated by independent experts or by standard measures or tests with clearly ascertainable results, not unreasonably subject to dispute.

Clearly, the cost of completion will be fundamental to the financial viability of the project. The lenders will need some mechanism to manage the risk that the project company's cost of completion increases as compared with that anticipated at financial close.

5.3.2 Force Majeure and Change in Law

It is important to note that the financing agreements will not include force majeure and change in law provisions. The obligation to repay the loans will continue in the event of force majeure or change in law. The lenders will want to review the force majeure and change in law provisions in the project documents and ensure that they are back to back (as far as possible) with the concession agreement.

5.3 Key Risks

5.3.3 Political Risk

As the market for project finance transactions has expanded into developing countries, concerns about political risk have grown. Commercial lenders may be prepared to take a degree of political risk (at a price), but in some countries the perceived political risk inhibits or even prevents the financing of projects that otherwise might be viable. Since the commercial insurance market can absorb only a limited degree of true political risk, many project sponsors have turned to multilateral or export credit agencies to shoulder some or all of this burden. Issues that commonly arise in relation to such cover include

- the scope of "political risk," including regulatory risk and administrative risk;
- whether or not political risk includes events in more than one country or different states of the host country;
- the relationship between political risk and other "normal" project risks (e.g., completion risk);
- the extent to which a shareholder (particularly a local shareholder) can influence events that comprise political risk; and
- the consequences of a political risk event occurring and how it affects, for example, shareholder obligations to achieve completion, liability of shareholders under indemnities provided to export credit agencies, or the basic liability of the borrower.

5.3.4 Environmental and Social Risk

Environmental and social laws and regulations will impose liabilities and constraints on a project. The cost of compliance can be significant and will need to be allocated between the project company and the contracting authority.

Environmental due diligence in respect of such projects and in respect of the legal regime within which they are being constructed and an appreciation of the environmental requirements of public agencies that will be involved with the project are crucial if the project company and lenders are to make a proper assessment of the risks involved.

Infrastructure projects generally have an important impact on local communities and quality of life, particularly in the delivery of essential services like water and electricity or land-intensive projects like toll roads. The impact of the project on society, consumers, and civil society, generally, can result in resistance from local interest groups that can delay project implementation, increase the cost of implementation, and undermine project viability.[9] This social risk should be high on lenders' due diligence agenda, though it often is not. The lenders and project company often look to the contracting authority to manage this

---

[9] Jeffrey Delmon, "Implementing Social Policy into Contracts for the Provision of Utility Services," in A. Dani, T. Kessler, and E. Sclar (eds.), *Making Connections: Putting Social Policy at the Heart of Infrastructure Development* (World Bank, 2007).

> **Box 5.5 Equator Principles**
>
> The Equator Principles constitute a voluntary code of conduct originally developed by the IFC and a core group of commercial banks but now recognized by most of the international commercial banks active in project finance. These banks have agreed not to lend to projects that do not comply with the Equator Principles. They follow generally the IFC system of categorizing projects, identifying those that are more sensitive to environmental or social impact, and requiring specialist assessment where appropriate. During project implementation, the borrower must prepare and comply with an environmental and social management plan.[10]

risk. The contracting authority in turn may underestimate its importance, since the social risk paradigm for public utilities is very different and the contracting authority may not have experience of its implications for private investors.

Equally, in order to attract international lenders, in particular international finance institutions (IFIs), the project must meet minimum environmental and social requirements that may exceed those set out in applicable laws and regulations(see Box 5.5). This process is made easier where local law supports similar levels of compliance.

5.3.5 Currency Exchange Risk

Infrastructure finance debt is often sourced from foreign lenders, in foreign currencies, yet project revenues are generally denominated in local currency. Where the exchange rate between the currency of revenue and the currency of debt diverge, the cost of debt can increase, often dramatically. Though under the theory of purchasing power parity, inflation pressures on the devalued currency will eventually bring the foreign exchange rate back to parity, project finance lenders are generally not prepared to wait quite so long (with average periods of about ten years).

Where revenues are to be earned in some currency other than that in which the debt is denominated, lenders will want to see the revenue stream is adjusted to compensate for any relevant change in exchange rate or devaluation. If this is not available, they will want to see appropriately robust hedging arrangements or some other mechanism to manage currency exchange risk.

5.3.6 Interest Rate Risk

Interest may be charged at a fixed rate, at variable rates (usually based on the bank's lending rate or an interbank borrowing rate plus a margin),

---

[10] www.ifc.org.

5.4 Key Investor Concerns

or a floating rate (calculated by reference to cost of short-term deposits). The spread or margin is expressed in "basis points." One basis point is one-hundredth of 1 percent. Interbank borrowing rates include LIBOR (London interbank borrowing rate), EURIBOR (in the European Union), and NIBOR (in New York).[11]

Project finance debt tends to be fixed rate. This helps provide a foreseeable, or at least somewhat stable, repayment profile over time to reduce fluctuations in the cost of infrastructure services. If lenders are unable to provide fixed-rate debt and no project participant is willing to bear the risk, hedging or some other arrangements may need to be implemented to manage the risk that interest rates increase to a point that debt service becomes unaffordable to the project. The tension between local and foreign currency debt is often a question of balancing fixed-rate debt with foreign exchange rate risk or local currency debt subject to interest rate risk.

5.4 KEY INVESTOR CONCERNS

When a lender considers financing infrastructure, it will perform due diligence and test whether the risks and investment potential merit investment of time and money for due diligence. The following sets out a few issues that are critically important to lenders. The feasibility study and the project agreements should address these issues. Government should review projects from the perspective of the lender to understand better the lender's perspective and priorities in advance of the bidding process and to prepare for the kind of questions and concerns that the investors/lenders will likely raise.

The key concerns of the lenders will be discussed here around a series of key questions that potential investors will ask when considering a project. This is not an exhaustive discussion, but rather it is meant to help municipalities understand some of the key issues relevant to private investors.

5.4.1 Importance of Project

Lenders know that projects that are important to the government and to the people have a better chance of closing and of succeeding. Projects that are important only to a particular official or political party are probably less likely to succeed. Indications of the importance of a project include the project's presence on the priority list of the government, the assessment of economic impact that the project will have on the local community and on the country at large, and the level of engagement with the local community (in the identification and design of the project as well as its implementation).

---

[11] Since the various allegations of the manipulation of LIBOR, there is some question as to the future of interbank borrowing rates.

5.4.2 Project "Champion"?

Lenders realize that projects will require someone powerful and influential enough to "push" the project through the various obstacles that projects are bound to face through the process of development and bidding. Therefore, they would typically try and get a better understanding of who within the government is championing this project. (*Note*: This is not information that the lenders will get from the bid documents or other documents shared by the government; this is research that the lenders will undertake.) This assessment will include the context of the "champion," including timing of the next election and the likelihood of the champion remaining in power.

5.4.3 Project Approvals

Lenders will need to understand all of the permits and licenses that need to be obtained at different stages of the project, before implementation, during implementation, and throughout operation – which approvals the municipality will secure and which ones the lenders have to secure, and which of these approvals are sensitive or difficult/time-consuming to secure. Even though the municipality may take on the responsibility of securing key regulatory and legal approvals, lenders will need a solid understanding of the probability of getting all required approvals and the likely time frame for the same. They will assess the risks and associated costs of waiting to commence construction or commence operations after construction due to delays in securing approvals. The project agreements will need to explain how and under what conditions, if at all, the government will compensate the investors for any delays in securing these approvals or where the approvals require different performance obligations or investments than are anticipated in the project agreements.

5.4.4 Demand Levels

There is a tendency for demand assessments to suffer from optimism bias, in particular where the assessment is performed by a party incentivized to see the project implemented. A municipality, for example, is likely to assume a much higher level of demand for a project than would other more conservative project parties. Studies of traffic forecasts and similar demand forecasts show a consistent overestimation of demand by the government, investor, and lenders, with lenders being the most conservative.

Potential investors will discount any demand forecast provided by the contracting authority (even if produced by an expert) to protect itself from the impact of optimism bias. Potential investors often undertake their own demand assessment. Even if they do not undertake a comprehensive assessment (e.g., if the government has undertaken a comprehensive study through a reputable expert), lenders would undertake a quick assessment of demand to validate the

5.4 Key Investor Concerns

study and to determine how much they should discount it. Even for demand forecasts, potential investors want to dig deeper on the factors that would affect demand positively and negatively in the years ahead. For example, lenders will assess any new urban area under development that would increase demand or a new industrial zone or township on the outskirts of the city under development that would result in an increase in demand. More often than not, just a population growth-driven assessment of demand is not adequate for lenders and they typically need more granularity with respect to demand projections.

5.4.5 Source of Demand

Potential investors need to understand the sources of demand. Are the high-demand segments located in some specific geographical areas or is the demand based on some demographic parameters, such as age or income? For example, for a water supply distribution project, potential investors would need a detailed breakdown of demand across the service area to assess the robustness of the demand from various segments and also its likely projected growth. This information is also used to design the project better and also plan operation of the project to fit actual needs.

Potential investors take seasonal variations in demand into account because it directly affects cash flows of a project and consequently debt servicing and other payout obligations. Moreover, if the seasonality is high enough, lenders also look at seasonality of labor demands and operating costs across different seasons. This can help design operating cost efficiencies.

5.4.6 Revenues

Just as demand forecasts are often optimistic, so too are revenue forecasts. Potential investors would like to understand the basis of determination of the tariff for the services being provided by the project, how the tariff is regulated, any administrative or bureaucratic approvals required, and whether users/people are likely to pay the proposed tariff (affordability and willingness to pay). Investors will compare proposed tariffs with similar services offered in neighboring municipalities and countries. They will also make an assessment of how strong the government is and whether they would be able to withstand any resistance against tariffs from citizens/users.

The potential investor will carefully assess revenue forecasts and will question all assumptions and discount forecasts provided by the government. Just like demand forecasts, revenue forecasts are subject to optimism bias – that is, those promoting the project will have a tendency to interpret data to show more healthy revenues than might be merited, whether this optimism is conscious or unconscious.

Lenders would like to understand how tariff revisions will take place. The project agreements will establish a baseline tariff and generally an agreed formula for tariff increases. Where there is a regulator (whether or not independent), the parties will need to agree how to resolve situations where the regulator sets a tariff that is inconsistent with the agreements. If tariff revisions for the entire period of the project are already set by regulation and that regulation cannot be modified, the agreements will use this as its baseline. Potential investors will assess the risk that tariffs are not increased or that those increases do not meet expectations. Their financial models will likely test for scenarios where tariffs do not meet agreed levels and the impact this will have on project financial viability.

5.4.7 Government Creditworthiness

Particularly for projects where the government pays for the service – for example, supply of treated bulk water to the government or operation and maintenance contract for a public sanitary landfill site – potential investors are entirely dependent on the availability of finances with the government to pay for the services provided and their actual payments. Investors need to understand the credit position of the government, its history of paying bills on time, its management of its finances, and so on. Where possible, the government should share whatever financial information it can to help potential investors understand the risk involved and create confidence among potential investors. Investors will make higher provisions for working capital (assuming delayed payments) and build into the operating costs, when preparing their bids, any perceived risk associated with the government fulfilling its financial obligations.

5.4.8 Project Configuration

Potential investors would like to understand whether the project structure is mandated or are only some aspects mandated, or is there a minimum specification of various elements. Lenders would like to explore different project configurations to maximize revenue while still delivering the specified service levels of the basic service. For example, in a bus terminal, while maintaining basic standards of making a bus bay available within say two minutes of a bus arriving, the potential investor will want the flexibility to ensure maximized space for retail outlets or restaurants or office space. Use of space outside of operating hours can also provide some interesting opportunities, for example, using the bus terminal as a parking facility for buses as well as other vehicles at night. Can the facilities include a hotel or other associated facilities?

Potential investors would typically undertake a thorough investigation into the proposed engineering design, in particular where the design has been mandated or only some elements of the basic project engineering design are mandated. The due diligence process will assess whether the mandated elements of the engineering design are appropriate given the specific project site conditions and service requirements. Investors also prefer to have the opportunity to

5.4 Key Investor Concerns

propose value additions or cost reduction to establish their competitive advantage and also maximize investor returns.

5.4.9 Time for Construction/Implementation

Potential investors are keen to complete project construction/implementation as early as possible to commence operations and start revenue flows. However, the time allowed for construction, testing, and commissioning needs to provide sufficient space for the construction to be delivered to the quality desired. The investor will also need to understand the process for approval of different stages of construction, who within the government will review, test, and approve, and the likelihood of delays in approvals. Governments need to think through which stages are really critical from a technical point of view and how to monitor and approve in the most efficient manner possible – the "must haves" rather than the "good to haves."

5.4.10 Materials/Inputs Required

Potential investors will perform extensive due diligence on project construction/implementation costs and the time required for the completion of the construction/implementation. They will be concerned about an underestimation of construction costs and therefore undertake their own detailed assessment. Usually detailed engineering design is not done as part of the feasibility study, even when undertaken by reputed experts, and construction costs are arrived at based on quick and rough engineering design and estimation of bill of quantities. Material costs need to be based on competitive market rates, providing for inflation in material costs between estimation and actual project implementation (which generally involved a delay of as much as two to three years or more, which makes an accurate calculation almost impossible). Lead times required for material availability will affect the inventory of materials that the construction contractor needs to carry and consequently the working capital requirement, which also add to construction cost. Some construction requires long lead items, which must be ordered long before delivery (e.g., specialized steel, tunnel boring machines, and turbines). The procurement process and construction milestones should provide for such time constraints.

5.4.11 Access to Skilled Staff

The project will need access to skilled labor. It is advantageous to the government, and generally to the investors, to source such labor locally. However, such skilled labor may not be available, or may be more expensive, locally. Potential investors want to understand the availability and costs of relevant skilled labor in the vicinity of the project. Finding the right people for each project is absolutely critical to implement and operate projects.

5.4.12 Cost and Revenue Risk

Once costs, revenues, and demand are forecast, the potential investor will assess what might happen to cause costs to go up, revenues to go down, or otherwise undermine the financial projects for the project. Investors will assess the likelihood of such events and their potential impact and apply sensitivity analysis to the project financials to assess the impact on the project if the event or series of events occurs. For example, where will the project source cement? Is the cost of cement likely to go up? How easy is it to access labor with the requisite skills and experience? Are income taxes likely to increase? Or might tariffs for project services be reduced by law? By considering these risks in advance, governments can address them in advance to reduce their impact on potential bids; for example, they may want to set up an experienced and independent regulator with the power to set tariffs and impose performance standards. Also, lenders will need to understand the implications of local content rules and what local content is most appropriate to include in project planning.

5.4.13 Security Structure

Lenders need to be willing to lend to the project based primarily on its financials and structure. They will test whether the project financials are adequate to enable debt servicing (interest and repayment of principal) comfortably and also whether the lenders have a security structure that enables them to ensure recovery of their loan.

Because assets typically cannot be repossessed in case of default of the loan and are often immoveable (such as a road or a bus terminal) or have limited value when moved away from their location, lenders will want security over the project cash inflows instead, that is, over revenues. Lenders often ask the investors to create an escrow account where all project revenues flow. They also seek, in addition to the escrow account, the creation of a debt service reserve account with cash equivalent to, say, three months' payment obligation of the government.

Lenders will also want step-in rights; where the investor is not performing its obligations, the lender has the right to replace the investor with another investor with similar or better technical and financial credentials.

Governments can offer different forms of support; for example, they may contribute capital to the project as a subsidy or as equity to reinforce project financials. They may offer guarantees or other credit enhancement to protect the lenders in the event of certain risks (such as demand shortfall) to make the project less risky. Such credit enhancement and security structures enhance the confidence of the potential investors and lenders in the project. If governments offer this in the project bid documents, it bolsters the lenders' ability to provide financing at more competitive rates and better terms, which in turn allows investors to make more and more price competitive bids.

5.4 Key Investor Concerns

5.4.14 Foreign Exchange Risk

Revenues from public services are generally denominated in local currency. Financing available for infrastructure is more often foreign sourced. In many cases, foreign financing offers longer tenor and lower interest rate. But if the exchange rate between the local currency and the currency of financing changes, this may limit the ability of the project to repay debt. Local currency debt mitigates the foreign exchange risk, but generally the amounts available are lower, for shorter tenor, and with higher interest rate.

5.4.15 Minimum Service-Level Obligations

The bid documents need to outline the required service levels, how they will be measured, and what penalties will be imposed for nonachievement, in as much detail as possible. The desired service levels need to be realistic given the other supporting infrastructure and in line with the typical levels of operation and maintenance in other infrastructure. Lenders are keen to understand how service levels will be monitored and measured, for example, with support from an independent engineering consulting company or by government staff. The monitoring official's identity, compensation arrangements, and terms of reference will create specific incentives to ensure delivery of the service levels, which the lenders will want to understand. Finally, the penalties to be levied for nonachievement of service levels need to be specified and realistic, that is, in line with the project revenues.

5.4.16 Government Obligations

The investor will feel vulnerable in the face of a government that has so much power over the project and its context. Governments may decide not to comply with their obligations, may change rules or regulations, may impose new permits or licenses, or create other constraints, in particular in the event of a change in government or after an election. Lenders will have little power to resist such changes, even where they are fundamental to the success of the project. Potential investors will review the government's history of respecting contracts and of using its power to deprive investors of assets or opportunities, as well as the frequency and transparency of the regulatory and permitting authority wielded by the government.

5.4.17 Reliability of Courts and Arbitration

Even if the project provides protection to the private investor, those protections are legal and contractual in nature. Local courts may not be perceived as trustworthy. In some countries, the courts are viewed as likely to take the side of the government over the private sector, or of local investors over foreign investors. Arbitration can be perceived as a more independent way to resolve disputes. Once the dispute is resolved, the award must be enforced. Local court decisions or local arbitration will need to be enforced based on local laws. International arbitration in many countries is enforced in accordance with international treaties and is therefore preferred by most investors.

5.4.18 Program/Pipeline

Bids are expensive to develop. A potential bidder will assess its likelihood of winning the bid before incurring the expense of bidding. If there is a large program of projects that will be let over the short to medium term by the government or in the country, then the potential bidder will assess whether it might win one of the projects when deciding whether to bid. The potential bidder can disperse the cost of bidding for one project across the likelihood of winning one or more of multiple projects. This will result in more and better bidders entering the market and pursuing individual projects. Therefore, a large program of projects offers better opportunities for potential bidders.

5.4.19 Open, Transparent, and Fair Procurement

Lenders will be concerned to know if the investment required to develop a bid and perform due diligence on a project will provide a fair opportunity to win the project. If another bidder has an unfair advantage, or may be able to steal the project even if it does not win the bid process, then potential bidders will be less likely to bid, and lenders may not want to invest the time and effort in supporting a bidder.

5.5 PROJECT FINANCE

One of the most efficient financing arrangements for private financing for infrastructure projects is project financing, also known as "limited recourse" or "nonrecourse" financing. Project financing normally takes the form of limited recourse lending to a specially created project vehicle that has the right to carry out the construction and/or operation of the project. One of the primary advantages of project financing is that it can provide off-balance sheet financing, which will not affect the credit of the shareholders or the contracting authority, and shifts some of the project risk to the lenders in exchange for which the lenders obtain a higher margin than for normal corporate lending. Project financing achieves a better/lower WACC than pure equity financing. It also promotes a transparent risk-sharing regime and creates incentives across different project parties to encourage good performance and efficient risk management.

5.5 Project Finance

5.5.1 Off-Balance Sheet

Project financing may allow the shareholders to keep financing and project liabilities "off-balance sheet." Project debt held in a sufficiently minority subsidiary is not consolidated onto the balance sheet of the respective shareholders. This reduces the impact of the project on the cost of shareholders' existing debt and on their debt capacity, releasing such debt capacity for additional investments. Clearly, any project structure seeking off-balance sheet treatment needs to be considered carefully under applicable law and accountancy rules.

To a certain extent, the contracting authority can also use project finance to keep project debt and liabilities off-balance sheet, taking up less fiscal space. Fiscal space indicates the debt capacity of a sovereign entity and is a function of requirements placed on the host country by its own laws or by the rules applied by supra- or international bodies or market constraints, such as the International Monetary Fund and the rating agencies. Those requirements will indicate to what extent project lending will be treated as off-balance sheet for the government.

It should be noted that keeping debt off-balance sheet does not necessarily reduce actual liabilities for the government and may merely disguise government liabilities. Knowing this, rating agencies and other similar oversight authorities will monitor project finance transactions and consider associated government liabilities in their assessments.

5.5.2 Limited Recourse and Sponsor Support

One of the advantages to the shareholders of project financing is the absence, or limitation, of recourse by the lenders to the shareholders' assets. The project company is generally a limited liability special purpose project vehicle; therefore, the lenders' recourse will be limited primarily or entirely to the project assets (including any completion and performance guarantees and bonds).

Nonrecourse (also, more accurately called "limited recourse") financing limits the lenders' recourse to the assets of the project at hand in case of default by the project company. A key question in any limited recourse financing is whether there will be circumstances in which the limited recourse nature of the borrower's liability is to fall away and the lenders are to have additional recourse to part or all of the shareholders' assets. Generally, the type of breach of covenant or representation that gives rise to this consequence is a deliberate breach on the part of the shareholders, in particular, the shareholders not using appropriate efforts to ensure that the project is successful by, for example, committing a breach of the operating or joint venture agreement that governs the running of the project. It should also be noted that applicable law will restrict the extent to which liability can be limited, for example, liability for personal injury or death.

Difficult questions arise in relation to the obligations of the shareholders to take up the participation of joint venturers who drop out or default on their obligations and, in particular, the question of when the shareholders are to be entitled to abandon the project in the event of catastrophe or in the event that the project no longer proves financially viable. These issues will be resolved either in the drafting of the financing agreement or at law (generally through the law of tort or contract).

Where some portion of the project involves more risk than another, recourse may be provided to the lenders to the extent of that risk or until that high-risk period has passed. Alternatively, the amount of recourse allowed to the lenders may be limited in value. The extent to which some recourse is provided is commonly called "sponsor support." In project financing, the construction phase involves particular risks for the lenders. The value of the project against which the lenders provide financing is usually in the operation and the payment stream supported by the concession agreement and not in the equipment and materials, the physical assets of the project. Since the lenders will bear more risk until construction is complete, sponsor support is sometimes provided for the period up to completion of the works, which will generally be defined in the concession agreement and marked by the issue of a certificate or the passing of specified tests. It may also be provided for the period until certain financial ratios are attained or until the works have achieved a period of operation at a certain level. Another approach is to provide the lenders with limited recourse to sponsor assets in the event of certain breaches of the financing agreements by the project company or the shareholders.

Sponsor support may include, where a shareholder agrees to provide:

- shortfall guarantees, to protect against the risk that the banks, after enforcing all other security rights, experience a shortfall;
- buydown undertakings, to prepay project debt to ensure specified ratios, in certain circumstances;
- price guarantees, to ensure pricing of offtake;
- market price purchase guarantees, to purchase a minimum quantity of product at market price over a set period;
- tax loss purchases, to purchase certain tax losses from the project company;
- technical support, to provide extended warranties, and maintenance arrangements; and
- contingent equity or subordinated debt commitments, to cover construction or other price overruns.

The project company will want to limit the type of breaches resulting in recourse to the shareholders, such as egregious or intentional breaches of essential covenants or representations that may alter the lenders' risk matrix. Sponsor support may involve the establishment of a fund, normally pledged or secured, which can be used, for example, where there is a deficiency of funds or an increase in costs during the period of limited recourse.

5.5 Project Finance

5.5.3 Bankability

Lenders' recourse for repayment of debt will be limited primarily to the revenue flow from the project. Due to the limited recourse and highly leveraged nature of project financing, any interruption of the project revenue stream or additional costs not contemplated in the project financial plan will directly threaten the ability to make debt service payments. This makes lenders extremely risk-averse. Lenders will want to ensure that the risks borne by the project company are limited and properly managed and that the project involves a solid financial, economic, and technical plan. Therefore, before committing themselves to a project, they will perform an in-depth review of the viability of the project (their "due diligence"). This is commonly known as verifying the project's "bankability."

Bankability requirements will vary based on the identity of the lenders, who will have different interests and concerns and perceptions of risk. Lenders' vigilance is a key benefit of project finance, helping the contracting authority and shareholders alike to assess project viability. Clearly, an overly anxious lender can delay, complicate, or even undermine a project. Equally, a lender that is not sensitive to risk, for example, where the government provides a comprehensive guarantee of the debt, will not be as concerned about due diligence, and therefore the benefits of the lender's incentive to assess and monitor the project are lost. A lender's due diligence will include several factors, which are discussed in the following subsections.

5.5.3.1 Economic and Political

Lenders will wish to review the effect the local economy and the project will have on each other. Although it is the contracting authority and not the lenders who should be verifying that the project will have an overall beneficial impact on the site country and the local economy, the lenders will need to assess the net political and socioeconomic benefit the project can have on the site country generally.[12] A commonly used measurement is the economic internal rate of return (EIRR[13]), which means the project's rate of return after taking into account economic costs and benefits, including monetary costs and benefits. EIRR captures the externalities (such as social and environmental benefits) not included in financial IRR calculations.[14]

Lenders will also use this macrolevel assessment to ask certain fundamental questions about the project:[15]

---

[12] For further discussion of this issue, see Geoff Haley, *A-Z of Boot: How to Create Successful Structures for Boot Projects* (IFR Publications, 1996), p. 34.
[13] EIRR is the project's internal rate of return after taking into account externalities (such as economic, social, and environmental costs and benefits) not included in normal financial IRR calculations.
[14] FIRR is the discount rate that equates the present value of a future stream of payments to the initial investment. See also EIRR.
[15] As modified from United Nations Industrial Development Organisation, "Guidelines for Infrastructure Development through Build-Operate-Transfer," 1996, p. 130.

- historical and likely future trends in prices, costs, production, availability, quality, competition, demand, and the nature of the demand;
- identification and location of the input supplier and other service providers;
- flexibility, sophistication, skill, and depth of the labor market;
- historical and likely future trends in inflation rates, interest rates, foreign exchange cost, and the availability of labor, materials, and services (such as water, power, and telecoms);
- condition of local infrastructure; and
- administrative burden placed on imports, in particular specialized labor and equipment.

5.5.3.2 *Legal/Regulatory*
Lenders will want to consider the legal system (including regulation and taxation) applicable to the project in view of

- the viability of a long-term commercial arrangement based on undertakings by the public sector, which normally involve property rights, asset management, management of tax exposure and governance of the project company through corporate structures;
- the likelihood of changes in law and taxation during the project;
- whether and to what extent the legal system is accessible to the project company and the lenders, including the time and resources required to access judicial review and whether such decisions can be enforced (courts or arbitration); and
- the availability of security rights and priority given to creditors.

5.5.3.3 *Financial*
In asset financing, it is the value and rate of depreciation of the underlying assets that define lenders' security and willingness to finance a project. In project financing, it is the viability of the project structure, the business plan, and the forecast revenue stream that will convince lenders to provide financing. The revenue stream is only as secure as the credit position of the offtaker (e.g., the power utility that plans to buy the electricity generated), so lenders will assess carefully the credit risk of different project counterparties, including of course the project shareholders. Financial due diligence will include issues associated with financing risk such as historical information on exchange rate movements, inflation, interest rates, availability of hedging and swaps, availability of insurance and reinsurance, and remedies available against different counterparties for losses or damages.

Lenders will develop their financial model from the information available. This model will identify the various financial inputs and outflows of the project. By considering the project risk in the financial model, lenders will be able to test project sensitivities, that is, how far the project can absorb the occurrence of a given risk, for example, a 10 percent increase in construction costs

5.5 Project Finance

> **Box 5.6 Financial terms**
>
> A number of financial ratios are used to test financial viability, which include the following:
>
> - *debt-to-equity ratio* – compares the amount of debt in the project against the amount of equity invested;
> - *debt service cover ratio (or DSCR)* – measures the income of the project that is available to meet debt service (after deducting operating expenses) against the amount of debt service due in the same period. This ratio can be either backward or forward looking; and
> - *loan life cover ratio (or LLCR)* – the net present value of future project income, available to meet debt service over the maturity of the loan against the amount of debt.

or a 10 percent reduction in revenues. When assessing financial viability, they will use the financial model to test a number of financial ratios, in particular debt-to-equity, debt service cover, loan life cover, and rates of return (some of these concepts are defined in Box 5.6 and in the glossary).

5.5.3.4 Technical

The review of a project carried out by its lenders will also focus on the technical merits of the design or intended design and the technology to be used in the project. The lenders will prefer not to finance projects using cutting edge or untested technology. They will want to have relatively accurate performance forecasts – including operation, maintenance, and life-cycle costs, the capacity of the technology to be used and its appropriateness for the site, and the type of performance required from the project – and will therefore prefer tried and tested technology used in similar projects with well-documented performance. Technical due diligence will also consider administrative issues, such as the likelihood of obtaining permits and approvals using the technology in question and the reasonableness of the construction schedule and price.

5.5.4 Taking Security

Lenders want to be protected in the event of insolvency of the project company. In the event the company can no longer meet its obligations, the lenders do not want to rely on the discretion of the courts under bankruptcy proceedings and will therefore want to appoint an administrative receiver to manage the allocation of project company assets to the benefit of its senior creditors. Under certain legal systems, a lender holding security over all project company assets, including receivables and future receivables, can appoint such an administrative receiver. In other legal systems, the extent to which lenders can take security over all project assets, in the event of insolvency or failure of the project company, may be limited, and therefore sophisticated structures must be implemented to achieve the level of security needed by project finance lenders.

Lenders will want to put in place as much security for the financing as possible. Security is both "offensive" and "defensive": offensive to the extent the lenders can enforce the security to dispose of assets and repay debt where the project fails; defensive to the extent that senior security can protect the lenders from actions by unsecured or junior creditors. Complete control requires comprehensive fixed and floating charges (which terms differ by country) over all project assets. If such comprehensive security rights are not available, the lenders may seek to use ring-fencing covenants in an effort to restrict other liabilities, security over project company shares to allow the lenders to take over control of the company, or the creation of a special golden share that provides the lenders with control in the event of default. Security rights may also allow the lenders to take over the project rather than just sell the project assets, since the value of the project lies in its operation and not in completed assets.[16]

A fixed charge attaches to the assets immediately, and such asset can be disposed of only subject to that charge. Under a floating charge, the asset may be managed in the ordinary course of business without reference to the holder of the charge. The charge does not attach to an asset until a specified event occurs, at which point the charge crystallizes and becomes a fixed charge over the relevant assets. Charges may be registerable, which provides the lenders with additional comfort.

The principal lenders issues in relation to securing their lending include

- share pledge or retention (where the lenders can take over ownership of shares);
- security over all (or substantially all) of the project assets and project agreements;
- security over insurance proceeds (as permitted), bonds, guarantees, and liquidated damages obligations of the project participants;
- collateral agreements and direct undertakings between the lenders and the parties to the more significant project agreements;
- standby equity or debt;
- legal rights and receivables (in particular the revenue stream) of the project company;
- bank accounts including retention and reserve accounts;
- sponsor support undertakings;
- guarantees from parent companies for their subsidiaries;
- government guarantees;

---

[16] Lender rights to run the project rather than just sell off the assets will require consideration of the applicable legal system and its treatment of security and insolvency. Rights over project company shares may achieve the desired security but may also involve the lenders taking on project risk.

5.5 Project Finance

- default, cross-default, and step-in rights so as to give the lenders maximum control over the possible termination, and cure, of any default related to any of the project documents; and
- comprehensive insurances either as coinsureds or assignable to the lenders.

The nature of the security taken over project assets will depend on the provisions of applicable law and negotiations between the lenders and the project company.

The security rights sought by lenders also include practical control mechanisms, such as reserve discretions (where the project company is limited to the discretion that it can exercise without lender approval). Lenders will also have trigger events, which allow lenders additional rights and powers in the event of their occurrence.

Since the types of security provided will often relate to either real property in the host country or movable property found within the territory of the host country, the host country's legal system will generally apply to the ownership, seizure, and security over such property. Insolvency and bankruptcy laws may also restrict the enforceability of security rights.

The project company may be a wholly owned subsidiary of a shell company that in turn is owned by the shareholders. This can permit shareholder issues to be addressed in a more favorable jurisdiction for providing lender security, voting rights, and management arrangements.

5.5.5 Financial Ratios

Given the importance of leverage and the sensitivity of lenders to the security of the project revenue stream, a number of financial ratios will be key to the analysis of a project-financed transaction. Financial ratios can quantify many aspects of the project company's business and operations and are an integral part of analyzing its financial position. For instance, profitability ratios (e.g., return on equity) measure its rate of return, liquidity ratios (e.g., DSCR) measure how much cash is available to pay down debt, and debt ratios (e.g., LLCR) measure the project company's ability to repay long-term debt.

During due diligence, before financial close, lenders will run these ratios using various sensitivities, for example, testing the financial ratios in the event construction costs increase by 20 percent or revenues fall by 10 percent. After financial close, the lenders will use these ratios as part of the project monitoring and control functions. Where ratios do not achieve the levels required, the lenders will have a series of possible interventions including blocking distributions, sweeping cash from existing accounts, applying reserve account money to debt service, taking control of additional rights of the borrower or its shareholders, and other measures to ensure that the company continues to be managed in a manner focused on successful implementation of the project and earns revenues sufficient to cover debt service. If these breaches persist, eventually, they will amount to events of default permitting the lenders to accelerate, cancel outstanding loan amounts, or suspend existing loans. Such breaches may also permit the lenders to increase the interest rate and require compensation for additional investigation costs and other fees and fines they incur. The following sets out some of the main ratios of interest to lenders.

5.5.5.1 Debt-to-Equity Ratio

A company's debt-to-equity ratio is calculated as its long-term debt divided by the shareholders' equity. Lenders will prefer a lower debt-to-equity ratio in order to obtain a greater investment from the shareholders, ensure shareholder commitment to the project, increase the net value of project assets, and provide the lender with greater security arising from the additional equity capital injection into the project, thus increasing the net value of project assets. Shareholders, on the other hand, will want an increased debt-to-equity ratio, decreasing the amount of investment they will need to supply and, since the return on debt contributions is fixed, increasing the potential return they can obtain from their equity contributions.

The actual agreed debt-to-equity ratio will be the result of a compromise between the project company and the lenders, based on the overall risk to be borne by the lenders, the project risk generally, the nature of the project, the identity of the sponsors, the industrial sector and technology involved, the value of the project, and the nature of the financial markets. For example, debt-to-equity ratios for power projects in developing countries tend to be in the order of 80:20 to 70:30, while other projects with higher market risks may not exceed 50–60 percent debt.

5.5.5.2 Loan Life Cover Ratio

The LLCR is the net present value of available cash for debt service over the full length of the credit facilities divided by the principal outstanding. It is expressed as a ratio representing the number of times the cash flow (over the scheduled life of the loan) can repay the outstanding debt balance.

To verify that the total outstanding debt is not at risk from a shortfall, lenders will apply a minimum LLCR to ensure that the total revenue available to the project company over the life of the loan is adequate to repay and service the total amount of debt outstanding.

5.5.5.3 Debt Service Cover Ratio

The amount of payment due to the lenders by the project company at any given time is called debt service, and making those payments is known as servicing debt. Lenders will want to be sure that as and when each payment obligation of the borrower arises, the borrower will have the money available to pay that amount. The lenders will therefore analyze, through the project financial model, the ratio of the total amount of revenues available for debt service (e.g., net of operating costs, insurance premiums, taxes, etc., but

5.5 Project Finance

before equity distributions) during a period and compare this to the amount of debt service owed. The DSCR measures the amount of cash flow available to meet periodic interest and principal payments on debt. Unlike the LLCR, it examines the project company's ability to meet its debt payments with reference to a particular period of time, for example, annually or semiannually, rather than over the life of the loan. This assessment can be made forward or backward looking.

5.5.5.4 Rate of Return

Rate of return or "return on investment", or sometimes just "return", is the ratio of the money gained or lost on an investment relative to the amount of money invested, usually on an annual basis. It includes the return earned on both debt and equity. IRR is the discount rate that results in a net present value of zero of revenues over the project period, which shows the annualized effective compounded rate of return that can be earned on the invested capital (again, both debt and equity).

Return on equity, on the other hand, strips out the return committed to debt servicing, providing equity investors with a picture of their return over the period of the project. Private sector shareholders will expect a high rate of return when they provide equity funding for a project because of the risk they will bear (the return reflects the risk premium). The actual rate of return achieved by the project company can be influenced by

- exchange rates between the local currency and any currency in which debt will be made available, including the cost of exchange and any applicable or potential currency restrictions;
- the willingness of private sector lenders, the capital markets, or other interested lenders to provide debt to the project, the interest rates and maturities available for such debt, the debt service cover ratios that they will require, and other conditions that the private sector lenders will impose;
- the availability of bilateral, export credit, multilateral, governmental, and other funding for the project;
- the leverage of debt to equity that the project company can withstand (see the discussion of WACC in Section 5.5.5.5); and
- the tax and accounting regime applicable to the project, including methods of calculating depreciation, treatment of off-balance sheet financing, and tax treatment of interest payments relating to debt exceeding certain legislatively prescribed debt-to-equity ratios.

Project financing assists investors in maximizing debt leverage, increasing the debt-to-equity ratio, and reducing the WACC.

5.5.5.5 Weighted Average Cost of Capital

The WACC is used to measure the project company's cost of capital: the value of its equity plus the cost of its debt. It is calculated by multiplying the cost of each capital component, such as share capital, bonds, and long-term debt, by its proportional weight and then adding these components together. Assuming that the interest charged on debt is much lower than the returns sought by equity investors, increasing the amount of debt also increases equity return. This is because the total amount paid by the project company in respect of its debt and equity (measured by its WACC) will be lower compared to a project fully equity financed, thereby leaving the project company with more funds for distribution and an increased return on equity. It also allows investors to spread precious equity capital over a greater number of projects (as total equity investment required for each project decreases through better leverage), allowing investors (in particular those with specialist sector expertise – sponsors) to undertake more projects and thereby deliver more infrastructure. Consider the following two scenarios where USD 400 is invested in a project company. In scenario 1, the amount is invested fully as equity with a return of 10 percent. The WACC would be (USD 400 × 10%)/USD 400 = 0.1. In scenario 2, the project company uses the leverage offered by a 3:1 debt-to-equity ratio and so the USD 100 equity investment is accompanied by a debt of USD 300 at a cost of say 7 percent. The WACC in scenario 2 would therefore be [(USD 100 × 10%) + (USD 300 × 7%)]/USD 400 = 0.078. The lower WACC in scenario 2 illustrates that the project company will have a lower threshold or cost to overcome before its cash flows create value for shareholders, increasing the return on equity investment.

5.5.6 Refinancing

After completion of construction, and construction risk in the project has been significantly reduced, the project company will look to refinance project debt at a lower cost and on better terms, given the lower risk premium. Less expensive and longer-term debt can significantly increase equity return, with the excess debt margin released, where the project performs well and where credit markets are sufficiently buoyant

In developed economies, the capital markets are often used as a refinancing tool after completion of the project, since the bondholders prefer not to bear project completion risk but are often able to provide fixed rates at a longer tenor and lower margin than commercial banks. Refinancing can be very challenging, in particular for lesser developed financial markets, where debt may not be as readily available and where lenders may not be experienced in refinancing infrastructure projects.

While wanting to incentivize the project company to pursue improved financial engineering, in particular through refinancing, the contracting authority will want to share in the project company's refinancing gains, often in the form of a 50–50 split. The contracting authority may also want the right to require refinancing in certain circumstances.

6

Climate Finance

Climate finance mobilizes capital to deliver climate change mitigation and adaptation activities.[1] Mitigation refers to actions that seek to reduce or avoid the release of greenhouse gas (GHG) emissions or to remove emissions, for example, through increasing the capacity of carbon sinks, to slow the pace of

---

[1] This chapter benefitted from work by Maria Lucila Serra Lahunsembarne, provided in the context of country assessments to access climate finance. Additional sources of information on climate finance include: The Project Preparation Resource Directory, https://citiesclimatefinance.org/project-preparation-resource-directory/; The NDC Partnership Climate Finance Explorer, https://ndcpartnership.org/climate-finance-explorer#:~:text=The%20Climate%20Finance%20Explorer%20is,can%20help%20you%2C%20click%20here; Compendium of Climate Finance Reports and Tools, https://e-lib.iclei.org/finance/Climate%20finance%20reports%20and%20tools-Website3.pdf; Toolkit to Enhance Access to Climate Finance, https://unfccc.int/sites/default/files/resource/Toolkit_to_Enhance_Access_to_Climate_Finance_UPDF.pdf; A Resource Guide to Climate Finance, https://actalliance.org/wp-content/uploads/2018/06/ENGLISH-quick-guide-climate-finance.pdf; Accessing Climate Finance: A Step-by-Step Approach for Practitioners, www.climasouth.eu/docs/E_Handbook_N8_EN.pdf; Good Climate Finance Guide, https://pubs.iied.org/sites/default/files/pdfs/2021-01/10207IIED.pdf; Green Climate Fund (GCF), www.greenclimate.fund; GCF Private Sector Facility, www.greenclimate.fund/sites/default/files/document/green-climate-fund-s-private-sector-facility_0.pdf; UNEP Report Demystifying Private Climate Finance, www.unepfi.org/fileadmin/documents/DemystifyingPrivateClimateFinance.pdf; The USAID: A Quick Guide to Climate Change Adaptation Funds, www.climatelinks.org/sites/default/files/asset/document/2017_USAID%20Adapt%20Asia%20Pacific_A%20Quick%20Guide%20to%20CC%20Adaptation%20Funds.pdf; Global Landscape of Climate Finance 2021: Report from the Climate Policy Initiative (CPI), www.climatepolicyinitiative.org/publication/global-landscape-of-climate-finance-2021/#:~:text=As%20measured%20in%20the%20Global,warming%20to%201.5%20%C2%BoC; OECD, *The OECD DAC Blended Finance Guidance* (OECD Publishing, 2021), https://doi.org/10.1787/ded656b4-en; Good Climate Finance Guide, https://pubs.iied.org/sites/default/files/pdfs/2021-01/10207IIED.pdf; Climate Bonds Initiative, www.climatebonds.net/; The Climate Finance Portal, https://unfccc.int/climatefinance?home; The Role of National Development Banks in Catalyzing International Climate Finance, IDB, https://publications.iadb.org/en/role-national-development-banks-catalyzing-international-climate-finance.

global warming. Adaptation refers to efforts to enhance or improve the resilience of infrastructure, communities, economies, and ecosystems and adjust to both the current adverse effects of climate change and the predicted future impacts.

Government resources alone cannot provide the amount of finance needed for infrastructure, in particular where that infrastructure is designed to meet climate transition aspirations, making private sector capital fundamental to achieving transformational and long-term impacts across all economies. Key advantages of climate finance include expanding the pool of available financing for projects and opportunities to leverage climate-related and risk-sharing mechanisms to increase viability at the project level. Climate finance can play a catalytic role in mobilizing private investments in mitigation and adaptation activities and aligning public and private investment incentives.

Climate finance can provide access to dedicated funds (international and in some cases national), multilateral and bilateral development institutions, and strategic private investors (such as pension funds), as well as nongovernmental and philanthropic organizations that are committed to investing in climate mitigation and adaptation efforts. These entities may also offer low-cost financing, such as grants, seed funding, and concessional loans. Climate finance can in principal provide lower rates of interest, better terms and longer tenors than typical commercial finance, due to the high demand for climate finance investments in the market and also by blending different sources of financing (see Chapter 8 for a discussion of blended finance).

This chapter describes the different climate finance instruments, the sources of such instruments, and the roles of different parties. While the process for accessing climate finance will vary depending on the source of financing, the flow chart in Figure 6.1 presents a typical nonexhaustive overview of the usual process for mobilizing climate finance. The different elements and considerations are explained in the following sections.

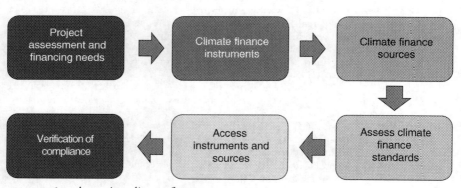

FIGURE 6.1 Accessing climate finance

6.1 FINANCING INSTRUMENTS

Climate finance is, first and foremost, finance; it uses common financial instruments such as debt, equity, credit enhancement, and risk transfer but is climate aligned. The difference between a typical financial instrument and a climate finance instrument is that funds raised under climate finance sources are ringfenced for the purpose of achieving specific climate-related objectives or the terms of the financing are linked to climate objectives.

The appropriate financial instrument(s) selected by the borrower will depend on the project's specific attributes, such as the type of infrastructure, sector, scale, financing and cofinancing needs, and mitigation and/or adaptation objectives, as well as the borrower's characteristics, investor appetite for risks and returns, and the type and sources of financing available. Depending on the selected climate finance source (public or private) and financial instrument(s), the financier's key criteria will be different, with specific requirements to be followed by the climate finance proponent.

The most common form of climate finance is green bonds, and for this reason this chapter will use green bonds as a practical example to describe the different elements and characteristics of climate finance. The typology of green bonds may be based on the nature of the borrower, for example, those issued by corporations (corporate green bonds), by governments (sovereign green bonds), and by municipalities (municipal green bonds). Asset-backed green bonds are backed by specific assets, such as wind farms or solar power plants, and the proceeds of the bond are used to finance the construction, refurbishment, expansion, and/or operation of the assets.

Climate finance instruments can be categorized further by the results against which the funds are lent. Specifically, some climate finance is based on the greenness of the investment to be financed – that is, the focus is on use of proceeds. "Use of proceeds" bonds are focused on activities such as climate adaptation, climate mitigation, social impact, ocean conservancy, biodiversity, community support, transition to a low-carbon economy, and sustainable development goals. These bonds are normally priced as conventional instruments. The issuer of a green bond typically states in the bond prospectus that the proceeds of the bond will be used for environmentally beneficial projects. For example:

- Green bond proceeds are designated to finance projects with a positive environmental impact. Blue bonds, a subcategory of green bonds, finance projects aimed at ocean and marine conservation.
- Social bonds raise funds for projects that address societal inequalities, like employment generation, food security, and access to affordable basic infrastructure (clean drinking water, energy, sanitation), health, education, financial services, and housing. Gender bonds are a subcategory of social bonds that focus on gender equality.
- Sustainability bond proceeds support a combination of green and social projects or activities.

A framework will set out a methodology for implementation and validation, based on agreed (often common) principles. A second-party opinion is usually required to verify use of proceeds.

In theory, a use of proceeds bond can be issued by a borrower that does not otherwise exemplify green practices. However, climate finance is sensitive to market perception, and borrowers may find it beneficial to be transparent about their green practices.

Other climate finance is linked to climate results that must be achieved by the borrower – either the interest rate goes down if the borrower meets the climate target or the interest rate goes up if it does not. "Target driven" (sustainability-linked) bonds (SLBs) are priced based on achieving ambitious climate targets (usually corporate environmental, social, and governance metrics). The targets need to be material and ambitious compared to business as usual. Compliance is verified based on a common methodology at an agreed point in time. A second party is often involved to verify compliance. Interest rates and fees are linked to compliance – for example, stepping down if compliance is achieved or stepping up if compliance is not achieved by the specified date.

SLBs provide capital to issuers that commit to meeting predefined key performance indicators usually related to verifiable and ambitious environmental or social objectives. If the key performance indicators are not met, the borrower must increase (step up) the coupon payment to investors or the coupon payments are reduced once the performance indicators are met. SLBs involve financial and/or structural characteristics (i.e., coupon, maturity, repayment amount) that vary depending on whether the issuer achieves identified sustainability, environmental, social, and/or governance objectives within a predefined timeline. Project categories can include renewable energy, energy efficiency, pollution prevention and control, environmentally sustainable management of living natural resources and land use, terrestrial and aquatic biodiversity conservation, clean transportation, sustainable water and wastewater management, climate change adaptation, circular economy and/or eco-efficient projects, and green buildings.

SLBs involve a number of key characteristics, for example, selection of key performance indicators, calibration of sustainability performance targets, bond characteristics, reporting, and verification.[2] The issuer must establish a governance framework to identify eligible assets and expenditures, track the allocation of bond proceeds, and report the allocation of bond proceeds and the impact of the projects supported. Standards have been developed to support consistency across the climate finance market, including by the International Capital Market Association (ICMA; see Box 6.1).

---

[2] International Capital Market Association, "Green Bond Principles Guidance Handbook," 2022, www.icmagroup.org/assets/GreenSocialSustainabilityDb/The-GBP-Guidance-Handbook-January-2022.pdf.

6.1 Financing Instruments

> ### Box 6.1 The Green Bond Principles
>
> The Green Bond Principles (GBP) are a set of guidelines that provide best practices for issuing green bonds. They were developed by a group of financial market participants in 2014, including the ICMA, and are voluntary. The ICMA subsequently released the Social Bond Principles, Sustainability Bond Guidelines (SBGs, see Box 6.6), the Sustainability-Linked Bond Principles, and the Climate Transition Finance Handbook, in an effort to provide the market with more consistency and transparency. The GBP consist of four core components:
>
> - The proceeds of the green bond must be used for environmentally beneficial projects, with a clear and specific use of proceeds statement in the bond prospectus.
> - The issuer must have a clear and transparent process for evaluating and selecting the projects that will be financed by the bond, as disclosed in the bond prospectus.
> - The issuer must have a clear and transparent process for managing the proceeds of the bond to ensure that they are used for the intended purpose, as set out in the bond prospectus.
> - The issuer must provide regular and transparent reporting on the use of proceeds, the management of proceeds, and the impact of the financed projects.
>
> The GBP only provide a broad, suggested, and nonexhaustive list of eligible green and social projects. Issuers are allowed to reference existing standards and taxonomies and/or develop their own framework.[3]

A bond can adopt both use of proceeds and sustainability-linked approaches if an issuer chooses to earmark the proceeds of an SLB to specific green and/or social projects.

Green bonds have the same characteristics as traditional bonds, such as a fixed coupon rate, currency, and a maturity date, but they are different in that they are specifically earmarked for use in environmental projects. Green bonds have become increasingly popular in recent years as investors seek to align their investments with their environmental, social, and governance values. They also provide a way for investors to support the transition to a low-carbon economy.

Issuers of thematic bonds must set up governance processes distinct from conventional bonds (see Box 6.2). These processes can result in additional costs due to the complexity of close collaboration between the debt management office, line ministries, and other government departments. Even where

---

[3] International Capital Market Association, "Green Bond Principles Guidance Handbook."

> **Box 6.2 The Climate Bonds Initiative**
>
> The Climate Bonds Initiative (CBI) is a not-for-profit international organization that promotes and certifies investment in low-carbon and climate-resilient projects and infrastructure. It offers certification for green bonds, the Climate Bonds Standard and Certification Scheme (CBSCS), including an independent assessment of the bond issuer's use of proceeds, management of proceeds, and reporting, as well as an assessment of the environmental impact of the financed project. The CBI operates a Climate Bonds Taxonomy, which classifies different types of climate-related projects; it also launched sector-specific criteria for different sectors such as transport, buildings, and agriculture.[4]

the government framework follows internationally accepted standards, the entire preparation and issuance process is expected to take at least six months.[5]

Rating agencies will assess the creditworthiness of the issuer and the use of proceeds in order to assign a rating to the bond. Third-party certification schemes, such as the GBP, provide guidelines and best practices for issuing green bonds to ensure that the proceeds of the bond are used for environmentally beneficial projects.

Green bonds may be particularly attractive to issuers because they can benefit from a green premium (sometimes called a "greenium"), interest rates charged to bond issuers that are lower than conventional bonds. A recent systematic review of the available literature estimates that an average green premium ranging from -1 to -9 basis points exists for green bonds on the secondary market.[6] Green bonds appear particularly advantageous for emerging markets, with an average emerging market green premium of -3.4 basis points as compared to conventional bonds by the same issuer.[7]

There is potential for the emerging market green premium to widen. The negative premium is mostly a result of the imbalance between the supply of green bonds and investors' demand.[8] Climate finance boasts a sustainability

---

[4] International Capital Market Association, "Green Bond Principles Guidance Handbook."
[5] "Sovereign Green, Social and Sustainability Bonds: Unlocking the Potential for Emerging Markets and Developing Economies," World Bank, 2022.
[6] S. MacAskill, E. Roca, B. Liu, R. A. Stewart, and O. Sahin, "Is There a Green Premium in the Green Bond Market? Systematic Literature Review Revealing Premium Determinants," *Journal of Cleaner Production* 280, part 2 (2021), https://doi.org/10.1016/j.jclepro.2020.124491.
[7] Amundi Asset Management and International Finance Corporation, *Emerging Market Green Bonds Report 2020: On the Road to Green Recovery* (IFC, 2021), www.ifc.org/en/insights-reports/2021/emerging-market-green-bonds-report-2020. Please note that this is based on a relatively small sample size.
[8] Ibid.

factor; it is credit positive; the issuance of the bond is perceived to improve sustainability, which in turn should result in lower overall risk of the issue (issuer) and thereby a lower yield (higher price) relative to the normal curve (i.e., green premium).[9]

As the green premium becomes wider, issuers will have greater incentive to issue green bonds, which should support the "greening" of the emerging market debt market. Overall, the green bond market presents a promising opportunity for organizations, in particular those operating in emerging markets, to finance large-scale sustainable investments across a wide variety of industries and green technologies, potentially at a lower cost of debt.

6.2 SOURCES OF CLIMATE FINANCE

There is a wide variety of climate finance sources, with different financiers having different priorities, objectives, criteria, processes, and instruments. These sources often have the ability to partner with the business world to mobilize institutional investors at scale to fund climate action and to encourage the development of the local private sector in emerging markets and developing economies to deliver climate solutions.

On one end of the spectrum are purely private and purely commercial investors, which are motivated primarily by the expected risk-adjusted rate of return on their investment. This type of market-driven investment is from a purely financial perspective, virtually indistinguishable from commercial lending for any other type of project. From the lender's perspective, the climate impacts may be viewed as an added benefit, but they are generally not the principal driver of the decision to invest.

At the other end of the spectrum are nonprofit investors, including nongovernmental and philanthropic organizations, which may provide grant funding for climate activities with little or no expectation of realizing a financial return. These programs are driven by access to development capital (e.g., grants) and the evolving requirements of those entities providing such capital.

This spectrum covers a huge array of public and private financiers that place varying degrees of emphasis on achieving climate outcomes versus realizing financial returns. Climate finance solutions will need to adapt to market appetite and the context on the ground and be structured accordingly.

Different climate financiers, mechanisms, and funds have specific operational modalities and differing requirements, which should be assessed prior to determining whether to seek climate finance. Access, eligibility criteria, and monitoring, reporting, and evaluation frameworks currently differ considerably across the myriad climate finance sources. The proliferation of approaches

---

[9] United Nations Development Program, "Identifying the 'Greenium'," *UNDP Blog*, April 25, 2022, www.undp.org/blog/identifying-greenium.

and criteria requires time, effort, and costs for the actors involved; more harmonization and coordination in this area are needed.

When deciding whether to pursue climate finance, practitioners need to weigh the additional transaction costs against the likely availability of the desired financing and its key characteristics, including terms, pricing, and conditions. The likelihood of accessing any specific climate finance source will vary and depend on the specific aspects of the transaction (such as sector, project size, availability of cofinancing, and risks), as well as the chosen financial instrument.

Different climate finance sources have diverse focuses and criteria that bear on the kinds of project activities they will finance. The following are a few of the more common characteristics to consider:

- Thematic area focus: Some financiers may support only mitigation actions or only adaptation efforts, though most of the largest sources finance both.
- Results area focus: Some financiers lend only to specific sectoral activities – for example, energy generation and access (renewable energy and energy efficiency), transport, forest and land use, blue carbon, agriculture, health, or food and water security – or for activities that engender specific outcomes – for example, ecosystem services, biodiversity, land degradation, and disaster risk management.
- Geographic focus: This includes, for example, dedicated funds that invest only in specific countries and/or regions or in specific groups of countries (e.g., small island developing states or least developed countries).
- Borrower focus: Some sources lend only to public sector actors, some only private, and some prefer public–private partnership projects.
- Direct lenders versus intermediaries: Some sources lend and accept proposals at the project level (i.e., direct access), while others invest through public or private funds or bodies (at the national, regional, or global level or through development financiers like the World Bank Group) that in turn invest in projects and programs (i.e., intermediaries).
- Types of support: Some financiers may support project or program preparation or delivery, while others focus on technical assistance and capacity building to improve the overall enabling environment for accessing climate finance.[10]

While the divergent sources of climate finance can seem daunting, by understanding the typical motivations of different categories of sources, practitioners can better assess the likelihood that any given project may be able to obtain climate finance and on what terms.

---

[10] See, for example, Barbara Buchner et al., *The Role of National Development Banks in Catalyzing International Climate Finance*. (Inter-American Development Bank, 2013), https://publications.iadb.org/en/role-national-development-banks-catalyzing-international-climate-finance.

6.2 Sources of Climate Finance

6.2.1 Public Sources

Traditionally, public sources have been the main source of capital available for climate finance, including financial resources from multilateral and bilateral financiers, other types of multilateral and bilateral organizations and aid agencies, governments, and dedicated climate funds.

<u>Bilateral sources and channels</u>: Bilateral financial institutions are agencies or funds primarily belonging to or governed by individual countries. This includes bilateral financiers and development cooperation agencies of individual countries. These institutions are capitalized through the public budget of the donor country, supplemented by own-source funds and funds raised on global capital markets.

<u>Multilateral sources and channels</u>: Multilateral financial institutions and funds have several governing members, including both borrowing developing countries and developed donor countries. This includes multilateral development banks, which may be global (e.g., the World Bank Group) or regional (e.g., the African Development Bank, the Development Bank of Latin America, and the Asian Infrastructure Investment Bank) in focus. Funds for these multilateral institutions are raised from a variety of sources and donors, including capitalization from member governments, fees for services, and income from different financial instruments such as concessional and nonconcessional loans.

<u>Climate funds</u>: Sometimes referred to as carbon funds, climate funds are dedicated climate-specific funds, often multidonor, set up and managed by national, bilateral, and multilateral organizations that usually provide trustee and administrative services. These funds may have a specific thematic focus, such as climate change mitigation and adaptation, and specific sectoral focuses, such as transport, energy, forestry, or land use, among others. In addition to money pledged from donors, many of these funds leverage significant sums of finance, frequently from development finance institutions and by derisking investments to mobilize additional private finance.

6.2.2 Private Sources

There is a global need to mobilize more private investment to ensure transformational and long-term impacts across all economies. The sources of private finance include funds and savings of individuals and corporations, institutional investors, asset managers, corporate actors, institutional funds, philanthropic organizations, and nonprofit organizations.

In many cases, the primary motive of private climate investors is to realize a risk-adjusted rate of return on their investment. A secondary motive may be climate impact and/or cobenefits such as sustainable development, gender-related, or social outcomes, which may be explicitly or implicitly included in their mandate as related filters for investment decisions. Nonetheless, private sources vary in their risk appetites and objectives. Some of the general categories of private finance sources are as follows:

- Commercial investors: These financiers make investments primarily to generate financial returns and comprise the largest share of private sector climate finance. This category includes private equity firms, commercial banks, bond issuances, and other common and established sources of commercial finance. As compared to other categories of private investors, discussed in the bullet points below, these investors primarily target more proven and less risky projects that promise a commercially viable rate of return, meaning financing is priced on market terms. Large commercial banks and infrastructure funds (often capitalized by institutional investors) are among the main actors that provide private sector financing for infrastructure.
- Angel investors/venture capitalists: These investors target early stage projects with a relatively high appetite for risk (as compared with commercial investors) and a commensurately high rate of failure. Due to the potential for failure, however, they seek a correspondingly high return on investment for those projects that succeed.
- Impact investors: Impact investing aims to generate both financial returns and positive environmental and/or social impacts, inhabiting a critical space between investors looking for a relatively high risk-adjusted return and those who can absorb more risk and expect less return. While impact investors need some return on investment to maintain financial sustainability, their return expectations may be more flexible, especially if they can achieve significant environmental and/or social impacts.
- Philanthropic investors: These are donor-based organizations seeking to generate positive social, environmental and/or climate-related impacts and outcomes but with relatively little or no expectation of financial return on invested funds.

6.2.3 Green Blended Finance

Blended finance is the strategic use of development finance for the mobilization of additional commercial finance toward sustainable development (see Chapter 8). Green blended finance refers to the use of development and commercial financing together for projects that contribute to low-carbon and climate-resilient interventions and achieving sustainable development outcomes, but where actual or perceived risks are too high for commercial lenders to bear on their own. Development financing is used to reduce investment risks for commercial financiers and to reduce the cost of financing. To this end, blended finance aims to (a) finance projects that would otherwise not be financed by pooling of resources and (b) ensure a high leverage effect on limited development resources. Blended finance can play an essential role in unlocking, scaling up, and channeling commercial finance toward sustainable development in developing countries.

Blended finance makes it possible, for example, for a government agency, a private equity investor, and an impact investor to all invest alongside each other while achieving their own objectives. Impact investors often, but not always, invest in blended finance transactions alongside other kinds of capital. Similarly, climate funds and development financial institutions are increasingly seeking to cofinance projects alongside private investors, to increase flows of private capital into projects that support sustainable development and increase the development impact of public monies invested. Accordingly, the financial leverage ratio, here referring to the amount of commercial capital mobilized as compared to the amount of development investment, is an increasingly important criteria for many of these climate finance sources.

However, it can be difficult for different public, private, and nonprofit groups to collaborate in existing structures, particularly across borders.[11] Preparation costs associated with blended financing can be high, making it more challenging, particularly for small projects. These challenges, coupled with the overall inadequacy of concessional finance resources relative to climate investment needs, have contributed to a decline in blended finance projects in recent years. Specifically, the USD 14 billion in tracked blended finance deals in 2019–2021 reflects a steep drop from USD 36.5 billion in the previous three-year period.[12] Accordingly, more must be done to improve coordination between the public and private sectors to realize the significant leverage potential promised by blended finance transaction structures.

6.3 IDENTIFICATION OF CLIMATE FINANCE SOURCES

Assuming climate finance may be available and, if so, is needed or desired, the financing proponent should review the public and private climate finance sources available and identify those sources most likely to be accessible for the specific asset recycling transaction, in light of the project type, themes, results area(s), and jurisdiction, among others. Once all reasonable options are identified, the available sources should be reviewed in terms of their criteria, due diligence requirements, and decision-making processes to narrow the options and facilitate identification of the right source of climate finance.

To understand the landscape of available climate finance, the financing proponent should assess the local jurisdiction's readiness and access to international climate funds. This includes identifying any comparable local actors, public

---

[11] Gillan Tett, "The Flood of Green Finance Must Be Diverted from the West," *Financial Times*, October 27, 2022, https://on.ft.com/3TKb8Rq.
[12] Shabtai Gold, "Blended Finance for Climate Fell 60% Despite Calls for More Funds," *Devex*, October 26, 2022, www.devex.com/news/blended-finance-for-climate-fell-60-despite-calls-for-more-funds-104317.

> **Box 6.3 Green bond for 500 kV Mantaro–Nueva Yanango–Carapongo interconnection and associated substations, Peru**
>
> The central zone of Peru is a large nucleus of hydroelectric power generation. The USD 164.4 million green bond for Mantaro–Nueva Yanango–Carapongo will help connect several renewable energy sources to the National Interconnected Electric System. Third-party assessments were obtained from Moody's Investors Service and S&P Global Ratings, which evaluated the transparency, governance, and anticipated mitigation impacts related to the use of proceeds. Both assessments scored the bond issuance toward the high end of their respective ratings systems, including alignment with ICMA's GBP. This was the first nonfinancial corporate international green bond issuance from Peru in 2019 and the first to specifically finance energy transmission projects in Peru to increase the use and reliability of renewable energy sources.
>
> The net proceeds of green financing will support the installation of electricity transmission lines for the connection of renewable electricity generation sources, energy efficiency improvements to transmission infrastructure, and energy storage systems to allow renewable energy sources to deliver energy needs on a timely basis.

or private, that have successfully accessed climate finance and whether there are local accredited intermediaries that can facilitate access to different climate finance sources (see Box 6.3). While there is an increasing number of climate funding and financing sources, this does not directly translate into easier access and availability where the local policy framework is not conducive to access.

Ultimately, the financing proponent should select the best sources of climate finance according to the transaction's needs and the desired financial instrument(s). Depending on the transaction (specific objectives, technology, sector, theme, need for climate finance, etc.) and country readiness to access climate finance, a decision must be made whether to commence engaging with the identified financiers. There are a number of common principles that bear on securing climate finance, including the capacity of the borrower (e.g., creditworthiness, reputation, and experience), expected return on investment, making use of collaborative action, communicating the rationale for action, and building local capacity.

Accessing bilateral or multilateral sources generally requires the preparation of an initial concept note, which is followed by a full project proposal once the concept passes the assessment criteria of the financing source being approached. It is fundamental to make a strong case for justifying the need for financing by the financial source targeted for the transaction being proposed. In some cases, it is useful to prepare the full proposals as bankable documents (i.e., functionally ready for financial close, with all material terms defined). If several sources are being accessed, this may entail an iterative process with multiple financiers to reach financial close. In addition, larger projects or programs that need to blend different financial sources and mechanisms often go through multiple rounds, either in succession or in parallel.

6.4 ROLES OF THE PUBLIC AND PRIVATE PARTNERS

In some cases, in particular where a concession is issued over infrastructure, financing risk will be assumed by the private sector partner (e.g., the concessionaire), meaning the responsibility for considering and seeking climate finance sources and instruments rests primarily with the private partner. Even in this case, the public sector project owner should play a cooperative and supportive role, for example, by sharing any data, information, studies, or planning documents relevant to the asset that may inform a climate finance proposal and facilitating any government approvals or letters of support that may be required by the climate financier. In addition, in its role as contract manager, the public partner may be well positioned or required to help monitor, report, and verify the achievement of results set by the climate finance instrument.

In other cases, however, the public sector may bear the financing risk and seek climate financing, for example, where a particular climate source (a climate fund) will lend only to the public sector, not only for project preparation but also to finance the project itself. There may be advantages to the public sector project owner undertaking the preparatory work needed to access climate finance alongside the other project preparation activities, prior to commencing the tender process. Where a project appears to be a good candidate for climate finance and some form of climate finance is likely necessary for the transaction to be commercially viable, the public partner may consider completing studies needed for the climate finance proposal, or even completing the preliminary or full climate finance proposal, as part of the project preparation activities. This is especially true if the public partner can access project preparation assistance at the domestic or international level that can provide funding and other resources to support project preparation. These resources may be more accessible to public sector project proponents, particularly those in emerging markets and developing economies. In addition to the possibility of obtaining support for project preparation, this approach permits the expected climate finance source and instrument to influence the transaction structure and may reduce overall financing costs.

6.5 TRANSACTION CHARACTERISTICS

Initially, the public and private parties to an infrastructure transaction should assess its likely eligibility for climate finance predominantly in view of its expected mitigation and/or adaptation impacts or focus, while also considering indirect benefits and other criteria that may bear on eligibility. To access climate finance, an infrastructure transaction should provide clear climate benefits, which can be assessed, measured, and reported by the borrower. That is, initial screening should focus on whether the project produces the right kind of outcomes – direct (reduced or avoided GHG emissions, reduction in harm, reduction in the risk of harm, or the realization of benefits to address climate variability and change), indirect (market development, capacity building, leveraging effects, sustainable development potential), or both.

While eligibility criteria will vary across climate finance sources, some of the most common and broadly applicable criteria are outlined in Box 6.4.

Box 6.4 Early stage screening criteria for climate finance eligibility

Practitioners, both public and private, should understand some of the key criteria and requirements for assessing the likelihood that a project or intervention will be able to access climate finance sources. As with most aspects of project preparation, this process is necessarily iterative and subject to change as more data and details about the project become known. Nonetheless, understanding these basic criteria can help practitioners identify projects with climate finance potential and guide decision-making as projects develop.

Practitioners should understand some of the key criteria, including:

1. <u>Mitigation and adaptation</u>: An essential element for any climate finance proposal is the ability to demonstrate verifiable impacts in terms of mitigation action, adaptation efforts, or both. In this regard, practitioners should consider both direct effects (e.g., a renewable energy project that avoids emissions from fossil-based power generation) and indirect effects (e.g., projects that contribute to market development and thereby create new opportunities for additional climate-positive investments in the future).
2. <u>Monitoring, reporting, and verification</u>: Climate benefits must be readily and reliably forecast, monitored, and verified. The clearer the impacts and the more easily they can be quantified, evaluated, and reported, the more likely the project is a good candidate for climate finance.
3. <u>Cofinancing/blended finance</u>: Practitioners should consider how conducive the project size and risk profile are to cofinancing or blended finance transaction structures. Size simply relates to the amount of investment needed – bigger investments create more space

for multiple investors – while risk profile considers issues like the use of new technologies or project types that may attract impact investors, venture capitalists, or concessional finance.
4. <u>Replicability</u>: Pilot or demonstration projects can unlock further similar investments or catalyze investment in proven sectors that so far have not developed in the specific jurisdiction. Climate financiers may see such projects as attractive to increase market opportunities and/or improve the financiers' position in the market.
5. <u>Scalability</u>: Opportunities for scaling up, including through successive rounds of financing, can increase the appeal of a project to some climate finance sources. Practitioners should consider whether there are options to build on and expand climate benefits after any immediate needs for operating, maintaining, and monetizing an asset are met.

In addition to initial screening for climate finance eligibility, at this stage the financing proponent (public or private) should undertake a reasonable transaction assessment based on relevant and reliable data to determine the transaction amount and establish the financing needs. This will help establish whether there is an opportunity for climate finance and, if so, begin to indicate what available instruments can best fill this need.

The financing proponent should also decide on the need for engaging a climate finance transaction expert as early in the process as possible, which will depend on the availability of in-house expertise and that of potential partners. Another option is to identify potential dedicated project preparation facilities and sources that may be able to provide support with preparing a climate finance transaction.

6.6 COMPLIANCE WITH CLIMATE FINANCE STANDARDS AND REQUIREMENTS

The financing proponent will need to ensure that the transaction complies with the specific standards, criteria, and requirements of the selected climate finance sources according to the terms of the financial instrument, which may include the use of funds, as well as specific documentation and methodologies to follow throughout the process of reaching financial close and over the life of the project.

Climate finance standards and principles differ according to the type of financial instruments, sources, and sectors. When developing a green bond, the issuer may wish to adopt a set of globally accepted criteria, certain of which also provide certification (see Box 6.5 for an example).

> **Box 6.5 The CBSCS**
>
> Developed by the CBI, the CBSCS is a labelling scheme for thematic bonds to be verified as Certified Climate Bonds. It is used globally by bond issuers, governments, investors, and financial markets to prioritize investments that contribute to addressing climate change.
>
> - Certification is available for assets and projects that meet the CBSCS requirements. Certified Climate Bonds are fully aligned with the GBP.
> - To receive the "Climate Bonds Certified" stamp of approval, a prospective issuer must appoint a third-party approved verifier, such as Bureau Veritas, Deloitte, Carbon Trust, KPMG, or EY.
> - A bond can be certified prior to its issuance, enabling the issuer to use the Climate Bonds Certification Mark in marketing efforts and investor roadshows.
> - The CBSCS Standard Board confirms Climate Bonds Certification once the bond has been issued and the proceeds have been allocated to the projects and assets.

6.7 VERIFICATION OF COMPLIANCE

The financing proponent should provide information for verification of compliance of the climate and/or social objectives that allowed access to climate finance (see Box 6.6). The use of qualitative performance indicators and, where feasible, quantitative performance measures (energy capacity, electricity generation, GHG emission reductions, avoided GHG emissions, etc.) should be included in the compliance report according to the specific requirements of the climate finance providers and financial instruments used. All sources request quantifiable and measurable impacts in terms of either mitigation (reduced or avoided GHG emissions) or adaptation (increased resilience to the adverse impacts of climate change) that can be reliably measured, reported, and verified.

Third-party verification of compliance may be required, especially where climate finance is sourced internationally. However, this will depend on the particular jurisdiction, including the location of the project as well as the jurisdiction where the financing is procured.

The SBGs include additional disclosure requirements such as the use of an external review, project-level information, and the choice of a framework or standard to assess the environmental and social impact of the financed projects.[13]

---

[13] International Capital Market Association, "Green Bond Principles Guidance Handbook."

6.8 Barriers to Accessing Climate Finance

> **Box 6.6 The SBGs**
>
> The SBGs are a set of guidelines developed by the ICMA that provide best practices for issuing bonds that finance or refinance projects and activities that have positive environmental or social impacts.[14] These are voluntary and consist of three core components:
>
> - Use of proceeds must be used for environmentally beneficial or socially beneficial projects, such as renewable energy, energy efficiency, sustainable transportation, and affordable housing. The issuer must provide a clear and specific use of proceeds statement in the bond prospectus.
> - The process for project evaluation and selection of projects to be financed by the bond must be clear and transparent and disclosed in the bond prospectus.
> - Reporting on the use of proceeds, the management of proceeds, and the impact of the financed projects must be regular and transparent; the information should be disclosed on the official website or on a recognized platform.

6.8 BARRIERS TO ACCESSING CLIMATE FINANCE

While offering significant opportunities, climate finance involves challenges and barriers too. The level of effort involved in mobilizing and managing climate finance can be substantial, particularly if the climate impacts are difficult to quantify and evaluate. Identifying and applying to an appropriate climate financier involves time and resources, including obtaining any required certifications and/or accreditations.

Some common barriers to accessing climate finance include the following:

- Climate finance is more complex than traditional financing. While the additionality of climate finance merits this complexity, borrowers need to prepare themselves for this complexity and mobilize the funding and expertise to manage this process. Prospective borrowers must submit specific project proposals and supporting technical documents that satisfy investor criteria, the specific requirements of climate investors, and the criteria applied by the sector. This is a complex space, and the time and cost associated with understanding and applying these requirements can be significant; such costs will need to be budgeted and planned. It is often difficult for borrowers to mobilize funding to pay for project preparation for traditional and commercial financing transactions; it may be easier to mobilize such funding for climate finance where subsidies and development funding may be available.

---

[14] International Capital Market Association, www.icmagroup.org/sustainable-finance/the-principles-guidelines-and-handbooks/sustainability-bond-guidelines-sbg/.

- Gathering and processing climate-related data and information as required by climate financiers and their verification agents (e.g., weather data covering wind, sun radiation, and precipitation; information on the nature, likelihood, and intensity of meteorological and hydrological implications of climate change) will require time, cost, and patience. This is a rapidly evolving space, with new instruments and methodologies being developed to help implement the due diligence required.
- Methodological issues around evaluating climate-related needs and impacts, for example, how to calculate energy savings from investments in energy efficiency, can create additional cost and delay when seeking to attract climate finance. This can be particularly tricky in relation to uncertainty over, or unfamiliarity with, new technologies, new project types, and innovative transaction structures.
- Enabling conditions (legal/regulatory environment, intuitional arrangements, local market development) for climate finance often face gaps or challenges that may require project-specific adjustments or larger reform programs – for example, the availability of reliable third-party verifiers and legal frameworks for defining and certifying green financing instruments and projects. Accessing climate finance can involve multiple layers of governance and institutional arrangements (at the domestic and/or international level), public and private actors and institutions, and an array of financial instruments that may be mobilized to deliver the funds.
- Borrowers will need to understand global markets for climate finance and international standards and to understand options and value propositions as they are driven by investor expectations. Financial markets may not have the experience with climate finance, may not offer the instruments and services needed to mobilize climate finance, or may not be sufficiently liquid or flexible to respond to the demands of climate finance markets. Macroeconomic volatility (fluctuations in exchange rates, hyperinflation, shifts in interest rates, etc.) brings an additional layer of risk that will need to be managed, which process may involve costs and delays.

7

Islamic Finance

The Islamic finance market can serve as a complementary source of finance for infrastructure development in emerging markets.[1] Even though Islamic finance accounts for a tiny percentage of global financial markets, it has been demonstrating strong growth,[2] nearly double-digit annually over the past six decades.[3]

The asset-backed nature of public–private partnership (PPP) infrastructure projects make them a natural fit for Islamic finance.[4] Islamic finance structures can be aligned with conventional finance; although the two are documented separately, the terms and conditions are structured to benefit both sets of financiers (Islamic and conventional) from the same or very similar commercial terms.[5] Successful PPPs using Islamic finance have been developed in countries such as Bangladesh, Djibouti, Indonesia, Kazakhstan, Malaysia, Mali, Morocco, Nigeria, Pakistan, Saudi Arabia, Turkey, and Uzbekistan.[6]

---

[1] This chapter provides a brief introduction to Islamic finance for infrastructure; it is informed by reports on the topic produced by Delwar Hossain, Najd AlHasan, and Abdulrahman Almajthoob of Baker & Mckenzie and by Fida Rana and Aijaz Ahmad of the World Bank. For a more thorough treatment of the topic, please refer to two excellent texts: World Bank, PPIAF, and ISDB, *Mobilizing Islamic Finance for Infrastructure Public Private Partnerships* (World Bank, 2017), and World Bank, PPIAF, and ISDB, *Reference Guide: Islamic Finance for Infrastructure PPP Projects* (World Bank, 2019).

[2] World Bank, PPIAF, and ISDB, *Reference Guide: Islamic Finance for Infrastructure PPP Projects*.

[3] The IFSB in their latest Islamic Financial Services Industry Stability Report (IFSB, 2017), www.islamicfinance.com/wp-content/uploads/2017/06/IFSB-IFSI-Stability-Report-2017.pdf.

[4] World Bank, PPIAF, and ISDB, *Reference Guide: Islamic Finance for Infrastructure PPP Projects*.

[5] Ibid.

[6] World Bank, PPIAF, and ISDB, *Mobilizing Islamic Finance for Infrastructure Public Private Partnerships*.

> **Box 7.1 Islamic finance glossary**
>
> *Ijārah* (asset based) – A contract that permits one party (the lessee) to use an asset or property owned by another party (the lessor), for an agreed price, over a fixed period.
>
> *Istiṣnā'* (sale based) – A contract to manufacture goods, assemble or process them, or build a structure according to exact specifications and a fixed timeline. Payments are made as work is finished; the sale price may be amortized or deferred.
>
> *Mudārabah* (equity based) – A contract between two parties; one provides the capital and the other provides the labor, profits are shared in agreed proportions, and any financial loss is borne only by the capital owner, unless the provider of labor has been grossly negligent or acted in willful default of its duties.
>
> *Murābahah* (sale based) – A sale contract of a good or property with an agreed profit against a deferred or a lump-sum payment.
>
> *Mushārakah* (equity based) – A contract between two or more parties to establish a commercial enterprise based on capital and labor. The profit and loss are shared at an agreed proportion, usually according to the amount of contribution.
>
> *Sukūk* – "Islamic bonds," financial instruments representing an undivided ownership share in an underlying asset or interest held by the issuer. They are based on certificates representing a proportionate ownership interest in underlying assets services or other activities that generate a cash flow.
>
> *Takāful* – Islamic version of insurance.

Islamic finance is driven by the avoidance of *ribā* (an unjustified increase) and *gharar* (uncertainty) and by a focus on what is religiously permissible (*ḥalāl*), and it adheres to certain key principles (see Box 7.1):[7]

- Transactions should be free from speculation, gains from luck, or gambling (*maysir*) or uncertainty (*gharar*). Transactions where the price, time of delivery, or the subject matter are not determined in advance may not be compliant with *shari'ah* principles. For this reason, returns to Islamic financiers should generally be linked to the profits of an enterprise and derived from the commercial risk taken by the financier. Islamic financiers should be partners in the project to share the profits and risk in the business, instead of being pure creditors, and fixed returns on investment should not be guaranteed.

[7] Ibid.

7.1 Overview of Islamic Finance Structures

- Fees or charges should be rendered only when an actual service has been provided, excluding things like commitment fees, late payment fees, and default fees. Islamic financiers are generally required to direct the late payment amount to a charitable purpose on behalf of the project company after deducting any actual and direct costs incurred by them due to such late payment.[8]
- Islamic finance solutions are in no way restricted to countries with sizable Muslim populations. They can be deployed in any jurisdiction if the financing arrangement can fit within the local legal and regulatory environment. But investments relating to alcohol, drugs, gambling, weapons, or other activities prohibited by *shari'ah* are not permitted.
- Tangible or physical assets, such as infrastructure, serve as the basis for Islamic finance structures. A variety of creative structures are used to adapt Islamic financing in cases where governments place restrictions on ownership of strategic assets (e.g., where public ownership is required).
- The transaction need not be wholly *shari'ah* compliant. Islamic finance tranches can be structured alongside conventional tranches.

The flexibility of *shari'ah* structures can accommodate the needs specific to the country, sector, and project. However, there are additional costs and time for developing innovative structures within the boundary of *shari'ah* tenets. The due diligence process should include a *shari'ah* compatibility analysis with the aim of identifying and resolving any potential *shari'ah* breaches. In certain countries, an external *shari'ah* audit may be required before an asset recycling transaction can be described as being *shari'ah* compliant.[9]

This chapter will provide a summary of key Islamic Finance structures (Section 7.1) followed by a more detailed discussion of sale and leaseback, one of the key commercial structures in Islamic finance (Section 7.2), and *Sukūk*, one of the key Islamic financing instruments (Section 7.3). The chapter will next discuss Islamic climate finance (Section 7.4), Islamic financial institutions, (Section 7.5), and finally legal issues and documentation (Section 7.6).

7.1 OVERVIEW OF ISLAMIC FINANCE STRUCTURES

The most common form of Islamic finance for large and long-term financing arrangements combines *istiṣnāʿ* for the construction and procurement stage and *ijārah* for the operations stage.

Istiṣnāʿ financing involves the borrower procuring or constructing assets by a certain date, on behalf of the Islamic financier (see Figure 7.1 and Box 7.2). The contract price payable by the Islamic financier must be fixed and is paid to the borrower in stages, to match payment obligations under construction

---

[8] World Bank, PPIAF, and ISDB, *Reference Guide: Islamic Finance for Infrastructure PPP Projects*.
[9] Ibid.

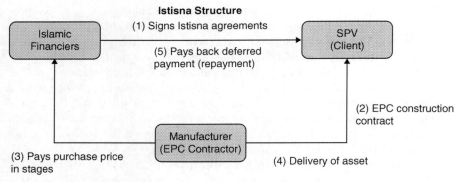

FIGURE 7.1 *Istiṣnāʿ* structure

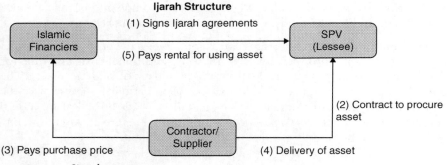

FIGURE 7.2 *Ijārah* structure

contracts. Title to the assets is transferred to the Islamic financier at the end of the construction period. The finance parties take construction risks as opposed to sales-based or *ijārah* structures, where the suppliers, not the financing parties, take the risk in constructing or manufacturing assets.[10]

Under the *ijārah*, the project company (as lessee) and the Islamic financier (as lessor) contemporaneously with the *istiṣnāʿ* agreement enter into a lease agreement to lease the assets under construction (see Figure 7.2). During the construction phase, the lessee pays advance rentals to the lessor with respect to the asset that is under construction, though these rental payments will be relatively small before the assets are constructed and when revenues are low. During the operational phase, the rental payment will include a fixed element (equivalent to the principal, in conventional facilities) and a variable element, generally on the basis of a reference, plus a margin (equivalent to the applicable margin under conventional facilities).[11]

[10] Ibid.
[11] Ibid.

7.1 Overview of Islamic Finance Structures

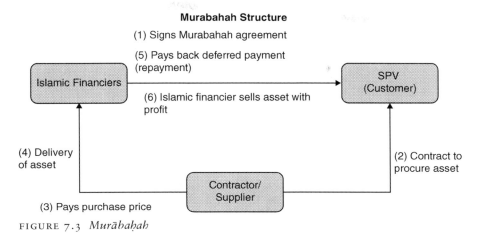

FIGURE 7.3 *Murābaḥah*

Infrastructure projects also use *Murābaḥah* (though more often in shorter-term financings), a contract between the Islamic financier and the client for the sale of goods on a cost-plus-mark-up basis – either as a percentage of the cost price or a lump sum, paid over a defined period of time (see Figure 7.3). The Islamic financier will purchase the goods and sell them to the client with an agreed mark-up. The client repays the Islamic financier, hence the justification for the mark-up. *Murābaḥah* is valid only where the exact cost of the assets can be ascertained. The profit in a *murābaḥah* can be determined by mutual consent of the parties, either in lump sum or through an agreed ratio of profit to be charged. All the expenses incurred by the seller in acquiring the assets (e.g., freight, custom duty, or tax) are included in the cost and the mark-up is applied on the aggregate cost.

A widely used variation of the *murābaḥah* contract is the *tawarruq* (monetization) structure. Under a *tawarruq* structure, following the obligor's acquisition of the assets (generally commodities traded on the London Metal Exchange) from the financiers, the obligor appoints an agent (usually one of the financiers, who acts as agent of the financiers in relation to the financing) to sell the same assets to a third party and thereby receives cash.

Mushārakah is a partnership between two or more parties that provide capital toward the financing of new or preexisting projects. The parties share the profits on a preagreed ratio, with losses being shared on the basis of equity participation (Figure 7.4). While used by Islamic financiers in certain countries such as in Malaysia and Pakistan, this mode is not very common in other countries for infrastructure projects.

Unlike loan-based conventional financing techniques, Islamic finance is asset based and generally involves (a) an equity-based/sharing-based structure, such as *mushārakah* (partnership) and *mudārabah* (partnership in profit) (Figure 7.5); (b) a sale-based structure, such as *murābahah* (sale with profit),

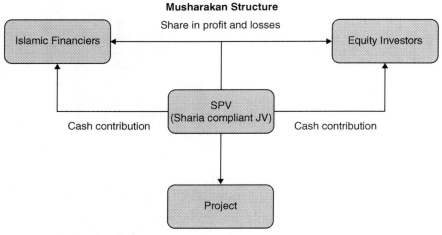

FIGURE 7.4 *Mushārakah*

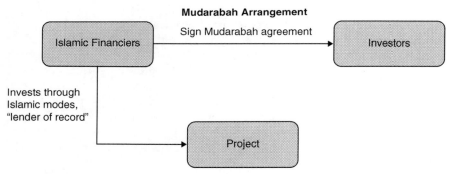

FIGURE 7.5 *Mudārabah*

istiṣnā'a (build/manufacture), and *salam* (advance purchase); (c) a lease-based structure, such as *ijārah* (leasing); or (d) a fee-based structure, such as *wakalah* (agency), *kafalah* (guarantee), and *ju'alah* (service contract).

Hedging in general is permitted by the principles of *shari'ah*. From an Islamic finance point of view, hedging is an attempt by a party to mitigate or reduce the level of risk inherent to a financing transaction. *Shari'ah*-compliant hedging instruments currently available in the market include Islamic foreign exchange forward, Islamic options, Islamic profit rate swaps, and Islamic currency swaps. The Bahrain-based International Islamic Financial Market and the International Swaps and Derivatives Association have jointly developed certain types of *shari'ah*-compliant hedging instruments (including Islamic foreign exchange forward, Islamic cross-currency swaps, and profit rate swaps).[12]

---

[12] Ibid.

In Islamic finance, the *takāful* contract performs an insurance function. It works based on the principle of mutual insurance; each participant in *takāful* contributes to the fund and receives payment if he or she incurs a loss due to the covered risks. Only a handful of institutions offer *takāful* products for infrastructure PPP projects, for example, the Islamic Corporation for the Insurance of Investment and Export Credit, a member of the Islamic Development Bank Group.

While the use of *takāful* is recommended, *shari'ah* scholars allow conventional insurance to be used in infrastructure projects that are financed wholly or partially by Islamic finance, if Islamic insurance products are not available or are not economically feasible.

This market is still evolving, which partly explains why *takāfuls* are underperforming compared to their conventional counterparts. In addition, *takāfuls* have higher expenses, less capital, lower employee productivity, and less income on assets. However, they also have higher retention ratios and solvency margins.[13]

7.2 SALE AND LEASEBACK

The sale and leaseback plays an important role in Islamic finance. In a sale and leaseback arrangement the obligor sells certain specified assets that it owns to the financiers for an agreed price and then the obligor (as lessee) takes the same assets back on lease from the financiers (as lessor). The result is an immediate cash inflow for the obligor (in the form of the sale price of the assets). In the context of an assets recycling financing, the obligor (typically a government) will ring-fence the sale price and invest it in new or existing infrastructure assets. The obligor continues to use the assets and makes rental payments to the financiers who now own the assets.

Ijārah or lease is the transfer of the usufruct (or a legal right to use) of an asset to another person in exchange for a rent, derived from the profit or benefit of the assets. An *ijārah* must be transparent and detailed, the terms must be agreed prior to execution, and the lessor must maintain legal and beneficial ownership of the asset and bear responsibility for risks associated with ownership of the asset. An *ijārah* arrangement must comply with all of the following:

1. The financiers (as lessor) must have ownership of (or the usufruct right in) the assets before entering into a lease agreement.
2. The leased assets must continue to exist throughout the period of the lease and any assets that are consumed during that period cease to be leasable.
3. The period of the lease and amount payable therefor in the form of rent must be certain and specified in advance.

[13] Ibid.

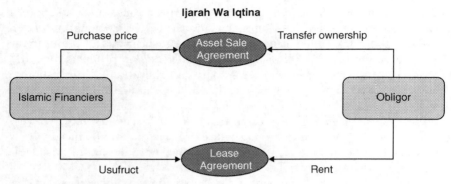

FIGURE 7.6 *Ijārah wa iqtina*

4. The lessee must use the leased asset only for the purpose specified in the lease, or, absent a specified purpose, in conformity with common practice, and such activities must be lawful under *shari'ah*; for example, leasing a property for selling alcohol would be unlawful under *shari'ah*.
5. The liabilities arising from the ownership of the leased asset, such as any harm or loss, are borne by the lessor (as the owner of the asset).

The form of *ijārah* typically used is known as an *ijārah wa iqtina* (i.e., a lease-and-purchase or buyback leasing), which includes a promise by the financiers, as lessor, to transfer the ownership of the leased asset to the obligor, as lessee, either at the end of the lease period or in stages during the term of the *ijārah*.

An *ijārah wa iqtina* is essentially the Islamic equivalent of a conventional equipment lease contract outlined in Figure 7.6.

In accordance with *shari'ah* principles, unlike in conventional operating leases, the financiers (in their capacity as owners of the assets or lessors) are responsible for all major maintenance – typically repair, replacement, and maintenance, for example, basic wear and tear, without which the assets could not reasonably be used by the lessee. In addition, the financiers will be responsible for the insurance of the assets and payment of ownership-related taxes.

To limit the financiers' liabilities and to ensure that third parties do not have any claims on the financiers or their assets, the obligor and the financiers enter into a service agency agreement pursuant to which the obligor is appointed as the agent of the financiers for the purpose of carrying out major maintenance, procuring insurance, and paying ownership-related taxes. If the obligor fails to implement any repairs or replacements, or obtain insurance, the financiers may do so and will be indemnified by the obligor for all amounts paid or costs incurred by the financiers. If the obligor is found negligent in the use or maintenance of the assets, or in procuring insurance or performing any of its obligations listed under the service agency agreement, it assumes principal liability for and will be required to indemnify the financiers for any related losses.

Box 7.2 Prince Mohammad Bin Abdulaziz International Airport in Saudi Arabia

A PPP concession was awarded to a consortium to rehabilitate and expand the Prince Mohammad Bin Abdulaziz International Airport (Madinah Airport) in Saudi Arabia, in particular to increase the capacity from five million to eight million and potentially to sixteen million passengers per year initially.

Two Islamic finance modes were used (see Figure 7.7):

Istiṣnāʿ – The special purpose vehicle (SPV) transferred certain rights contained under the concession agreement to the financiers. When the construction of the assets was complete, the ownership of the project assets was transferred to the public authority, while beneficial rights were transferred to the SPV through the concession agreement.

Hybrid *istiṣnāʿ* – During operations, the financiers gradually transferred the ownership of the asset to the SPV against rental payments through a lease agreement with a put and call option for sale and purchase undertaking. The SPV is designated from the outset as the manager of the project. Because the SPV did not own the project assets, a leasing (*ijārah*) structure based on the ownership of project assets could not be used. Therefore, an innovative structure combining the *istiṣnāʿ* structure during the construction phase and the assignment of commercial rights during the operations phase was successfully employed. The financiers also obtained direct agreement with the SPV and the government authority in case of default of the SPV, in which case the government authority will pay the financiers.[14]

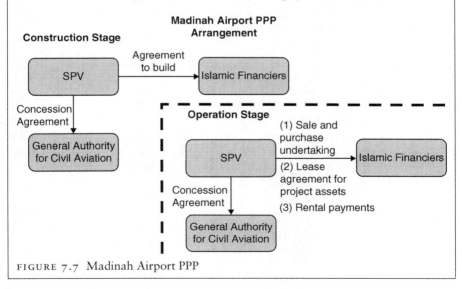

FIGURE 7.7 Madinah Airport PPP

---

[14] World Bank, PPIAF, and ISDB, *Mobilizing Islamic Finance for Infrastructure Public Private Partnerships.*

The financiers usually undertake to sell all or part of the assets to the obligor (a call option) in the event of a partial or full cancellation and following the discharge by the obligor of all outstanding payments owed to the financiers.

If the obligor defaults, the obligor promises to purchase the assets (through a put option). If the financiers exercise their rights under the put option, the obligor must purchase the leased assets for a price equal to the aggregate amounts outstanding under the facility. The documentation normally stipulates that title to the assets does not pass to the obligor until the amounts owed to the financiers have been discharged in full.

Pursuant to *shari'ah* principles, a lease arrangement will be terminated with immediate effect upon the occurrence of a total loss of the leased assets (i.e., the underlying assets) and any purchase undertaking with respect to those assets becomes ineffective as a result. In order to mitigate this risk, financiers typically appoint the obligor as their service agent under a service agency agreement and require it, in such capacity, to maintain insurance with respect to the full replacement value of the leased assets. Upon the occurrence of a total loss, the obligor (as service agent) will be under an obligation, within a given timeframe, to provide the financiers with the proceeds of the insurance. In the event that the proceeds are less than the full replacement value of the assets, the obligor will have failed to comply with its strict insurance obligations (as service agent) under the service agency agreement and will be liable to indemnify the financiers for any shortfall.

While a structure based on sale and lease back is widely accepted by *shari'ah* scholars for Islamic finance, some *shari'ah* scholars and Islamic finance institutions consider a sale and lease back structure as a less preferred option for structuring an Islamic finance transaction.

7.3 SUKŪK

Sukūk, often referred to as "Islamic bonds," are more like Islamic trust certificates, representing an undivided beneficial ownership interest in an underlying asset wherein the return is based on the performance of that underlying asset (see Box 7.3). The assets themselves may be tangible or intangible, but they must be certain, income-generating, and not used for any non-*Shari'ah*-compliant purposes such as gambling or the sale of alcohol.

Like conventional bonds, *sukūk* are freely transferrable on the secondary market, pay a regular return, and are redeemable at maturity. Unlike conventional bonds, the return generated is justified as the certificate holder has an ownership interest in the underlying asset and is thus assuming ownership risks. The profit or benefit derived from the asset must be linked to the performance of a real asset and the risks associated with the ownership of that asset.

Like conventional project bonds, they have seen limited application in infrastructure projects, since they raise finances through a subscription process in the market; the amount and cost of money are established at a single point

7.3 Sukūk

> **Box 7.3 Indonesia's sovereign green *sukūk***
>
> In March 2018, Indonesia issued a five-year sovereign green *sukūk* for USD 1.25 billion, which was the world's first. It was issued under the Indonesia's Green Bond and Green Sukuk Framework. The underlying *sukūk* assets included state-owned land and buildings (accounting for 51 percent of the asset pool) and project assets that are under construction or to be constructed (accounting for the remaining 49 percent of the asset pool). The deal was oversubscribed by 2.4 times.[15]

in time, while the funds are released over a relatively long period of time. The whole amount of the money raised will accumulate mark-up/margin right away, known as "cost of carry," even though the funds may not be used for some time; hence *sukūk* (and project bonds) are used less often to finance greenfield infrastructure PPPs.[16]

7.3.1 *Sukūk* Structure

The Bahrain-based Accounting and Auditing Organisation for Islamic Financial Institutions has identified fourteen eligible types of *sukūk*, of which *sukūk al-ijārah* and *sukūk al- murābahah* are the most common. In order to explore specific issues and structures, the *sukūk al-ijārah* will be discussed here. It includes two Islamic finance techniques, namely sale and *ijārah,* which structure may consist of the following:

1. *Incorporation of an SPV*: The originator creates an SPV to act as issuer, trustee, or agent (as relevant) and lessor.
2. *Issuance of sukūk*: The SPV issues the *sukūk*, the SPV represents an undivided ownership interest in the underlying *sukūk* assets.
3. *Subscription to sukūk and creation of a trust (or declaration of agency)*: The investors subscribe to the *sukūk* and pay the proceeds to the SPV (as issuer). The SPV declares a trust or agency (as relevant) over the proceeds and acts as a trustee or agent (as relevant) for the investors.
4. *Sale and purchase arrangement of the underlying assets*: The originator as the seller enters into a sale and purchase arrangement with the SPV, as trustee or agent (as relevant), and transfers the underlying assets to it. The SPV (as trustee or agent) pays the purchase price of the assets, as consideration for the sale, to the originator using the proceeds from the issuance of the *sukūk*.

---

[15] World Bank, PPIAF, and ISDB, *Reference Guide: Islamic Finance for Infrastructure PPP Projects.*
[16] Ibid.

5. *Ijārah (lease back) arrangement*: The SPV (as lessor) then leases the assets back to the originator under *ijārah* arrangements for an agreed period.
6. *Rental payments and periodic distribution amounts*: The originator (as lessee) agrees to make periodic rental payments to the SPV, as lessor and trustee or agent (as relevant).
7. *Payment of distribution amount*: The SPV (as issuer) uses the rental payments received from the originator to pay the periodic distribution amounts to the investors.
8. *Sale and purchase agreement of the underlying assets at maturity*: At maturity of the *sukūk* or upon an option call, the SPV (as trustee or agent, as relevant) will sell and the originator will buy the underlying assets at the exercise price, which will be equal to the face amount plus accrued but unpaid periodic distribution amounts.
9. *Payment of the dissolution amount*: The SPV (as issuer) will then use the exercise price it has received to pay the dissolution amount due to the investors under the terms and conditions of *sukūk* certificates.
10. *Reimbursement of servicing costs*: The SPV (as trustee or agent, as relevant) will appoint the originator as its service agent to carry out or procure performance of the lessor's obligations under the *ijārah* arrangement, which include undertaking, obtaining, or paying any major maintenance, insurance, and ownership taxes relating to the *sukūk* assets.

7.3.2 *Sukūk* – Asset Backed and Asset Based

Sukūk al-ijārah can be categorized into asset-backed and asset-based structures. Although *sukūk* are generally issued by an orphan SPV, typically the investor will not bear exposure solely to the credit risk of that SPV, and there will be some sponsor support from the obligor. *Sukūk* may however be structured as nonrecourse, ring-fencing the underlying *sukūk* assets. Whether (a) the investors will have legal recourse to the underlying *sukūk* assets (what is generally referred to as asset-backed *sukūk*) or (b) the investors have recourse only against the obligor will depend on whether the *sukūk* assets underlying the funding arrangement have been permanently transferred to the SPV.

In asset-backed *sukūk*, there is a real (true) sale and absolute transfer of the underlying *sukūk* assets to the third party, which is an SPV. The SPV acts as a trustee or agent on behalf of *sukūk* holders and collects rental from the lessee of the assets and transfers the same to the *sukūk* holders. An asset-backed *sukūk al-ijārah* permits the holders of *sukūk* to liquidate the underlying assets in any case of default to recover their investments.

Under the asset-based *sukūk*, the *sukūk* holders do not have legal ownership of the underlying assets. If there is a deficit in the payment, the *sukūk* holders have recourse to the obligor but not the underlying assets. The investors rely on the credit strength of the obligor rather than the underlying *sukūk* assets.

7.4 ISLAMIC CLIMATE FINANCE

There is growing awareness among global investors of the synergy between environmental, social, and governance (ESG) investing and Islamic finance, contributing to the rising appetite for *Shari'ah*-compliant investments as investors look for greater portfolio diversification and an alternative to more traditional ESG investments.

Sukūk are structured to avoid high degrees of leverage and speculation. *Shari'ah* compliance demands high levels of transparency. The outcome of transactions must not be entirely dependent on chance and all rights and obligations relating to an investment must be clear. The green *sukūk* market is one key response to this growing confluence of Islamic finance and ESG investing, even in the face of high issuance costs (see Boxes 7.4–7.6). The Islamic Development Bank has been one of the leading Islamic financial institutions to promote and participate in green and sustainable *sukūk*.

Islam promotes shared management of natural resources; it is therefore perceived that emissions reduction credits could be considered as *Shari'ah*-compliant assets and thus a significant opportunity for Islamic ESG investment.[17] However, it should be noted that there is currently no consensus among *Shari'ah* scholars on the matter.

Box 7.4 Corporate green *sukūk* in the United Arab Emirates

In 2019, the United Arab Emirates' Majid Al Futtaim listed the world's first benchmark corporate green *sukūk*, raising USD 600 million, closely followed by a second raising another USD 600 million. The underlying *sukūk* assets included hotels, offices, and a number of shopping malls. The issuance financed existing and future green projects, including green buildings, renewable energy, sustainable water management, and energy efficiency, as part of the company's strategy aimed at significantly reducing the company's water consumption and carbon emissions, resulting in a positive corporate carbon footprint by 2040.[18]

Box 7.5 Green *sukūk* in Malaysia

In Malaysia, the birthplace of *sukūk* in the 1990s, the Securities Commission introduced the Sustainable and Responsible Investment Sukuk Framework in 2014. This was followed by the issuance of the first social impact *sukūk* by its sovereign wealth fund, Khazanah Nasional Berhad.

---

[17] See Section 3.4 on emissions reduction credits.
[18] Ibid.

> **Box 7.6 Quantum Solar Park, Malaysia**
>
> In 2017, Quantum Solar Park (Semenanjung) issued the largest solar project linked to green *sukūk*, to build three large-scale solar photovoltaic plants in the states of Kedah, Melaka, and Terengganu in Malaysia at a total cost of RM 1.25 billion. The projects are collectively expected to generate and supply about 282,000 megawatts of electricity annually to Malaysia's electric utility company, Tenaga Nasional, under the respective power purchase agreements over a period of twenty-one years. In terms of social impact as well as the sustainability aspects of the projects, it mitigates about 193,000 tons of carbon per year. The assets used for this project were *Shari'ah*-compliant commodities (excluding *ribawi* items in the category of medium of exchange such as currency, gold, and silver). The project has proven successful, with the *sukūk* earning a local AA rating in 2021.[19]

7.5 ISLAMIC FINANCE INSTITUTIONS

Underpinning global Islamic finance is a variety of institutions that form part of the ecosystem for the Islamic finance industry, helping to standardize global Islamic finance practices and establish sound policies and procedures:[20]

- Credit rating agencies are critical players in conventional financial markets and Islamic financial markets alike. Globally, the big three credit rating agencies (S&P, Moody's, and Fitch Ratings) have Islamic windows and rate Islamic financial assets, with specific guidelines and methodologies to assess Islamic financial institutions and instruments. In addition to a number of domestic rating agencies active in Islamic finance, the Islamic International Rating Agency started operations in 2011 and is hosted by Bahrain.[21]
- The *shari'ah* adjudication system will differ in each country; for example, in some countries each Islamic finance institution has a *shari'ah* advisor/committee that gives an opinion on each transaction and product, whereas in others, *shari'ah* rulings and principles are centralized and regulated.
- Several organizations have been working to provide broad principles and guidelines. While only advisory in nature, they seek to standardize Islamic financing:
    - The Accounting and Auditing Organization for Islamic Financial Institutions,[22] established in 1991 and based in Bahrain, develops and issues standards for the global Islamic finance industry.

---

[19] www.bixmalaysia.com/news-announcements/announcement-details?id=56196.
[20] World Bank, PPIAF, and ISDB, *Reference Guide: Islamic Finance for Infrastructure PPP Projects*.
[21] Ibid.
[22] http://aaoifi.com.

7.6 *Legal Issues and Documentation* 173

- The Islamic Financial Services Board (IFSB),[23] an international standard-setting organization that started operations in 2003, also conducts research and coordinates initiatives on industry-related issues and organizes roundtables, seminars, and conferences for regulators and industry stakeholders, culminating in the annual Islamic Financial Services Industry Stability Report.
- The International Islamic Financial Markets focuses on the standardization of Islamic financial contracts and product templates relating to the capital and money market, corporate finance, and trade finance segments of the Islamic financial services industry.[24] It also creates industry awareness by organizing specialized seminars and workshops, as well as publishing research reports.
- The International Islamic Fiqh Academy,[25] headquartered in Saudi Arabia, studies contemporary issues from the *shari'ah* point of view and tries to find *shari'ah*-compliant solutions.
- The International Islamic Rating Agency provides independent assessments to issuers with a special focus on the development of local capital markets.[26]
- The International Islamic Center for Reconciliation and Arbitration focuses on settling disputes according to Islamic *shari'ah* principles, through reconciliation and arbitration services.[27]
- The International Islamic Liquidity Management Corporation,[28] established in 2010 by central banks, monetary authorities, and multilateral organizations, creates and issues short-term Islamic financial instruments to facilitate effective cross-border Islamic liquidity management. By creating more liquid Islamic financial markets for institutions offering Islamic financial services, it aims to enhance cross-border investment flows, international linkages, and financial stability.

7.6 LEGAL ISSUES AND DOCUMENTATION

Legal and regulatory frameworks can be adapted to make Islamic financing more easily available. For example, Islamic finance transactions often require multiple title transfers of underlying assets, which may trigger double or even triple tax charges in some jurisdictions (see Box 7.7). These transactions may be subject to withholding tax or may be accounted for as both an equity and debt financing arrangement for the obligor and for the financiers (for accounting

---

[23] www.ifsb.org.
[24] www.iifm.net.
[25] www.iifa-aifi.org.
[26] http://iirating.com/corprofile.aspx.
[27] http://iicra.com.
[28] www.iilm.com.

Box 7.7 Doraleh container terminal project in Djibouti

A consortium of local and foreign investors was awarded a thirty-year concession for the design, construction, operation, and maintenance of a greenfield container port terminal in the city of Doraleh, Djibouti (Figure 7.8). The Islamic project financing combines four Islamic finance instruments:

- *Mushārakah* – The SPV and the project financiers agree to procure assets for the project jointly and commit to making respective capital contributions according to the debt-to-equity ratio of the financing plan.
- *Istiṣnāʿ* – The parties appoint the SPV as their agent to procure and construct the container terminal and ensure delivery of assets at the end of the construction period. Capital contributions under the *mushārakah* are paid to the SPV, which is equivalent to multiple drawdowns under a conventional lending arrangement.
- *Ijārah* – The project financiers lease their coownership interest in the project to the SPV in exchange for periodical rental payments. During the construction phase, the documentation allows the project financiers to receive advance lease rentals. During operations, the project financiers receive periodic rental payments based on both floating and fixed rates, reflecting amortization of the loan.
- *Takāful* – The World Bank's Multilateral Investment Guarantee Agency issued guarantees totaling USD 427 million against the risks of restrictions on currency transfers, expropriation, breach of contract, and war and civil disturbance. The Islamic Corporation for the Insurance of Investment and Export Credit, a member of the Islamic Development Group, provided *takāful* reinsurance for USD 50 million to the agency.[29]

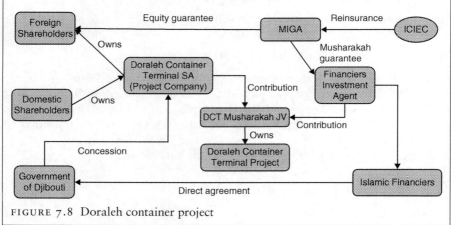

FIGURE 7.8 Doraleh container project

[29] World Bank, PPIAF, and ISDB, *Mobilizing Islamic Finance for Infrastructure Public Private Partnerships*.

7.6 Legal Issues and Documentation

and tax deduction purposes). Clarification of such issues in a country's legal framework to ensure a level playing field with conventional financing can make Islamic financing transactions more attractive. Some jurisdictions have amended their tax laws so that Islamic finance products are taxed in the same way as equivalent conventional financial products.[30]

A quick overview of the legal documentation for different Islamic finance structures helps understand the key dynamics among the parties. The following provides an overview of legal documentation for a sale and leaseback transaction:

1. *An assets sale agreement*: The obligor sells the underlying assets to the financiers (or to a special purpose vehicle for the benefit of the financiers).
2. *A lease agreement*: The financiers (as owner) lease the assets to the obligor against periodic rental payments (which include both the principal amount of the financing and the profit).
3. *A service agency agreement*: The financiers appoint the obligor as the service agent to (a) carry out structural and major maintenance and repair of the assets; (b) procure insurance; and (c) pay ownership taxes.
4. *A purchase undertaking* (put option): It is given by the obligor in favor of the financiers in the case of (a) illegality, (b) a mandatory prepayment, or (c) the occurrence of an event of default, at a purchase price to be determined in accordance with a preagreed formula.
5. *A sale undertaking* (call option): It is given by the financiers in favor of the obligor in the case of (a) a voluntary early payment by the obligor in accordance with a preagreed formula or (b) full and final maturity of the financing facility at a nominal price.

---

[30] World Bank, PPIAF, and ISDB, *Reference Guide: Islamic Finance for Infrastructure PPP Projects*.

8

Blended Finance

Blended finance is an innovative approach to the use of development finance for the mobilization of additional commercial finance by using the low pricing, high-risk tolerance, and perceived risk management of development finance (and the technical assistance and project preparation that comes with it) to bring commercial lenders and borrowers together.[1]

---

[1] There are a number of different definitions of blended finance, reflecting the priorities of different interest groups. This text adopts a simple definition in an effort to cover the different issues, challenges, and opportunities of blended finance in all of its variations. There is also often confusion between blending and other concepts like mobilizing, leveraging, catalyzing, and enabling. The latter are goals, while blending is the instrument; in particular, blending is the cofinancing of a project by development and commercial financing to achieve these goals. Further reference should be made to the various texts on blended financing, including: Emelly Mutambatsere and Philip Schellekens, *The Why and How of Blended Finance: Recommendations to Strengthen the Rationale for and Efficient Use of Concessional Resources in Development Finance Institutions' (DFI) Operations* (International Finance Corporation, World Bank, 2020), www.ifc.org/en/insights-reports/2020/202011-bf-discussion-paper; World Bank, *The International Finance Corporation's Blended Finance Operations: Findings from a Cluster of Project Performance Assessment Reports* (Independent Evaluation Group, World Bank, 2020), https://ieg.worldbankgroup.org/evaluations/ifcs-blended-finance-operations; Convergence, *The State of Blended Finance 2021*; DFI Working Group on Blended Concessional Finance for Private Sector Projects, Joint Report, 2021, www.convergence.finance/reports/sobf2021/assets/The_State_of_Blended_Finance_2021.pdf; Javier Pereira, *Blended Finance: What It Is, How It Works and How It Is Used*, Report delivered to Oxfam and Eurodad, 2021, https://policy-practice.oxfam.org/resources/blended-finance-what-it-is-how-it-works-and-how-it-is-used-620186/; Irene Basile and Jarrett Dutra, "Blended Finance Funds and Facilities – 2018 Survey Results: Part I: Investment Strategy," OECD Working Paper, 2019, www.oecd.org/dac/financing-sustainable-development/blended-finance-principles/blendedfinancefundsandfacilities.htm; Convergence, *The State of Blended Finance 2019*, www.convergence.finance/resource/13VZmRUtiK96hqAvUPk4rt/view; A. Koenig and E. Jackson, "Mobilising Private Capital for Sustainable Development," *Great Insights*, October 6, 2016, https://ecdpm.org/great-insights/2030-smart-engagementbusiness/mobilising-private-capital-for-sustainable-development/; *Making Blended Finance Work for the Sustainable*

- Development finance includes debt, equity, and grants from governments, development financiers, foundations, and philanthropic investors. Development financiers include bilaterals (owned by a single country) and multilaterals (owned by a number of countries, e.g., the World Bank).
- Commercial finance is provided by commercial actors such as institutional investors, commercial banks, private equity funds, venture capital funds, hedge funds, and companies (e.g., on a vendor finance basis).

Blended finance can mobilize commercial finance where such investments would be too risky for private finance alone, especially where the project involves "frontier" countries, technologies, or business models, which are otherwise below investment grade. Markets alone can fail to produce socially desirable outcomes in these cases. Blended finance, which combines concessional public funds with commercial funds, can help rebalance risks, enable investment, and ensure focus on developmental priorities.

The potential for blended finance is huge. Developing countries need to mobilize financing from all sources, public, development, and commercial. Unless we leverage these different sources of financing, we will never get close to the levels of investment needed globally to lift developing countries out of poverty or to set them on track to achieve middle-income or upper middle-income status. Specific issues like global health and climate change also rely on blended finance to mobilize more commercial finance to fill the gaps in available development finance (see Box 8.1). In March 2002, the Monterrey Consensus recognized "the value of exploring innovative sources of finance" and sparked a broad effort to pilot and implement a variety of new financing mechanisms, catalyzing developing countries to pursue the Millennium Development Goals.[2]

Despite its potential, commitments to blended finance remain limited, at around 2 percent of official development assistance and USD 10–15 billion of project volumes annually.[3] Blended finance needs to scale up significantly in a much broader range of countries and sectors. Its role is critical for creating the conditions for greater investment in low-carbon solutions, to make them competitive with high-carbon alternatives (which have been subsidized for decades) on key dimensions (e.g., cost, convenience, social acceptability).

Development Goals, OECD, 2018, https://assets.ctfassets.net/4cgqlwde6qyo/77K8guUYE wekieaIWmiSqm/8a2472bac649affc93e8558200c994ec; OECD__Making_Blended_Finance_ Work__2018.pdf; *Blended Finance Funds and Facilities 2018 Report*, OECD, 2019, www.kfw-entwicklungsbank.de/PDF/Download; *Unlocking Infrastructure Investment: Innovative Funding and Financing in Regions and Cities*, OECD Report for the G20 Infrastructure Working Group, 2021. www.oecd.org/regional/unlocking-infrastructure-investment-9152902b-en.htm.

[2] *Report of the International Conference on Financing for Development*, United Nations, 2002.

[3] *Blended Finance for Scaling Up Climate and Nature Investments*, Report of the One Planet Lab, 2021.

> **Box 8.1 Blended finance for community lending in Bolivia**
>
> Approximately 35 percent of Bolivians live below the national poverty line. Poverty is more concentrated in rural areas, where people are dependent on subsistence farming and have only very limited access to markets and financial services. These market failures affect women and indigenous communities in particular. The Dutch bilateral, FMO, provided USD 3 million in debt and USD 2 million in equity to the Bolivian lender, Sembrar Sartawi, to provide microloans to people living in rural areas. By combining long-term debt and equity funding, with reasonable interest rates, in local currency, with technical assistance the financiers were able to offer a variety of additional advantages compared to fully commercial finance. The development financing allowed Sartawi to engage with risky rural community loans. A study among 600 dairy farmers who received these microloans and technical assistance found a 11 percent increase in daily milk production and a 16 percent increase in income.[4]

In 2017, a collection of development finance institutions (DFIs) led by the International Finance Corporation (IFC) calling itself the DFI Working Group on Blended Finance for Private Sector Operations issued a set of Enhanced Principles for Using Concessional Finance in Private Sector Investment Operations. This DFI Working Group issued a joint report, the State of Blended Finance 2021, which identifies nearly 680 blended finance transactions, representing aggregated financing of over USD 160 billion, from over 5,300 financial commitments by over 1,450 unique organizations across the public, private, and philanthropic sectors. Sub-Saharan Africa continues to be the most common destination for blended finance flows, with Asia mobilizing an increasingly large part of blended resources.[5]

8.1 BLENDED FINANCE INSTRUMENTS

The right blended finance instruments should be used to achieve the right impact. Instruments should be selected to address directly the underlying obstacles. But too much structure can reduce the impact and responsiveness of blended finance. Blended finance (like any project finance) needs to respond to changes in needs of the project and circumstances surrounding the project. This section explores a few of the key challenges and opportunities of blended finance.

---

[4] *DFI Working Group on Blended Concessional Finance for Private Sector Projects, Joint Report.*
[5] It should be noted that the lack of consensus of the definition of blended finance makes it difficult to compare the amounts reported for blended finance. For this reason, we will not focus much on these data points in this text. Convergence, *The State of Blended Finance 2021.*

8.1 Blended Finance Instruments

8.1.1 Desire for Lower Income, Bias toward Middle Income

Blended financing uses development financing to address constraints that otherwise impede commercial financing. By definition, lower-income countries suffer from more constraints than do middle-income countries, and therefore blended financing in lower-income countries requires a larger proportion of development finance than do investments in middle-income countries. This can result in a bias (conscious or unconscious) among development financiers for projects in middle-income countries, where they can show a larger proportion of commercial finance leveraged. This said, in lower-income countries, where development finance plays a larger role, development financiers will have more influence in the transaction and commercial financiers are generally more comfortable with the standards and requirements imposed by development financiers.

8.1.2 Who Is Whom?

The divide between entities providing commercial and development finance is often not entirely clear. Some development financiers, for example, the IFC and Asian Development Bank (ADB) private sector, exhibit attributes of both commercial and development financiers – with terms and pricing similar to commercial financiers but risk appetite closer to development financiers. Some commercial financiers have a greater appetite for risk, for example, angel funds (investors that support start-ups at initial stages, where risks of the start-ups failing are relatively high, and when most investors are not prepared to back them – also known as a business angel, informal investor, angel funder, or seed investor) and impact funds (investors whose goal is to generate a social or environmental impact – such as renewable energy, housing, healthcare, education, microfinance, and sustainable agriculture – alongside a financial return).

8.1.3 When to Blend?

Blended finance is meant to bring commercial financiers into projects/investments that would otherwise be too risky for them and where the pricing of commercial finance would not be affordable for the borrower and where development financiers are motivated to support that project or borrower, given its developmental impact (see Box 8.2). However, it is easy for blended finance to stray into projects that could be financed by private capital alone. There is no clear and bright line.

The fact that certain investments can be enabled by blended finance does not necessarily mean that they should. A number of factors should be taken into account when considering blended finance:

- *Sustainability* – commercial and economic sustainability beyond the presence of blended finance;

> **Box 8.2 Blended finance for low-income countries, Haiti**
>
> Haiti is one of the poorest countries on the planet. It suffers from rampant poverty, inequality, and a lack of access to basic public services. It is estimated that 70 percent to 85 percent of Haiti's population has no access to electricity. USD 8 million in senior debt was provided by the Clean Technology Fund (CTF) in 2020 to blend with USD 1.5 million of commercial financing from Inter-American Development Bank (IDB) and Climate Investment Fund (CIF) to support an electrical minigrid located in Haiti's northwest with 2.9 megawatts of clean generation capacity, 1.1 megawatts of battery storage, and associated distribution infrastructure. The project targets 6,600 connections (an estimated 20,000 individuals) with no or intermittent access to electricity. While the level of concessionality is significant, mobilizing commercial financing into economies such as Haiti can be extremely difficult.[6]

- *Proportionality* – a proportional use of development finance (or concessional funds) will ensure balance and avoid unnecessary windfalls for commercial financiers;
- *Complementarity* – appropriate for the challenges faced and the variety of interventions needed to address those challenges (not just availability of credit);
- *Additionality* – mobilize commercial finance where it would not otherwise have been mobilized, at a cost that represents value for money and in a way that achieves developmental goals consistent with the goals of the development financier.

It may also be that when the blended financiers assess the investment and make investment decisions, the project is sub-investment grade and therefore blended finance is appropriate, but later, as the financing is being arranged, the situation changes (maybe because of the efforts of the blended financiers), and the project becomes one that could attract commercial-only financing. The criticism will fly, even if unfair. Blended financiers need to be prepared for this and to adjust the balance of commercial and development financing as the project context changes and as the project can absorb more commercial finance. This is of course easier said than done; development finance can take time to organize and approve, and once approved, after the cost of mobilizing it, it may not be easy to reduce the amounts or change terms, in particular where grants are mobilized to help prepare the development finance. Commercial financiers for their part would see part or all of the development cofinancing withdrawn, which may be very difficult to explain to their credit committees, forcing them to reconsider the investment based on its new context.

---

[6] Ibid.

8.1.4 Need for Commercially Viable Projects

Project selection for blended finance is often influenced by the government. Blended financiers may be convinced to support projects that are not only sub-investment but may not be a good idea at all, or they may be purely politically driven projects. Such projects are unlikely to succeed and often attract harsh criticism from future governments who will see the project as the white elephant that it is, but also one driven by a previous (possibly competitor) government.

8.2 THE COMMUNITY OF PRACTICE AROUND BLENDED FINANCE

A number of global entities and communities focus on the topic of blended financing, looking to improve its efficiency and increase its use, in the belief that blended finance holds an important role in scaling up investment in developing countries, in particular in the area of infrastructure. The Organisation for Economic Co-operation and Development (OECD), for example, adopted the five Blended Finance Principles for Unlocking Commercial Finance for the Sustainable Development Goals in 2017, which were referenced by the G7 and the G20 as these groups in turn sought to improve the use of blended finance. In 2018, the OECD also launched the Tri Hita Karana Roadmap for Blended Finance programs.[7] Also in 2018, the Global Impact Investing Network launched a Blended Finance Working Group, which has assembled a series of materials to support blended financing.[8] In 2021, the United Kingdom launched the COP26 Blended Finance Platform.[9]

Most multilateral and bilateral lending agencies are searching for a better way to blend financing, to mobilize more private capital using scarce concessional and grant resources. They have set up initiatives to share important lessons learned and designs for blended finance structures, including the One Planet Summit,[10] United Nations/Interagency Task Force on Financing for Development,[11] Climate Finance Leadership Coalition,[12] Tri Hita Karana/OECD,[13] Convergence/DfID (UK Department for International Development, now the Foreign, Commonwealth, and Development Office),[14] and Climate

---

[7] www.oecd.org/dac/financing-sustainable-development/development-finance-topics/tri-hita-karana-roadmap-for-blended-finance.htm.
[8] www.thegiin.org.
[9] www.convergence.finance/news-and-events/news/8UshDGgKoVo3p1yyRNlVB/view.
[10] *Blended Finance for Scaling Up Climate and Nature Investments.*
[11] United Nations, *Financing for Sustainable Development Report 2020.*
[12] *Climate Finance Leadership Initiative, Financing the Low-Carbon Future: A Private-Sector View on Mobilizing Climate Finance,* 2019.
[13] *Tri Hita Karana Roadmap for Blended Finance, Summary of Outputs,* 2020.
[14] Convergence, *How to Mobilize Private Investment at Scale in Blended Finance,* The DfID Impact Programme, 2020. www.convergence.finance/resource/how-to-mobilize-private-investment-at-scale-in-blended-finance/view.

Policy Initiative/Blended Finance Task Force.[15] The DFI Working Group on Blended Concessional Finance and the OECD Development Assistance Committee have established important guidelines for the governance and implementation of blended finance.[16] Blended finance design innovations are being generated by the Green Climate Fund, the CIFs, the DFIs, and numerous public–private initiatives, such as the Global Innovation Lab for Climate Finance.[17] Data are being collected, in particular, by the OECD, the DFIs, and Convergence, though there is general agreement that transparency and reporting, especially at project level, remain inadequate and make analyses of the impact and efficiency of blended finance very difficult.

These bodies have produced important guidance and toolkits and coordinated discussions among development and commercial financiers in an effort to improve the effectiveness of blended finance and to raise awareness of its importance. Much has been done, but so much more is left to do.

8.3 DRIVERS OF BLENDED FINANCING

Blended finance is often driven by development financiers seeking to mobilize more commercial finance to stretch available development financing, have greater impact through better commercial efficiencies, and help developing country governments improve their ability to engage with commercial financiers on complex financings.

But blended finance is also often driven by commercial financiers seeking to develop opportunities in developing countries, where the project financials are too weak or the risk (or perception thereof) in the project is too great for them to engage alone and where development financing can be used to address constraints and make the project commercially viable (see Box 8.3).

In other cases, borrowers may drive blended financing in an effort to stretch scarce development financing resources, attract more commercial financing, capacitate local commercial financiers, expand local financial markets, and get more investment.

Mobilizing more blended finance will require a number of changes to current practices:

---

[15] Bella Tonkonogy, Jessica Brown, Valerio Micale, Xueying Wang, and Alex Clark, *Blended Finance in Clean Energy*, Climate Policy Initiative, 2018; Barbara Buchner et al., *Global Landscape of Climate Finance 2021*, Climate Policy Initiative, www.climatepolicyinitiative.org/publication/global-landscape-of-climate-finance-2021/.

[16] *DFI Working Group on Blended Concessional Finance for Private Sector Projects, Summary Report*, 2020, Annex 1, www.ifc.org/en/insights-reports/2020/bf-dfi-ifc-annual-reports; OECD DAC, *Blended Finance Principles Guidance*, 2020, https://one.oecd.org/document/DCD/DAC(2020)42/FINAL/En/pdf.

[17] Global Innovation Lab for Climate Finance, www.climatefinancelab.org/the-labs/global/.

8.4 Blended Financing Funds and Facilities

Box 8.3 Blended climate finance in Chile

In Chile, in 2018, 5.45 GW of coal-fired power plants were still delivering 38 percent of all energy generated. To incentivize the early decommissioning of Units 14 and 15 in Tocopilla and CTM1 and CTM2 in Mejillones and replacing them with the Calama Wind Farm to supply an equivalent volume of clean energy, the CTF provided USD 15 million in senior loan in support of USD 110 million in commercial financing from DFIs (IDB and CIF). About 5.16 million tons of CO_2 are expected to be effectively displaced during the twelve-year loan life according to the methodology put in place. Up to 2.18 million tons of CO_2 would be eligible at maturity for credit under the CTF loan for a value of USD 6.54 million.[18]

- More risk taking by commercial financiers; there is a tendency for commercial financiers to see blended financing as a "free lunch," but sharing risk and cost needs to be a fundamental focus of commercial financiers;
- Improved governance frameworks around allocation of development finance and technical assistance, to improve incentives for bilaterals and multilaterals to engage with commercial financiers;
- Improved reporting to ensure value for development monies, testing proposals against benchmarks for impact, with better measurement frameworks and better data and transparency to provide comfort to development financiers;[19]
- Better understanding among development financiers, many of whom are still new to dealing with commercial financiers; they remain underinformed and concerned about the value and proper use of blended finance;
- Better understanding among commercial financiers, as many have little experience or patience in dealing with development financiers and the requirements of a public-policy-driven approach to investing.

8.4 BLENDED FINANCING FUNDS AND FACILITIES

Blending can happen at the project level or at the fund/facility level. Blending at the project level allows it to respond to the specific needs of the project and can be delivered more quickly; it can respond to the priorities of individual development financiers and commercial financiers, making investment approvals less complex.

Blended funds and facilities (BFF) can improve efficiency, achieving economies of scale; establishing a coordinated management, implementation, and

---

[18] *DFI Working Group on Blended Concessional Finance for Private Sector Projects, Joint Report 2020*, www.ifc.org/en/insights-reports/2020/bf-dfi-ifc-annual-reports.
[19] *Blended Finance for Scaling Up Climate and Nature Investments*.

> **Box 8.4 Benefits of blended funds and facilities**
>
> Blended funds and facilities can help
>
> - use government and development funding to leverage commercial finance;
> - reduce the transaction costs represented by government and donor funding for individual transactions by creating a wholesale mechanism;
> - increase transparency and consistency of government support by establishing an entity with governance mechanisms and operational guidelines establishing rules of the game;
> - adopt private sector salary scale to attract suitably skilled and expert staff and create a center of expertise based on larger volumes of transactions, with commercial selection criteria, where a public entity might not be able to provide sufficient salaries or attract skilled staff;
> - use the leverage available through a financial institution to increase the amount of support made available from a limited capital base – a BFF can achieve leverage of its capital far in excess of what public entities can normally achieve.

monitoring and evaluation framework for all projects supported by the BFF; and allowing for a larger amount of development financing to be mobilized (it is often difficult to mobilize smaller amounts of development financing due to the relatively high marginal cost of preparation), against which different amounts of commercial financing can be mobilized, including smaller amounts of local commercial financing(see Box 8.4). BFFs can also help mobilize commercial financing, providing different tranches of investment with more or less risk for commercial financiers with different risk appetites. They are also able to channel capital to sectors/investments that would have been unattainable as individual projects due to size, risk, and institutional constraints.

BFFs can help coordinate financiers, aggregate human and financial resources, and facilitate management of multiple investments across sectors and countries. The following are some examples of the financial instruments used by such BFFs:

1. *Debt funds* – with a subordinated donor tranche and mezzanine mid-risk tranche (for DFI and private investors) derisking a senior low-risk (A to BB) tranche for institutional investors; these funds would invest directly in debt for projects, including green debt securities(see Box 8.5). Debt funds may also include credit enhancement mechanisms, such as guarantees, first loss facilities, and insurance instruments to credit enhance the vehicle to attract more commercial financing that would otherwise be too risk-averse(see Box 8.9).

8.4 Blended Financing Funds and Facilities

Box 8.5 Emerging Africa Infrastructure Fund

The Emerging Africa Infrastructure Fund (EAIF) is a debt fund established in 2001, which provides loans to infrastructure projects in Sub-Saharan Africa to address the lack of available long-term foreign currency debt finance for infrastructure.[20] It was created through a joint venture of development institutions and commercial banks, mixing equity from donors, subordinated debt from development partners, and senior debt from commercial lenders. The EAIF has committed over USD 900 million to more than forty projects, mainly owned, managed, and operated by private sector businesses, in developing countries. It received its first-ever credit rating in 2022, from Moody's Investors Service – a foreign currency long-term issuer rating of A2 with a stable outlook.

The EAIF is managed by professional private sector fund managers, bringing knowledge of countries, sectors, and financial markets. The management team markets the EAIF, identifies projects, evaluates loan applications (including due diligence), manages transactions, and monitors the loan portfolio.

This public–private partnership (PPP) between development financiers wanting to take risk and commercial financiers with a more risk-averse approach to project selection created a particular challenge in the early days. The EAIF had to develop an appropriate incentive mechanism for the fund manager, staffed by commercial bankers who were less familiar with developmental risk appetite.

Box 8.6 Green Growth Equity Fund

The Green Growth Equity Fund (GGEF) is anchored by India's National Investment and Infrastructure Fund and the UK Foreign, Commonwealth and Development Office and is managed by a commercial fund manager. It uses a fund-of-funds structure that aims to raise funds from a mix of institutional investors and DFIs, supported by concessional funds in the form of subordinated equity from the Global Climate Facility. GGEF plans to invest equity capital through sectoral platforms in climate technology growth firms in renewable energy, e-mobility, energy services, and resource efficiency projects with strong innovation potential.[21]

---

2. *Equity funds* – with distribution waterfalls that support returns to the senior tranches up to a target level, to attract different tranches of equity; these BFFs invest equity directly in projects(see Box 8.6).

---

[20] www.emergingafricafund.com.
[21] Anthony Osae-Brown, "UK-Backed Africa Infrastructure Fund Plans to Raise $500 Million: Fund Gets First Rating since 2001 as It Seeks to Scale," *Bloomberg*, August 24, 2022.

> **Box 8.7 Climate Finance Partnership**
>
> The Climate Finance Partnership was launched in 2022 under the umbrella of the One Planet Summit. It is a USD 500 million fund managed by a commercial fund manager, with catalytic subordinated equity from development agencies and philanthropies. It aims to offer "narrower standard deviation of outcomes for institutional investors" and an "OECD-like risk-return profile" on climate investments in a range of developing countries.[22]

> **Box 8.8 Chilean Infrastructure Bonds**
>
> Chile successfully tapped the bond market for project finance debt through infrastructure bonds amounting to an average of USD 1 billion a year during 1996–2001. This situation was aided by government revenue guarantees and even foreign exchange guarantees in certain cases and political and regulatory risks were mostly insured by DFIs.[23]

3. *Credit enhancement/guarantee funds* – backed by a weighty balance sheet or support from entities with significant balance sheets, credit enhancement instruments can be managed through a BFF to support individual projects (see Box 8.8).
4. *Funds of funds* – can be used to aggregate debt and equity funds to allow for larger investment sizes, with different focus and requirements (see Box 8.7).

8.5 IMPLEMENTING BLENDED FINANCE FUNDS

Creating a BFF (whether from an existing entity or by creating a new venture) can be costly and time-consuming. There is no easy or standard approach. Each country will have different legal requirements, financial sector context, and the kind of infrastructure to be financed. BFF are often created through state-owned enterprises, which provide a convenient nexus between public, government support, and commercial/private context.

8.5.1 Functionality

Three key functions for the BFF that can help mobilize commercial finance are origination, liquidity, and refinancing.

---

[22] *Blended Finance for Scaling Up Climate and Nature Investments.*
[23] Marianne Fay and Mary Morrison, *Infrastructure in Latin America and the Caribbean: Recent Developments and Key Challenges* (World Bank, 2007).

8.5 Implementing Blended Finance Funds

Box 8.9 Investment Promotion and Financing Facility

The Investment Promotion and Financing Facility (IPFF) of Bangladesh is a publicly held vehicle in operation since 2006 that provides long-term funding through eligible financial institutions, who on-lend to qualifying PPP projects on market terms. The equity contribution of the sponsor (minimum of 30 percent) and the debt share of the local financial institution (minimum of 20 percent) ensure market-based incentives in selecting only commercially viable PPP transactions and their successful implementation.[24]

- *Origination*: BFFs originating infrastructure finance will assess a project, influence its design and structure, and then build a book of debt either alone, with a club of other lenders, and/or through syndication.
- *Liquidity*: Long-tenor funds can be made available to those financiers or as cofinancing (senior or subordinated) to the project. Other instruments, like take-out guarantees, can be used to extend tenors of debt.
- *Refinancing*: Liquidity constraints, risk ratios, single borrower limits, and other prudential requirements can constrain the amount of support that commercial financiers can provide to infrastructure markets. Refinancing involves the prepayment of part or all of a project's debt by borrowing from a new lender (possibly at a lower interest rate, longer tenor, or on easier terms).

8.5.2 Fund Structure

A BFF can be designed to have multiple tiers of capital. In such a structure, the highest-risk tier, typically subscribed by donors and development agencies, is structured to improve the risk-return of other tiers of capital to a "market-equivalent" investment risk-return profile that mobilizes commercial investors to invest (see Figure 8.1). Generally, "senior" tier investors are repaid first and do not bear losses suffered by the fund until the "junior" capital has been exhausted. When and how BFF proceeds are distributed to different tiers depends on the type of distribution waterfall that the BFF establishes to mobilize commercial investors:[25]

- Commercial investors usually rank senior to donors and sometimes development organizations.
- Senior investors usually have preference in the distribution of proceeds.
- Senior investments can have shorter maturities than development financing leading to a faster payback and lower risk.

---

[24] www.mof.gov.bd/en/budget/09_10/ppp/IPFF.
[25] Anja-Nadine König, Chris Club, and Andrew Apampa, *Innovative Development Finance Toolbox* (KfW, 2020).

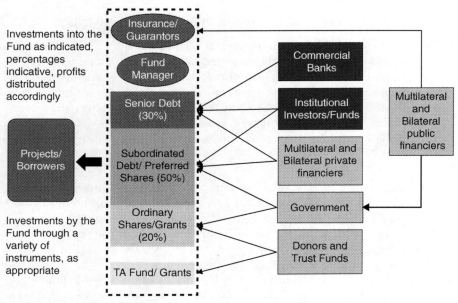

FIGURE 8.1 BFF structure

> **Box 8.10 Infrastructure Development Finance Company**
>
> Infrastructure Development Finance Company (IDFC) of India was set up in 1997 by the government of India along with various Indian banks, financial institutions, and IFIs. Its task is to connect projects and financial institutions to financial markets and by so doing develop and nurture the creation of a long-term debt market. It offers loans, equity/quasi-equity, advisory, asset management, and syndication services.[26]

This kind of structure allows the BFF to attract a larger variety of sources of commercial financing, from a diversity of entities (see Box 8.10).

8.5.3 A Few Challenges

A BFF can be particularly difficult to implement effectively. Some of the key challenges when creating an intermediary are discussed here.

Pipeline – A BFF can be very tricky to design well, setting up the framework is complex, and development financiers will often want a clear understanding of the eventual investments to be made (which may not be practical/realistic

---

[26] www.idfc.com.

8.5 Implementing Blended Finance Funds

for many such BFFs, and it is often necessary to create the BFF to attract investors and prepare projects).

Management of the BFF can be outsourced to a private fund manager, but this can be expensive and often those fund managers are as risk-averse as commercial financiers. Few of the fund managers have development experience. Another option is to create a new entity and hire in staff and consultants. This can take a lot of time and require significant investment to create such a new structure. It can also be difficult to attract experienced staff to join a new venture, such as a BFF.

Stay demand responsive – The BFF must address identified market gaps, with access to products and instruments designed to address those gaps but also with the flexibility to use other instruments or approaches that respond to the changing nature of such gaps and market needs (see Box 8.11). Rather than crowding out private investment, it must crowd in private lenders and investors to give them new opportunities. The Indonesian Infrastructure Finance Facility (IIFF, see Box 8.12) was created after much effort at market analysis and coordination with other market actors.

Box 8.11 Development Bank of Southern Africa

The Development Bank of Southern Africa (DBSA) is a development finance institution wholly owned by the government of South Africa that focuses on investments and joint ventures/partnerships in public and private sector financing. DBSA can raise money on local and international capital markets and is publicly listed on the New York Stock Exchange. Its bond ratings are the same as South African Sovereign Ratings. DBSA offers a variety of financial products, including grants, equity, debt (senior and subordinated), underwriting guarantees, and other credit enhancement.[27]

Box 8.12 The IIFF

The IIFF is a private nonbank financial institution, a commercially oriented fund with private sector governance, mandated and equipped to mobilize local currency private financing. It is capitalized through equity investments and subordinated loans from the government, the private sector, and multilaterals. It invests in PPP projects, with debt, equity, and/or guarantees and provides advisory services.[28]

---

[27] www.dbsa.org.
[28] www.iif.co.id.

Once a BFF is created, it is often difficult to get rid of it after it has served its purpose. Provision needs to be made for the BFF to be wound up, sold off, or absorbed into another entity or to evolve into some other mechanism that will be responsive to other market demands, relevant at that time.

Governance and management structures – Investment project selection must be based on sound commercial criteria and not driven by purely political priorities; the risk of capture of the intermediary by political interests is high. This is generally addressed by developing the BFF as a privately owned company, for example, the IIFF (see Box 8.12). At the same time, purely commercial motivation may be too risk-averse for the investments available. The EAIF (see Box 8.5) faced this challenge – a partnership between development financiers wanting to take risk and commercial financiers with a more risk-averse approach to project selection, creating a particular challenge in the early days searching for an appropriate incentive mechanism for the fund manager.

Amount and source of original capital – Any effort to make a significant impact on an infrastructure market is likely to require a large investment of capital in the BFF. Efforts to do BFFs on the cheap have often proven unsuccessful.

Skilled staff and resources – Newly formed BFFs are a risky bet for financiers, and so need a solid and experienced management team to give comfort to the financial market and politicians. They must be able to attract funding from institutional investors and display a keen understating of the infrastructure market. The management team also needs to be committed for a reasonable period; this is not the job for a political appointee, a retiree looking for something to keep them busy, or a short-term consultant. The role of the CEO is key and the candidate should preferably be a politically acceptable individual but with good finance experience and the right incentives to take calculated risks. The IIFF (see Box 8.12) had challenges with its management team in the early days, that is, in finding the right set of skills and personality. These skilled staff can also be sourced through secondments from shareholders as was done for IDFC (see Box 8.10) or through a management contract as was done for the EAIF (see Box 8.5).

Identifying a solid pipeline – It is often tempting to focus on the market gap to be resolved by the BFF. But the first investments, the demonstration projects, will be critical and must be carefully prepared as the BFF is being created (see Boxes 8.13 and 8.14). This creates a timing challenge as the market is unlikely to wait for the BFF. The IPFF of Bangladesh (see Box 8.9) addressed this challenge by focusing on a series of gas-fired power projects in its first phase, projects that were well developed, easy to market, and limited to one sector. Phase two expanded to other sectors and more risky projects. IDFC (see Box 8.10) and the IIFF (see Box 8.12) spent their first few years providing advisory services to the infrastructure sector and thereby developing their own pipelines of investments, the former by necessity and the latter by design.

Box 8.13 Fondo Nacional de Infrastructura (Fonadin) of Mexico

Fondo Nacional de Infrastructura (Fonadin) is housed within Banobras, Mexico's national development bank, and was created in response to the tight credit market of the financial crisis to address risks that the market was not able to handle. It began with a sum of over 40 billion pesos (USD 3.3 billion) in 2008 and has its own revenue source from existing toll road assets that were rescued in a government bailout in the late 1990s, and therefore it does not rely on government support for its financing base. Fonadin's role is to finance infrastructure. It offers a variety of instruments, including grants, subsidies, guarantees (for stock, credit, damage, and political risk), subordinated lines of credit, and technical assistance.[29]

Box 8.14 Tamil Nadu Urban Development Fund

Tamil Nadu Urban Development Fund (TNUDF) was created as a trust fund with private equity participation and without state guarantees, the first such structure in India. Paid-in capital combined with debt raised from a World Bank loan allowed TNUDF to issue the first nonguaranteed and unsecured bond issue by a financial intermediary in India, in 2000. The issue received a LAA+ rating due to credit enhancement and structured payment mechanism, low gearing, and strong repayment record. The proceeds from bonds are deposited in the fund and subsequently lent back to the participating local bodies as subloans to finance their infrastructure projects.[30]

8.6 CORE RECOMMENDATIONS FOR BLENDED FINANCE

Blended finance is a very simple concept but is extremely difficult to implement in practice. In the effort to design an effective approach to blended financing, the following principles emerge from best practices.

8.6.1 Is It Necessary?

Blended finance should not be used simply to make commercial financing more attractive or to give a commercial financier (whether private, DFI, or otherwise) a competitive advantage. It should be used only where commercial financing would not be available without blended financing or where significantly more commercial financing will be available through blended financing.

---

[29] www.fonadin.gob.mx.
[30] www.tnudf.com.

Commercial financing in developing countries can be challenging. It is tempting to leverage blended financing where possible to make commercial financing easier and cheaper. But blended financing is scarce. It should not be used as the icing on the cake; it should not be "wasted." It should be used for those countries, those sectors, where commercial financing would not otherwise be available, to address specific market failures. These market failures might include unstable political systems with frequent changes in policy or government strategy, poorly functioning local regulatory systems or application of law, weak protections for creditors and property rights, and poorly functioning local financial markets.

Equally, blended financing should not displace commercial financing; it should not be allowed to distort the commercial market or crowd out commercial capital. By definition, when blending finance, some development financing takes space in a project that could/would/should be delivered with commercial financing. This is a tricky balance to achieve. It is generally easy to find commercial financiers who say they would be interested in financing a project. It is much harder to find commercial financiers who will actually cut a check for the amount needed.

The question of whether blended finance is "necessary" is complex, and it will depend on the perception of necessity of the various actors, including the borrower, development financiers, commercial financiers, the developer, and key stakeholders. It is better to have this discussion openly and transparently. While this can take some additional time early in the project to ensure consensus, this can avoid questions and conflict later in the project if the "necessity" is challenged or proves illusory.

Once (if) the identified market failures are addressed, development financing should be phased out (through appropriate exit strategies), leaving commercial finance to take its rightful place. Setting such exit strategies can be challenging – knowing when market failures have been sufficiently addressed and how to withdraw development financing without undermining the project and exposing the commercial financiers to too much risk is extremely difficult to do well.

8.6.2 Manage Expectations

There is a tendency to perceive blended finance from the perspective of the commercial financier and to exaggerate the ease and impact of blended finance. Commercial financiers may see blended finance as cheap and easy development money to buydown the cost of commercial financing, with no other real change to the commercial transaction. The numbers and impact need to line up. Surprisingly high financial returns are just as unlikely as surprisingly high impact. Blended finance is by definition a transaction that requires a careful balance of impact and returns.

8.6 Core Recommendations for Blended Finance

8.6.3 Get the Incentives Right

Any transaction requires a balance of incentives and risk management among the key parties; the better the balance, the more likely the transaction is to succeed. A normal transaction requires balanced risk management between the financier and borrower, fitting the context of each. Blended finance is no different but adds a new complexity of two types of financiers – development and commercial. Those familiar with development finance focused on the private sector (e.g., from the IFC) will understand one level of this complexity, but blended finance includes concessional finance and grants, to buy down financing costs. These sources of finance (e.g., from the World Bank) involve risk perceptions and incentive frameworks very different from commercial finance. Incentives need to include development impact, financial returns, sustainability, and a series of what are increasingly common criteria such as environmental, social, and corporate governance and gender equality.

8.6.4 Impact

Blended finance should focus on development impact. It is easy to get lost in the complexity of making blended finance work between development and commercial entities and in the process lose the focus on the development goals for which the blended finance is intended. The development impact should meet the needs of the beneficiary country/community, not just the entities providing the finance (development and commercial).

8.6.5 Address Capacity Constraints

Commercial financiers, development financiers, governments, borrowers, and other stakeholders often lack experience working on blended finance transactions, which require an understanding of commercial and development drivers, a mix of skill that is rare in the market. This tendency for commercial and development financiers to speak past each other, to misunderstand the other's motivations and practices, is a fundamental challenge for blended financing.

Even those commercial financiers with experience in lending to public sector entities, while they may have a better understanding of public sector interests, may not have the full set of skills needed to implement blended financing. Equally, certain development financiers have a better familiarity with commercial financing and may have some background working with commercial financiers. Yet commercial financiers will tend to take a commercial perspective, development financiers will tend to have a public policy perspective, and these different perspectives have a specific influence on risk perception and aversity. Blended financing transactions will often involve higher commercial/financial risk than would a normal commercial financing, and it will be more sensitive to commercial/financial risk than would a normal development financing. Taking a blended approach to risk when analyzing a blended finance transaction may be challenging for all.

Blended finance transactions should build in capacity enhancement for all parties, bring in consultants with real expertise in blended finance, and take the time needed to develop the blended finance transaction well. This investment of time and effort will bear significant fruit in successful projects with fewer disputes.

Similarly, when looking to select a partner for a blended finance transaction, care should be given to choosing entities with the right experience and the right incentives to undertake such a complex transaction. Not every commercial financier is well suited to blended finance, just as not every development financier has the right experience or incentives. Some commercial partners will see blended finance as a less expensive and safer way to enter into a new market. There is some merit to this perception, but the challenges of blended finance should cause commercial actors to approach this carefully. Equally, some development financiers engage in blended financing only because of an institutional or national diktat to mobilize private capital. This is not a problem in itself but may indicate a suboptimal commitment to overcome the complexities of blended finance.

Some development financiers are required to support commercial entities from their country of origin, limiting the scope of commercial partners available to develop the project. For blended finance transactions, the number of commercial competitors with the right skills and experience is likely to be fewer, making the national preference more of a challenge. Because of this national preference, the development financier may seek to influence national commercial financiers to develop a blended finance transaction. This too can be problematic where that national commercial entity does not have the skills/experience, and may not have the commitment to the project, that is needed to deliver a blended finance transaction.

In some cases, lack of understanding is caused by lack of transparency. Financiers may seek to obfuscate information in an effort to convince other financiers to engage in blended financing, but this is generally a poor strategy that is likely to result in a deficient project. All parties should seek to be as transparent as possible with data, requirements, financial analysis, and technical assessments. Transparency should be adopted during project selection, preparation, and implementation. This requires a robust monitoring and evaluation framework focused on the impact and other characteristics discussed earlier to ensure that the reason for agreeing to blended finance in the first place is continually monitored and verified. This allows adjustments to the project over time where circumstances change or where the original project design is not as effective as hoped.

Development financiers need to expand their ambition when it comes to blended finance. Blended finance involves more effort, complexity, and risk

8.6 Core Recommendations for Blended Finance

for development financiers. More time, staff, and technical assistance must be dedicated to this topic if significant volumes of blended finance are to be mobilized. Some progress has been achieved through accounting for private capital mobilized by multilateral development banks. These reporting frameworks elevate the importance of blended finance and help to focus multilateral development bank management, but more needs to be done. Development financiers need to have strategies and even policies for mobilizing more commercial capital, including through blended finance.

8.6.6 Get the Structure Right

Blended finance is not a cut and paste. The right combination of instruments will help address many of the challenges mentioned here, but there is no quick and easy answer.

The DFI Working Group on Blended Concessional Finance noted that, in 2020, the most common DFI concessional instrument was senior debt (32 percent), followed by equity (19 percent), risk-sharing facilities and guarantees (19 percent), and subordinated debt (12 percent). Each has a specific role and place in blended finance. Debt and equity are well-known instruments that can be used to great effect. Less well known, but potentially even more impactful, are derisking instruments such as patient equity, subordinated debt (e.g., first loss facilities), refinancing commitments, standby facilities, derivative instruments (e.g., currency swap, put options), guarantees, and insurance. Such risk mitigation facilities hold specific potential, allow providers to maximize their balance sheets, and can be adapted to address specific risks.[31]

Higher risks and uncertainties associated with higher transaction costs will result from unproven technologies, nonexistent or untested policies and regulatory frameworks, anticipation of policy reversal, and so on, all of which are common challenges in blended transactions. Shallow capital markets in most developing countries (illiquid, limited refinancing, and exit options) will drive blended finance structures, as will inadequate institutions, limited public sector capacity, and incomplete price discovery.

---

[31] Convergence, *The State of Blended Finance 2021*.

Glossary

This glossary of terms, abbreviations, and acronyms is included exclusively for use as a reference aid and therefore should not be considered an exhaustive or complete discussion of any of the terms set out below, or indeed of all the terms relevant to innovative funding and finance.[1] Definitions are cross-referenced and generally given under their spelt-out form; the abbreviation refers to the spelt-out form.

acceleration After a default, the right of the lenders to make the loan immediately and fully due and payable. Repayments are accelerated to the present.

ADB Asian Development Bank, a multilateral agency with headquarters in Manila, the Philippines.

AfDB African Development Bank, a multilateral agency with headquarters in Abidjan, Côte d'Ivoire.

air rights The property interest in the space above ground. Generally speaking, owning land or a building includes the right to use the space above the land without interference by others, subject to specific limitations such as development rights, zoning and easements.

angel capital Investors, usually high net worth individuals, that provide early stage capital to certain types of businesses (e.g., clean energy, socially focused health and education) filling the capital gap between initial funding (e.g.,

---

[1] Terms in this glossary have been adopted and modified from several sources: Tinsley, *Advanced Project Financing* (2000); *Black's Law Dictionary* (6th ed., 1990); Finnerty, *Project Financing: Asset-Based Financial Engineering* (2007); Nevitt and Fabozzi, *Project Financing* (7th ed., 2000); UNIDO *Guidelines for Infrastructure Development through Build-Operate-Transfer* (United Nations, 1996); Merrett, *Introduction to the Economics of Water Resources: An International Perspective* (1997); Wood, *Project Finance, Securitisations and Subordinated Debt* (2nd ed., 2007); Yescombe, *Public-Private Partnerships: Principles of Policy and Finance* (2007).

from the entrepreneur, their friends and family) and other sources of funding (e.g., venture capital).

annuity Repayment of debt where the sum of principal and interest is equal for each period; also a term used in India for availability payments.

ARR See average rate of return.

arranger The senior tier of a syndication. Implies the entity that agreed and negotiated the project finance structure. Also refers to the bank/underwriter responsible for originating and entitled to syndicate the loan/bond issue. The arranger may not necessarily also be the agent and may not even participate in the transaction.

arranger fee The fee paid to an arranger of financing for its work in relation to a transaction.

asset All tangible and intangible property of a company including real property, chattels money, and debts owing to such company.

availability payment Where the contracting agency pays the project company for the services rendered (different from a user fee).

average debt service cover ratio (ADSCR) See debt service cover ratio (DSCR).

average rate of return (ARR) The ratio of average net earnings to average investment.

balance sheet The accounts that show assets, liabilities, and net worth/shareholders' equity.

basis point (BP) One hundred basis points equal one percentage point.

BBO Buy, Build, Operate (similar to BOO).

bid The technical proposal and financial proposal submitted by the bidder in response to the issuance of an RFP. In the case of single-stage bidding, the bid also contains the bidder's qualification documents. See also tender.

bid bond A bond of a fixed amount, usually 1–3 percent of the tender contract price, deposited by bidders with the tendering authority at the time of submission of their tenders as a form of guarantee that the bidder will enter into a contract and achieve financial close in conformity with the tender. The bid bond is generally returned to the successful bidder on effectiveness of the relevant contract or on financial close. Also known as a tender bond.

bid price The price offered.

bid process A procurement mechanism using competitive pressure among bidders to obtain the best price and terms.

bidder A private sector entity or consortium who has participated or intends to participate in the tender of the project.

bilateral agency An agency of one country, either public or private, that funds development in other countries. Also known as a "bilateral lending agency." See also export credit agency and multilateral agency.

bip One-hundredth of one percent.

BLO(T) Build, Lease, Own (Transfer). The contracting authority builds the project, then leases it to the project company, which operates it for the duration of the concession period.

bond The paper evidence of a legal promise by the issuer to pay the investor on the declared terms. Bonds are usually negotiable and customarily long term,

Glossary

such as five to twenty-five years. Short-term bonds are usually referred to as notes. See also bid bond; maintenance or retention bond; performance bond; and straight debt.

BOO Build, Own, Operate. The private entity will build, own, and operate the project just as in a BOT project, but there is no transfer back to the government. This method is often used where there will be no residual value in the project after the concession period or accounting standards do not permit the assets to revert to the contracting authority if the contracting authority wishes to benefit from off-balance sheet treatment.

BOOS Build, Own, Operate–Sell. Same as a BOT except that the contracting authority pays the project company for the residual value of the project at transfer.

BOOST Build, Own, Operate, Subsidize, Transfer (similar to BOT).

BOOT Build, Own, Operate, Transfer (similar to BOT).

BOR Build, Operate, Renewal of concession (similar to BOO).

borrower An institution or individual that raises funds in return for contracting into an obligation to repay those funds together with payment of interest either as capital appreciation (as in a discount security) or as a coupon payment or at determinable periods over the life of a loan facility.

BOT Build, Operate, Transfer. In this, the project is transferred back to the party granting the concession. The transfer may be for value or at no cost. See also constituent documents.

bridge financing Interim financing, before a long-term financing is put in place.

BRT Build, Rent, Transfer (similar to BOT).

BT Build, Transfer. The project company builds the facilities and transfers them to the contracting authority (similar to BOT).

BTO Build, Transfer, Operate (similar to BOT). This often involves the contracting authority paying for construction of the facility, separate from operations, at or before transfer.

bullet A one-time repayment, often after no/little amortization of the loan. A balloon.

business risk See commercial risk.

buyback A promise to repurchase unsold production. Alternatively, a promise to repay a financial obligation.

buyer credit Financing provided to a buyer to pay for the supply of goods or services, usually by an exporting country or the supplier company.

call option A contract sold for a price that gives the holder the right to buy from the writer of the option, over a specified period, a specified property or amount of securities at a specified price. Also known as a "call." For example, in a bond or loan, the call option may give the borrower a refinancing option if interest rates fall below the call option interest rate. The borrower will pay a higher coupon for this right.

capacity charge Payment by the purchaser to the project company for the available capacity of the project. This charge will cover fixed costs, including debt service, operating costs, and service fees. Also known as availability charge.

Glossary

capex See capital expenditure.

capital The amount invested in a venture, that is, capitalization.

capital appreciation The increase in the value of an asset over time.

capital costs Costs of financing construction and equipment. Capital costs are usually fixed one-off expenses.

capital expenditure (capex) Long-term expenditure on fixed assets such as land, buildings, plant, and equipment.

capital grant Funded support from government to offset construction costs and thereby reduce the amount of private finance needed for a project. See also government support and viability gap fund.

capital markets A term that includes tradable debt, securities, and equity, as distinct from private markets or banks.

capitalized interest Accrued interest (and margin) that is not paid but added ("rolled up") to the principal amount lent at the end of an interest period. See grace period.

carbon capture Removal of CO_2 from fossil fuels either before or after combustion. In the latter, the CO_2 is extracted from the flue gas.

carbon credits A credit or permit arising from a greenhouse gas emissions reduction scheme, such as emissions trading. Also known as emissions reduction credits.

carbon emissions trading scheme A scheme in which greenhouse gas emissions are controlled by setting a cap on total emissions and allowing the market sector(s) to reach an economically balanced response via trading of emissions allowances. Allowances are allocated initially, perhaps through a free distribution or through an auction, and the total allocation is adjusted (capped) periodically. See also carbon trading.

carbon storage The long-term storage of CO_2 (as at carbon capture) in forests, soils, ocean, or underground in depleted oil and gas reservoirs, coal seams, and saline aquifers. Also referred to as engineered carbon sequestration.

change in law The situation in which the law of the host country changes after the date of contract and in such a way as to have an impact on the project.

charge Security rights over an asset. For example, under United States or English law, a fixed charge refers to a defined set of assets and is usually registered, while a floating charge refers to other assets that change from time to time – for example, cash at bank and inventory – which become a fixed charge (crystallize) after a default.

clawback The ability (e.g., on the part of the contracting authority) to recover prior project cash flow that may have been distributed/paid away, for example, as dividends to the sponsors.

CMP The contract management plan.

CMU The contract management unit.

CO_2 Carbon dioxide, a greenhouse gas.

cofinancing Lending by different lenders under the same documentation and security packages, but where there may still be different interest rates, repayment profiles, and terms, perhaps via multiple tranches.

Glossary

collar A combination of a ceiling and a floor, for example, to an interest or foreign exchange rate, structured through swaps, options, hedging, or agreement. Also known as a tunnel.

collateral Assets pledged as security under a loan to assure repayment.

commercial bank A bank that both accepts deposits and grants loans and, under certain stipulations in some countries, pays interest on current accounts.

commercial close In a financing, the point at which the commercial documentation has been executed but before conditions precedent have been satisfied or waived; before financial close.

commercial risk The risk due to uncertainty about investment outlays, operating cash flows, supply, demand, and asset values. Also known as business risk.

commissioning The testing and inspection of the completed works to verify that the works are ready for commercial operation.

commitment fee A per annum fee applied to the portion of the unused financing (the amount not yet drawn down) until the end of the availability period.

completion In a project financing, the stage at which the project's cash flows become the primary method of repayment. It occurs after a completion test. Prior to completion, the primary source of repayment is usually from the sponsors or from the construction contractor. See also physical, or mechanical completion.

completion risk The risk that a project will not be able to pass its completion test within the time for completion.

completion tests Tests of the project's ability to satisfy the contract requirements, perform to a specified minimum standard, and generate the expected cash flows.

concession The right granted by the host government for a private company to undertake an otherwise public sector project and operate that project over a period of time.

concession agreement The agreement with a government body that entitles a private entity to undertake an otherwise public service. See also constituent documents and project documents.

concessional finance Debt provided on a subsidized basis, where the borrower (usually a sovereign entity) would not be able to access debt at such a low cost of money on the financial markets. The subsidized cost is generally provided to encourage specific activities or support certain borrowers. For example, the World Bank through IDA provides concessional financing to the poorest countries.

consortium Two or more parties acting together as a partnership or joint venture.

construction contract The contract between the project company and the construction contractor for the design, construction, and commissioning of the works. See also constituent documents and project documents.

construction contractor The project participant bearing the obligation to design, construct, and commission the works.

contingency An additional amount/percentage set aside against a cash flow item, for example, capital expenditure. For liabilities, those that do not appear on the balance sheet until they crystallize, for example, guarantees, supports, and dispute settlements.

contingent liability A liability that is uncertain as to its crystallization, for example, a guarantee or a contingent debt, in amount and/or timing.

contract management plan The contracting authority's plan for managing the PPP contract during implementation.

contract management unit The team established by the contracting authority to manage the PPP contract during implementation.

contract manager The primary point of contact of the contracting authority with the project company during the implementation of the PPP project.

contracting authority The public entity entering into a PPP agreement.

cost of debt Yield to maturity on debt, frequently after tax, in which event it is one minus the tax rate times the yield to maturity.

country risk The risk specific to a particular country, including political risk and economic risk. See also sovereign risk.

coupon The interest amount or rate payable on a bond. A coupon may be physically attached to the bond certificate.

covenant An agreed action to be undertaken (positive) or not done (negative). A breach of a covenant will generally constitute a default.

cover See cushion.

cover ratio The ratio of income to debt service requirements used as an indicator of the safety margin for servicing debt. Sometimes known as debt service cover ratio.

CPI Consumer Price Index.

credit rating agency See rating agency.

credit risk The risk that a counterparty to a financial transaction will fail to perform according to the terms and conditions of the contract (default), either because of bankruptcy or any other reason, thus causing the asset holder to suffer a financial loss. Sometimes known as default risk.

creditworthy An entity that is "creditworthy" is deemed to have a low risk of default on a debt obligation.

currency option A currency option entitles the holder to buy or sell an agreed amount of foreign currency at an agreed price until or on an agreed date.

currency risk The risk associated with changes in the exchange rate for a currency. See also transfer risk.

currency swap A swap in which the parties sell currencies to each other subject to an agreement to repurchase the same currency in the same amount, at the same exchange rate, and at a fixed date in the future. The exchange ensures that neither party is subject to currency risk because exchange rates are predetermined.

cushion The extra amount, for example, of net cash flow remaining after expected debt service. See also cover and residual cushion.

Glossary

D:E ratio See debt–equity ratio.

DBFO Design–Build–Finance–Operate. The contracting authority retains title to the site and leases the project back to the project company for the period of the concession. Similar to BOO.

DCMF Design–Construct–Manage–Finance, similar to BOO.

debenture A document evidencing actual indebtedness. Often also used to refer to a document creating a charge, mortgage, or other security interest. (It should be noted that the exact legal meaning of the term "debenture" is uncertain and there are differing views on whether or not documents such as loan agreements constitute debentures.) A legal security over the issuer's general credit/balance sheet.

debt An obligation to pay cash or other goods or to provide services to another. See also liability; straight debt; and subordinated debt.

debt capacity The total amount of debt a company can prudently support, given its earnings expectations and equity base.

debt leverage The amplification in the return earned on equity funds when an investment is financed partly with borrowed money. See debt–equity ratio and gearing.

debt rescheduling Adjusting the tenor, interest rate, or other terms and conditions of a debt agreement.

debt service cover ratio (DSCR) The ratio of income to debt service requirements for a period. Also known as the cover ratio.

debt service Payments of principal and interest on a loan.

debt service reserve An amount set aside either before completion or during the early operation period for debt servicing where insufficient revenue is achieved.

debt–capitalization ratio The proportion of a firm's debt to its capitalization. The higher this ratio, the greater the financial leverage and the risk.

debt–equity ratio The proportion of debt to equity, often expressed as a percentage. The higher this ratio, the greater the financial leverage of the firm. Also known as D:E ratio. See also gearing and debt leverage.

default The breach of a covenant by one of the parties. A default may be involuntary. See also cross-default; event of default; and latent default.

default interest A higher interest rate payable after default.

default risk See credit risk.

defects liability The construction contractor's obligation to cure defects that may arise after completion.

defects liability period The period during which the construction contractor is liable for defects after completion.

depreciation Amortization for accounting (book), tax calculations, or income calculations. A regular reduction in asset value over time. See also straight-line depreciation.

design and build See turnkey construction.

development finance institution (DFI) A multilateral or bilateral agency, either public or private, which funds development. See also bilateral agency (BLA); international finance institution (IFI); and multilateral agency.

DfID Department for International Development, the development aid agency of the United Kingdom; further to a recent restructuring, also UKAid.

direct agreement An agreement made in parallel with one of the main project documents, often with the lenders or the contracting authority. Step-in rights and other lender rights are often reinforced or established through direct agreements between the lenders and the project participants.

DOT Develop, Operate, Transfer (similar to BOT).

drawdown The obtaining by the borrower of some of the funds available under a credit facility.

due date The date on which payment of interest or principal becomes due and payable.

due diligence The analysis of a project to assess the viability of the project. The detailed review of the borrower's/issuer's overall position, which is supposed to be undertaken by the lead manager of a new financing in conjunction with the preparation of legal documentation.

ECA See export credit agency.

economic rate of return Also economic internal rate of return (EIRR). The project's rate of return after taking into account economic costs and benefits, including monetary costs and benefits.

EIA See environmental impact assessment.

EIRR See economic rate of return.

EIS See environmental impact statement.

End-user The final consumer of the output produced by a project.

environmental impact assessment (EIA) An assessment of the potential impact of a project on the environment that results in an environmental impact statement.

environmental impact statement (EIS) A statement of the potential impact of a project on the environment. The result of an environmental impact assessment, which may have been subject to public comment.

environmental risk The economic or administrative consequences of slow or catastrophic environmental pollution.

EPC contract Engineering, procurement, and construction contract (i.e., a turnkey construction contract or a design and build contract).

equity The cash or assets contributed by the sponsors in a project financing. A company's paid-up share capital and other shareholders' funds. For accounting purposes, it is the net worth or total assets minus liabilities.

equity kicker A share of ownership interest in a company, project, or property or a potential ownership interest in a company, project, or property in consideration for making a loan. The kicker may take the form of stock, stock warrants, purchase options, a percentage of profits, or a percentage of ultimate ownership.

Glossary

ERC See emissions reduction credit.

ERR Economically recoverable reserves.

event of default One of a list of events that would entitle the lenders, under the terms of the relevant credit facility or debt instrument, to cancel the facility and/or declare all amounts owing by the debtor to be immediately due and payable. Events of default typically include nonpayment of amounts owing to the lenders, breach of covenant, cross-default, insolvency, and material adverse change. See also default.

evergreen A contract that rolls over after each agreed (short-term) period until cancelled by one party.

exchange rate The price at which one currency trades for another. Also known as foreign exchange rate. See also floating currency.

expected NPV (ENPV) Weighted by probability of outcome.

export credit agency (ECA) An agency established by a country to finance its national goods, investment, and services. It often offers political risk insurance. Also known as a trade finance agency. See also bilateral agency and multilateral agency.

facility fee An annual percentage fee payable to a bank providing a credit facility on the full amount of the facility, whether or not utilized. See also front-end fee.

feasibility study A detailed assessment of the parameters of a PPP project used to prepare a project for transaction development. See also full business case.

featherweight floating charge A floating charge whose only purpose is to defeat the appointment of an administrator in relation to a company.

financial close In a financing, the point at which the documentation has been executed and conditions precedent have been satisfied or waived. Drawdowns become permissible after this point.

financial internal rate of return (FIRR) Also financial rate of return. See internal rate of return.

financial model A method of analyzing the revenues and costs of the project, identifying the need for contingencies, and allocating revenue to costs in accordance with the needs of the project and the project company's obligations toward the project participants and other contractors.

FIRR See financial internal rate of return.

fiscal risk The risk borne by the government (by the fiscal position of the country) due to liabilities associated with PPP transactions.

fiscal space The capacity in a government's budget (including borrowing capacity) that allows it to provide or access resources for a desired purpose without jeopardizing the sustainability of its financial position or the stability of the economy or otherwise breaching restrictions created by its own national laws or by supranational bodies or by lenders (in particular large lenders such as the IMF or World Bank).

fixed charge A charge usually contained in a debenture over a company's assets that prevents the company from dealing in any way with the property covered by the fixed charge without the consent of the chargee. See also floating charge.

fixed cost Any cost that does not vary over the observation period.

fixed rate An interest rate that is fixed (calculated as a constant specified percentage) for a defined period.

floating charge A form of security taken by a creditor over the whole or substantially the whole of a company's assets. The company can continue to use the assets in its business until an event of default occurs and the charge crystallizes. The holder of the floating charge can then generally appoint an administrative receiver. See also featherweight floating charge and fixed charge.

floating interest rate An interest rate that fluctuates during the term of a loan in accordance with some external index or a set formula, usually as a margin or spread over a specified rate. See also interest rate.

floor The level below which, for example, an interest rate or currency is ordained not to fall.

floor area ratio (FAR) The ratio of a building's total floor area to the size of the land on which it is built. The higher the floor area ratio, the higher the density.

floor space index (FSI) See floor area ratio.

force majeure Events outside the control of the parties and which prevent one or both of the parties from performing their contractual obligations.

foreign exchange rate (FX rate) The price at which the currency of one country can be bought with the currency of another country. Also known as the exchange rate.

foreign exchange risk The effect on project cash flow or debt service of a movement in the FX rate for revenue, costs, or debt service.

forex (FX) Foreign exchange.

forward contract (forwards) An agreement to exchange currency or interest obligations in the future. For tradable commodities or securities, an agreement to buy or sell at a future date. See also futures contract.

forward market A market in which participants agree to trade some commodity, security, or foreign exchange at a fixed price at some future date. Unlike futures and options, trading in forward markets does not occur on organized exchanges but through the forex traders of financial institutions. Forward currency contracts are not transferable instruments, and settlement is usually expected to be through actual delivery of currencies. See also futures market.

forward rate The rate at which forward transactions of some specific maturity are being made, for example, the US dollar price at which euros can be bought for delivery three months hence.

front-end fee A fee, calculated as a percentage of the principal value of an issue of securities, which is payable once at issue (front-end), as opposed to a percentage fee payable each year. See also facility fee.

full business case See feasibility study.

full recourse No matter what risk event occurs, the borrower's or its guarantor's guarantee to repay the debt.

Glossary

funding risk The impact that higher funding costs or lack of availability of funds can have on project revenue flow.

futures The sale and purchase at a price agreed upon in advance for delivery at a future date. Both buyer and seller are speculating on how prices will change in the future.

futures option The right of a buyer to buy from or sell to a writer a designated futures contract at a designated price at any time during the period stated. See also hedge and option.

FX Foreign exchange. Sometimes abbreviated to forex.

FX rate See foreign exchange rate.

FX risk See foreign exchange risk.

gearing The level of debt to equity. Interest-bearing debt divided by shareholders' equity. See debt–equity ratio and debt leverage.

GHG See greenhouse gases.

grace period The borrower does not have to pay interest or possibly any debt service, during the grace period, that amount being capitalized. This allows for periods when revenues are insufficient, such as during construction. See also capitalized interest.

grantor The party that grants a concession, a license, or some other right. See contracting authority.

green bonds Bonds with proceeds earmarked for projects aimed at generating positive environmental impact.

greenfield Often used to refer to a planned facility that must be built from scratch, without existing infrastructure.

greenhouse gases Gases that contribute to global warming. See also emissions and GHG.

guarantee An undertaking to fulfil the obligations of a third party (whether or not related) in the event of a default. It may be limited in time and amount and may be callable immediately on default or only after the beneficiary has exhausted all other remedies. See also subrogation.

guarantor A party that will guarantee repayment or performance of a covenant.

hard currency A currency considered by the market to be likely to maintain its value against other currencies over a period and not likely to be eroded by inflation. Hard currencies are usually freely convertible. See also soft currency.

hedge A method whereby currency (the risk of possible loss due to currency fluctuations), interest rate, commodity, or other exposure is covered or offset for a fixed period of time. This is accomplished by taking a position in futures equal and opposite to an existing or anticipated position or by shorting a security similar to one in which a long position has been established. See also swap.

host country The country of the site of the project, which is considered to be hosting the project.

hurdle rate The minimum acceptable rate of return on investment.

IBRD See International Bank for Reconstruction and Development.

ICC The International Chamber of Commerce, an organization based in Paris that represents the interests of the global business community. For example, it provides a variety of international dispute resolution services through its International Court of Arbitration.

ICSID International Centre for Settlement of Investment Disputes, a body created under the auspices of the World Bank but wholly independent. It provides dispute resolution services for investment disputes.

IDA See International Development Agency.

IDC See interest during construction.

IFC See International Finance Corporation.

IFI an international financial institution, such as the World Bank or the EBRD.

ijārah (asset-based) – Under Islamic finance, a contract that permits one party (the lessee) to use an asset or property owned by another party (the lessor) for an agreed-upon price over a fixed period.

IMF International Monetary Fund, a multilateral agency headquartered in Washington, DC.

incremental borrowing rate The interest rate that a person would expect to pay for a certain loan at a certain time.

indexed loan A loan with debt service repayment tied to some standard that is calculated to protect the lenders against inflation and/or currency exchange risk.

indexed rate An interest rate linked to an index.

infill The rededication of urban, usually open, space to new, higher density, development.

input supplier The project participant that will bear the market risk of purchase and transportation of the input necessary for operation of the project.

input supply agreement The agreement entered into by the project company and the input supplier that defines the rights and obligations in relation to the supply of input for the project. It will be used to allocate the market risk of input cost and provision. This agreement will often be on either a take-or-pay or a take-and-pay basis. See also constituent documents and project documents.

institutional investors Investors such as banks, insurance companies, trusts, pension funds and foundations, and educational, charitable, and religious institutions.

intensification The use of built-up areas with good existing or potential public transit links that can support redevelopment at higher densities.

intercreditor agreement An agreement between lenders as to the rights of different creditors in the event of default, covering such topics as collateral, waiver, security, and set-offs.

interest Cash amounts paid by borrowers to lenders for the use of their money. Normally expressed as a percentage. See also capitalized interest; compound interest; and simple interest.

Glossary

interest during construction (IDC) The interest accumulated during construction, before the project, which has a revenue stream to pay debt service and is usually rolled up and treated as the capitalized interest. See also grace period and capitalized interest.

interest rate The percentage payable to a lender calculated at an annual rate on the principal.

internal rate of return (IRR) The discount rate that equates the present value of a future stream of payments to the initial investment. See also financial internal rate of return and economic rate of return.

International Bank for Reconstruction and Development (IBRD) A multilateral agency focused on middle-income countries, based in Washington, DC, and part of the World Bank group. Also known as the World Bank.

International Development Agency (IDA) A multilateral agency focused on developing countries, based in Washington DC, and part of the World Bank group. Also known as the World Bank.

International Finance Corporation (IFC) The private sector arm of the World Bank group, based in Washington, DC.

international financial institution (IFI) See multilateral lending agency. See also development finance institution.

IRR See internal rate of return.

istiṣnāʿ (sale based) Under Islamic finance, a contract to manufacture goods, assemble or process them, or build a structure according to exact specifications and a fixed timeline. Payments are made as work on the property is finished; the sale price may be spot payable, amortized, or deferred.

joint venture Often used to describe any jointly owned corporation or partnership that owns, operates, or constructs a facility, project, or enterprise. More specifically, an arrangement between two or more parties for the joint management or operation of a facility, project enterprise, or company under an operating agreement that is not a partnership.

LDO Lease–Develop–Operate (similar to BOO).

LDs See liquidated damages.

lead arranger The senior tier of arranger.

lead bank The bank that negotiates a large loan with a borrower and solicits other lenders to join the syndicate making the loan.

lead manager A ranking of lenders and advisers according to the underwriting, final take, or number of project finance loans or advisory mandates.

legal framework The laws and regulations that create the enabling framework for a PPP program.

legal risk A risk that a defect in the documentation or legal structure will affect cash flow or debt service.

lenders The entities providing debt contributions to the project company.

lending agreements The documents that provide the terms of financing.

letter of credit A guarantee limited in time and amount. A letter of credit is a written undertaking by a bank (issuing bank) given to the seller (beneficiary) at the request and in accordance with the instructions of the buyer (applicant) to effect payment up to a stated sum of money within a prescribed time limit and against stipulated documents. See also confirmed letter of credit; revocable letter of credit; and standby letter of credit.

limited recourse Lenders have access to the sponsors' credit or other legal security for repayment (besides the project's cash flows) only under certain limited conditions (legal or financial). There is usually recourse in the event of fraud or misrepresentation/nondisclosure – thus "nonrecourse" is better described as "limited recourse." See also recourse.

line of credit A commitment of a bank to a borrower to extend a series of credits to the borrower under certain terms and conditions up to an agreed maximum amount for a specified period.

liquidated damages (LDs) A fixed periodic amount payable as a sanction for delays or substandard performance under a contract. Also known as a penalty clause.

liquidation The process of closing down a company, selling its assets, paying off its creditors, and distributing any remaining cash to owners.

liquidity The ability to service debt and redeem or reschedule liabilities when they mature and the ability to exchange other assets for cash.

local currency The official domestic currency (currency of issue) of any particular country.

long-term debt A borrowing over a long period, usually through bank loans or the sale of bonds. On balance sheet, any debt due for more than one year is classified as "long-term."

LPVR Least Present Value of Revenues; financial bids are based on the least amount of revenues over the period of the concession, discounted back to the date of issue.

LROT Lease, Refurbish, Operate, Transfer; the project company leases the project, refurbishes it, operates it for a period, and then transfers it back to the contracting authority. Similar to BOT.

maintenance (or retention) bond A bond to provide funds for the maintenance and repair of equipment or a facility. Maintenance bonds are used in connection with construction contracts to ensure that a construction contractor will repair mistakes and defects after completion of the construction. The retention bond may be used in lieu, leaving a portion of the contract price on deposit with the project company to ensure performance.

maintenance reserves Reserves set aside to make up for any lack of funds available to the project company when maintenance costs exceed forecasts or where, periodically, maintenance costs will be higher than during other periods of the project.

management contracting A structure whereby a private company takes on the management of the project, selecting contractors, setting prices, and overseeing construction and other services for the benefit of the contracting authority for a fee, generally based on performance or total cost.

Glossary

mandate An authorization or allocation of rights, for example, the authorization from a borrower to a lead manager to arrange a transaction on agreed (usually outline) terms.

margin The amount expressed as a percentage per annum above the interest rate basis or cost of funds. For hedging and futures contracts, it is the cash collateral that is deposited with a trader or exchange as insurance against default. See also spread.

marginal cost of capital The incremental cost of financing.

market risk Changes to the amounts sold or the price received that would have an impact on gross revenue. Sometimes known as sales risk.

market value The price at which an item can be sold at arm's length on the open market.

maturity The date upon which a given debt falls due for repayment.

medium-term Generally from two to six years.

mezzanine financing A mixture of financing instruments, with characteristics of both debt and equity, providing further debt contributions through high-risk and high-return instruments, subordinated debt, sometimes treated as equity.

MIGA Multilateral Investment Guaranty Agency, the political risk insurance (PRI) arm of the IBRD.

mixed-use development The pattern of development characterized by diversified land uses, typically including housing, retail shops, and private businesses, either within the same building space (vertical mixing) or in close proximity (horizontal mixing).

MLA Multilateral lending agency.

monitoring, reporting, and verification (MRV) The process of confirming that emission reductions are and have been achieved, according to applicable standards, to support the generation of carbon credits and/or to confirm that climate finance is appropriately green.

monoline Specialist insurers, whose business is the provision of financial guarantee insurance.

muḍārabah (equity based) – Under Islamic finance, a contract between two parties; one provides the capital and the other provides the labor to form a partnership to share the profits by certain agreed proportions, but any financial loss is borne only by the capital owner, unless the manager has been grossly negligent or acted in willful default of its duties.

multicurrency loan A loan in which the borrower has the option to choose to make borrowings in more than one currency. See also export credit agency.

multilateral agency Organizations jointly owned by a group of countries and designed to promote international and regional economic cooperation. In particular, these agencies may have such goals as aiding development and furthering social and economic growth in member countries. Also known as "multilateral lending agencies." See also bilateral agency and export credit agency.

murābahah (sale based) – Under Islamic finance, a sale contract of a good or property with an agreed profit against a deferred or a lump-sum payment.

mushārakah (equity based) – Under Islamic finance, a contract between two or more parties to establish a commercial enterprise based on capital and labor. The profit and loss are shared at an agreed proportion, usually according to the amount of contribution.

negative pledge The borrower agrees not to pledge any of its assets as security and/or not to incur further indebtedness.

net income Operating cash flows less overheads and depreciation, either before tax (BT) or after tax (AT) earnings.

net present value See NPV.

net worth Equity, total assets less liabilities.

NGO Nongovernmental organization.

nonrecourse The lenders rely on the project's cash flows and collateral security over the project as the only means to repay debt service, and therefore they do not have recourse to other sources, for example, shareholder assets. More often, nonrecourse debt is actually limited recourse debt. See also recourse.

NPV Net present value, the discounted value of an investment's cash inflows minus the discounted value of its cash outflows. To be adequately profitable, an investment should have a net present value greater than zero.

O&M Operation and maintenance.

ODA Official Development Assistance, a general term for assistance provided by developed countries to developing countries, whether in the form of grants, loans, or other assistance.

off-balance sheet liabilities Corporate obligations that do not need to appear as liabilities on a balance sheet, for example, lease obligations, project finance, and take-or-pay contracts.

offshore entity An entity operating outside the restrictions of the legal and tax regimes of a given country.

offtake purchase agreement The agreement whereby the offtake purchaser undertakes to purchase an amount of some or all of the project output, for example, the power purchase agreement in the context of a power project and a water purchase agreement in the context of a water treatment project. See also constituent documents and project documents.

offtake purchaser The purchaser of the product produced by a project. The term is often used in connection with take-or-pay contracts.

offtake The product produced by a project.

operating cash flow Project revenues accruing from the operation.

operating risk The risk related to cost, technology, and management components, including inflation, that have an impact on the opex and project output/throughput.

operation and maintenance agreement The agreement allocating to the operator the obligation to operate and maintain the project in accordance with its requirements. See also constituent documents and project documents.

Glossary

operator The project participant that undertakes the operation and maintenance obligations.

opex Operating expenditures, always expressed as cash.

option A contract under which the writer of the option grants the buyer of the option the right, but not the obligation, to purchase from or sell to the writer something at a specified price within a specified period (or at a specified date). See also purchase option; put option; hedge; and futures contract.

outline business case See prefeasibility study.

par Principal amount at which an issuer agrees to redeem its notes or bonds at maturity.

partnership An arrangement in which two or more persons place their money, efforts, labor, and skill in lawful commerce or business with the understanding that there shall be a proportional sharing of profits and losses between them.

payback period The amount of time required to recover the initial investment. It may be calculated on a discounted, nondiscounted, leveraged, or unleveraged basis.

penalty clause See liquidated damages.

performance bond A bond payable if a project is not completed as specified. Some performance bonds require satisfactory completion of the contract while other performance bonds provide for payment of a sum of money for failure of the contractor to perform under a contract.

physical or mechanical completion The project is substantially complete with only minor elements, usually identified on a punch list, left outstanding.

pip One hundredth of one percent of the market value of a security. It is used to express price differentials.

PMU Project management unit.

political risk The risk usually comprising currency inconvertibility, expropriation, war and insurrection, terrorism, nongovernment activists, and legal and administrative approvals. The first three are normally insurable. It often overlaps with the political component of force majeure risk. See also country risk and sovereign risk.

PPP See public–private partnership.

PPP agreement The contract signed between the contracting authority and the project company to implement the PPP project (see Sections 5.1 and 5.2).

PPP framework See public–private partnership framework.

PPP institutions Government institutions, units, and agencies that perform functions specific to PPP, in support of the PPP program, often including a PPP unit.

PPP laws Laws designed to support and regulate PPP transactions and program. See also BOT laws and concession laws.

PPP policy The government policy on the implementation of the PPP program.

PPP unit A government unit or agency focused on PPP, often located in a powerful central agency (e.g., planning or finance) able to enforce the PPP policy and provide the support needed to implement PPP transactions.

Glossary

prefeasibility study An assessment of the basic parameters of a PPP project used to decide whether to go forward with more in-depth and expensive studies – feasibility studies and transaction development. See also outline business case.

preferred bidder The bidder identified as providing the most advantageous bid but before commercial close and/or financial close (see Section 5.2).

prepayment A payment made ahead of the scheduled payment date.

prequalification The process whereby the number of qualified bidders is limited by reviewing each bidder's qualifications against a set of criteria, generally involving experience in the relevant field, capitalization, site country experience, identity of local partners, and international reputation.

present value The value today of a future payment, calculated by discounting at a specified discounting rate.

PRI Political risk insurance.

principal A sum on which interest accrues. It is capital, as distinguished from income or the par value of a loan, exclusive of any premium or interest that is the basis for interest computations. Also, a person on whose behalf an agent or broker acts.

procurement To obtain; gain access to. The process by which the contracting authority obtains infrastructure services on terms and price considered to be the best available as they were reached through a competitive process. See also bid process and tender process.

project company The incorporated entity of the private investor for the PPP project. Also referred to as the special purpose vehicle or "SPV."

project documents or project agreements The commercial agreements that are the subject of this book, including the concession agreement, the construction contract, the input supply agreement, the offtake purchase agreement, and the operation and maintenance agreement. See also constituent documents.

project financing A loan structure that relies for its repayment primarily on the project's cash flow, with the project's assets, rights, and interests held as secondary security or collateral. See also limited recourse and nonrecourse financing.

project management unit (PMU) The team appointed by the contracting authority to manage the PPP project.

project manager The person appointed by the contracting authority for the daily management of the PPP project.

project The asset constructed with, or owned via, a project financing, which is expected to produce cash flow at a debt service cover ratio sufficient to repay the project financing.

public–private partnership (PPP) A public sector service provided partially or wholly, directly or indirectly, by the private sector, where the private sector bears some combination of design, construction, operation, and financing risk in a manner more comprehensive than traditional public procurement of good and services.

Glossary

put-or-pay contract See supply-or-pay contract.

put or put option An option whereby one person has to sell an asset to another person at a set price at some established point in the future (European). A contract allowing the holder to sell some property to some person at a fixed price at any time within a given period (United States).

qualitative risk assessment The emotional and reactive assessment of risk, resulting from an individual's social, cultural, educational, commercial, and emotional context.

quantitative risk assessment The mathematical assessment of the likelihood and gravity of a given risk, for example, by probability analysis. An accurate quantitative risk assessment is rarely, if ever, possible due to risk noise.

rating agency or credit rating agency A private agency that assesses credit risk of sovereign entities, companies, or investments, such as Standard & Poors, Moody's, and Fitch. The agency applies a letter grade to indicate credit risk. Lenders and investors use the rating as an indication of the relative riskiness of a loan or investment.

receiver A person/entity appointed under the legal security documents to administer security on behalf of the project lenders.

recourse In the event that the project (and its associated escrows, sinking funds, or cash reserves/standby facilities) cannot service the financing or the project completion cannot be achieved, then the lenders have recourse to cash from either other sponsors and/or corporate sources or other nonproject security. See also full recourse; limited recourse; and nonrecourse.

refinancing Repaying existing debt by obtaining a new loan, typically to meet some corporate objective such as the lengthening of maturity or lowering the interest rate. See also rescheduling and restructuring.

request for proposals (RfP) The request issued by the contracting authority to potential bidders inviting them to submit a proposal (or bid) and setting out the terms and conditions of the bidding process.

request for qualification (RfQ) The request issued by the contracting authority for interested parties to submit applications to be prequalified as a potential bidder for a project, based on a defined set of criteria.

rescheduling In relation to debt obligations, the renegotiation and agreement of revised terms of a loan facility (usually involving the spreading of interest and capital repayments over a longer period) as a result of the borrower being unable to comply with the original terms. See also refinancing and restructuring.

reserve account A separate amount of cash or a letter of credit to service a payment requirement such as debt service or maintenance.

residual cushion The amount of net cash flow from the project after the project financing has been repaid. If it is expressed as a percentage of the original loan amount, it is the "residual cover." See also cushion.

residual value Sometimes used to indicate the value of the assets associated with a project at the expiry of the concession period, for example, the value of the assets transferred to the contracting authority at the end of the life of a PPP project. See also tail.

restructuring An arrangement by a borrower to replace debt of one maturity with debt of another (longer) maturity – and perhaps of a different type. See also refinancing and rescheduling.

retention An amount held back from construction contract payments until the construction contractor fulfils certain obligations, generally 5–15 percent of the contract price.

retention bond See maintenance (or retention) bond.

return on assets (ROA) Net profits after taxes divided by assets. This ratio helps a firm determine how effectively it generates profits from available assets.

return on equity (ROE) Net profits after taxes divided by equity investment.

return on investment (ROI) Net profits after taxes divided by investment.

revenue flow Net income, depreciation, and amortization during a given period. A measure of a company's liquidity. Also known as cash flow or "revenue stream."

revenues Sales or royalty proceeds.

revocable letter of credit A letter of credit that can be changed or cancelled by the issuing bank or by any party involved until the time payment is made.

revolving credit agreement or revolving line of credit A legal commitment on the part of a bank to extend credit up to a maximum amount for a definite term. The notes evidencing debt are short term, such as ninety days. As notes become due, the borrower can renew the notes, borrow a smaller amount, or borrow amounts up to the specified maximum throughout the term of commitment.

RFP Request for proposal.

RFQ Request for qualification.

risk Instability or uncertainty about the future; more specifically, the degree of uncertainty involved with a loan or investment.

risk aversion An unwillingness either to bear any risk or to bear risk without compensation of some form.

risk noise The combination of qualitative risk assessment and insufficiency of information that influences an individual's assessment of a risk and distracts from an accurate quantitative risk assessment.[2]

risk premium An additional required rate of return that must be paid to investors who invest in risky investments to compensate for the risk.

RLT Refurbish, Lease, Transfer (similar to BOT).

ROA Return on assets.

ROE Return on equity.

---

[2] Jeffrey Delmon, "Risk Noise: Increasing the Efficiency of Risk Allocation in Project Financed Public Private Partnership Transactions by Reducing the Impact of Risk Noise – Part II," [2015] ICLR 264; Jeffrey Delmon, "Risk Noise: Increasing the Efficiency of Risk Allocation in Project Financed Public Private Partnership Transactions by Reducing the Impact of Risk Noise – Part I," [2015] ICLR 134.

Glossary

ROI Return on investment.
ROO Rehabilitate, Own, Operate (similar to BOO).
ROT Rehabilitate, Operate, Transfer (similar to BOT).
royalty A share of revenue or cash flow or a fee paid to the government or contracting authority of the concession or license.
sale and leaseback A transaction in which an investor purchases assets from the owner and then leases such assets back to the same person. The lessee receives the sale price (and can return it to capital) and continues to enjoy the use of the assets.
sales risk See market risk.
secondary market After the initial distribution of bonds or securities, secondary market trading begins. New issue houses usually make a market in bonds or securities which they have comanaged.
secured creditor A creditor whose obligation is backed by the pledge of some asset and is therefore secured debt. In liquidation, the secured creditor receives the cash from the sale of the pledged asset to the extent of its loan.
secured debt The debt secured against specific assets or rights accessible to the lenders in the event of default.
securitization A process that changes bank loans or other nontradable financial transactions into tradable securities.
security A legal right of access to value through mortgages, contracts, cash accounts, guarantees, insurances, pledges, or cash flow, including licenses, concessions, and other assets. Lenders can act on security rights in the event of default by the borrower. It is a negotiable certificate evidencing a debt or equity obligation/shareholding.
security agreement An agreement in which the title to a property is held as collateral under a financing agreement, usually by a trustee.
senior debt The debt that, by agreement or legal structure, takes priority over other (junior) debt, allowing the senior lenders to have priority in access to amounts paid to the lenders by the borrower from time to time and to borrower assets or revenues in the event of default. This priority may be binding on liquidators or administrators of the borrower.
shareholder An equity holder in the project company.
shareholders' agreement The agreement entered into by the shareholders of the project company that governs their relationship and their collective approach to the project. See also constituent documents and project documents.
shareholders' equity The book value of the net assets (total assets less total liabilities). Also known as net worth.
short-term debt An obligation maturing in less than one year.
simple interest The charge for the loan of money or for a deferment of the collection of an account, computed by applying a rate of interest against only the amount of the loan or account. Contrasts with compound interest in that interest is charged only on the principal for the entire life of the transaction and no interest is charged on any interest already accrued. See also interest rate.

sinking fund A reserve fund established or set aside for the purpose of payment of a liability anticipated to become due at a later date.

social bonds Bonds with proceeds earmarked for projects aimed at generating positive social impact.

soft currency A currency perceived by the market to be reasonably unlikely to maintain its value against other currencies over a period. The convertibility of soft currencies is usually, or may become, restricted. See also hard currency.

solvency The state of being able to pay debts as they become due.

source country The country from which important materials, equipment, or one of the project participants originates. This country may provide financing or insurance to the project to promote exportation of materials, equipment, or services and thus assist its national economy.

sovereign immunity A historical doctrine of law in certain jurisdictions under which sovereign governments may not be sued or their assets seized.

sovereign risk Political risk caused by the fact that one of the parties is a sovereign entity. See also country risk.

special purpose vehicle (SPV) An entity created to undertake a single task or project in order to protect the shareholders with limited liability, often used for limited or nonrecourse financing. A corporate vehicle (also known as a project company) created to implement the project, whose sole purpose is the project, and therefore does not undertake obligations or liabilities outside of the project.

sponsor A party wishing to develop/undertake a project. A developer. A party providing financial support. A strategic investor, with technical and commercial skills needed to deliver the project, which often also provides some combination of equity and debt investment.

spot market An international market in which products are traded for immediate delivery at the current price (the "spot price").

spread In the trading or quotation of a security's price, the difference between the bid and the offered price. Also used in loans as a synonym for margin.

standby credit An arrangement to lend money on demand, usually at market rates and sometimes with a commitment fee. Overdraft facilities are sometimes used for standby credit by corporate borrowers.

standby letter of credit A letter of credit that provides payment to the beneficiary when it presents a certification that certain obligations have not been fulfilled.

step-in rights The right of a third party to "step in" to the place of one contractual party where that party fails in its obligations under the contract and the other party to the contract has the right to terminate the contract.

subordinated creditor A creditor holding a debenture having a lower priority of payment than other liabilities of the project.

subordinated debt The debt that, by agreement or legal structure, is subordinated to other (senior) debt, allowing those (senior) lenders to have priority

Glossary

in access to amounts paid to the lenders by the borrower from time to time and to borrower assets or revenues in the event of default. This priority may be binding on liquidators or administrators of the borrower.

subsovereign entities Emanations of a sovereign entity, such as regional, provincial, and municipal governments and state-owned enterprises.

sukūk – "Islamic bonds." Financial instruments representing an undivided ownership share in an underlying asset or interest held by the issuer. They are based on certificates representing a proportionate ownership interest in underlying assets services or other activities that generate a cash flow.

super-turnkey contract Based on a turnkey construction contract, the contractor is required to contribute to the financing of the construction, often by agreeing to the deferral of the payment due to it until after completion or during operation.

supply risk The risk that the availability of raw materials or input to a project (e.g., raw water) will change from those assumed/projected. In the case of a resources extraction project, this is called reserves risk.

supply-or-pay contract A contract under which a party agrees to supply a raw material, product, or service for a certain price during a stated period and agrees to pay for an alternative supply if it cannot perform. Also known as a put-or-pay contract.

sustainability bonds Bonds with proceeds earmarked for projects aimed at generating positive environmental and social impact.

sustainability-linked bonds Issuer makes a commitment to achieve predefined key sustainable performance targets and the financial characteristics of the bond depend on the achievement of key performance indicators (KPIs). Proceeds go toward general purposes.

swap The exchanging of one security, debt, currency, or interest rate for another. Also known as a switch. See also currency swap; hedge; futures contract; and option.

sweep All available cash flow used for debt service.

switch Sometimes used as a synonym for a swap; for example, buying a currency spot and selling it forward.

syndicate A group of banks participating in a single credit facility, a syndicated loan, or syndicated credit facility. A group of bond houses that act together in underwriting and distributing a new securities issue.

syndicated credit facility A credit facility in which a number of banks undertake to provide a loan or other support facility to a customer on a pro rata basis under identical terms and conditions evidenced by a single credit agreement.

tail The remaining reserves after the project financing has been repaid. Sometimes means the residual.

takāful – the Islamic version of insurance.

take-and-pay If the project's output is deliverable and can be taken, it will be paid for.

take-or-pay In the event the project's output is not taken, payment must be made whether or not the output is deliverable. Also known as throughput contract or use-or-pay contract. See also requirements contract.

tender bond See bid bond.

tender process See bid process.

tenor The number of years a loan is outstanding; the term or maturity. Also tenure or maturity of debt.

term The loan life or tenor; the period to a loan's maturity. "Term" also means a condition attached.

term loan A fixed-period loan, usually for one to ten years, that is paid back by the borrower in regular (often monthly) instalments with interest. This is the most common form of business loan; it may be secured or unsecured.

term sheet A document, not generally intended to be legally binding, setting out the main agreed terms and conditions to a transaction between the borrower and arranger.

termination The act of bringing the contract to an end by one of the parties in accordance with a right to do so granted by the applicable law or the contract.

trade finance agency Another term for export credit agency.

trade financing programs Another term for export credit incentive programs.

tranche A separate portion of a credit facility, perhaps with different lenders, margins, currencies, and/or term.

transfer risk The risk that a given currency will not be allowed to be sent out of the country, usually due to central bank restrictions or a national debt rescheduling. See also currency risk.

transformation Involves the redevelopment of larger urban areas to increase place value through better urban design, job concentration, improved services, and of course infrastructure investment.

transit-oriented development (TOD) Planning and design strategy for an urban development organized around transit stations and embracing the idea that place value is significantly improved by local jobs, shops, housing, improved user experience, and other economic activities.

translation risk A type of foreign exchange risk arising from the need to translate the assets and liabilities of a foreign subsidiary into the currency of the home country.

trust deed The deed in which an issuer of notes or bonds, any guarantor, and the trustee set out the obligations of the issuer and guarantor and appoint a trustee to represent the interests of the bond or note holders.

tunnel See collar.

turnkey construction Where one contractor is responsible for the design and construction of a project to completion, so that it is ready to produce cash flow. See also EPC contract or design and build.

underwriting A bank undertaking to buy a certain amount of a new debt issue if it is not taken up by third parties during an agreed period.

Glossary

unsecured loan A loan made on the general credit of a borrower. The lenders rely upon the borrower's balance sheet and the capability of the borrower's management to manage its assets and produce sufficient cash flows to repay the debt. No assets are pledged.

unsecured The financier has no security, merely the obligation/undertaking from the borrower to repay.

unsolicited bid; also unsolicited proposal (USP) A proposal submitted by a private investor to a contracting authority that was not solicited by the contracting authority and is not otherwise part of a formal bid process, in the hopes of securing the award of the project without competition, or with some advantage.

use-or-pay contract Another name for a take-or-pay contract or throughput contract.

user fee Where the project company receives payment from users for services delivered (different from availability payments).

value for money (VfM) The optimum combination of whole-of-life costs and quality of the good or service to meet the user's requirements and not the choice of goods and services based on the lowest cost bid; it extends beyond financial cost to include quality considerations, such as the ability to meet the service requirements of the users.

variable duration notes At the coupon payment date of a note, the holder elects to receive either payment or an additional note with identical terms.

variable rate loan A loan made at an interest rate that fluctuates with the prime rate, the LIBOR, or some other index.

variation or change A technical term in construction contracts referring to a variation of the client's requirements ordered by the client, generally entitling the contractor to a change in the contract price, the time for completion, and any other obligation affected by the variation ordered.

venture capital Equity and risk capital for new entrepreneurial ventures, invested in a stage earlier than other capital would normally be available.

viability gap fund (VGF) A programmatic approach to capital grants, using a fund to sequester budget allocations and roll them over from one year to the next and establish criteria for funding allocation. Used in India, Indonesia, and a few other countries, though with different rules and procedures. See also capital grants.

volatility The degree of fluctuation that occurs away from a value, such as the mean, of a series of figures. The greater the volatility in returns, the higher the risk.

WACC See weighted average cost of capital.

weighted average cost of capital (WACC) The total return required by both debt and equity investors expressed as a real posttax percentage on funds usage.

withholding tax A tax on interest, royalty, or dividend payments – usually those paid overseas. It may be deducted at source to mitigate the risk of avoidance, in particular by foreign recipients.

working capital The part of the capital of a company that is employed in its day-to-day trading operations. It consists of current assets (mainly trading stock, debtors, and cash) less current liabilities (mainly trade creditors).

working capital replenishment An undertaking by an industrial company sponsor and/or parent to make liquid funds available to a special purpose subsidiary or company to enable such a company to keep its working capital at sufficient levels to service debt and meet operating expenses.

World Bank Group A multilateral agency based in Washington, DC, made up of the IBRD, IDA, IFC, MIGA, and International Court of the Settlement of Investment Disputes. IBRD and IDA are together commonly known as the World Bank.

wraparound loan A long-term loan structured with a short-term loan in such a manner as to postpone payments of principal (and sometimes interest) on the long-term loan until the short-term and long-term wraparound may produce level debt service for both loans over the life of the long-term loan.

yield Rate of return, expressed as a percentage and annualized.

yield curve A curve showing several yields or interest rates across different contract lengths (two months, two years, twenty years, etc.) for a similar debt contract. The curve shows the relation between the (level of) interest rate (or cost of borrowing) and the time to maturity, known as the "term," of the debt for a given borrower in a given currency. The shape of the yield curve indicates the cumulative priorities of all lenders relative to a particular borrower. Lack of a yield curve of sufficient length makes it difficult for lenders to price debt at that maturity.

yield to maturity The rate of return yielded (e.g., by a debt security held to maturity) when both interest payments and the investor's capital gain or loss on the security are taken into account.

Index

affordable housing, 45, 55
African Development Bank, 149, 197
arbitration, 130, 173, 208

bankability, 108, 115, 133
betterment levies, 20
bonds, 110, 112, 141, 146, 156, 186, 198, 207, 218, 219

capital markets, 118
community engagement, 65, 87
construction contract, 120, 201, 204, 214, 216, 219
credit rating, 113, 172

DBSA. *See* Development Bank of Southern Africa (DBSA)
debt, 9, 105, 109, 113, 118, 135, 138, 184, 195, 197, 201, 217, 218
   capital markets, 118
   service cover ratio (DSCR), 135, 137–139, 198, 203
density bonus, 21
Derivatives, 164
Development Bank of Southern Africa (DBSA), 189
DFI, 117, 176, 178, 180, 182–184, 191, 195, 204
domestic capital markets, 119
DSCR. *See* debt, service cover ratio (DSCR)

educational facilities, 49, 50
engineering, procurement and construction, 204

EPC, 204, 220
Equator Principles, 122
equity, 9, 92–94, 96–98, 105, 109, 119, 185, 212, 221

finance, xvi, 9, 16, 17, 20, 22, 37, 40, 41, 43, 48, 58, 64, 68, 82, 83, 93, 96, 98, 105–107, 109, 110, 130, 133, 141, 145–148, 150, 154, 159–162, 164, 165, 167–169, 171, 172, 174–176, 178, 180–183, 186–191, 195, 197, 203, 208, 209, 222
FIRR, 133, 205
fiscal space, 108, 131
foreign exchange risk, 129
funding, xv, 2, 3, 13, 19, 20, 22, 23, 52, 82, 86
FX risk, 207

global capital markets, 118
green bond, 143
guarantee, 174

ICSID, 208, 222
IDFC, 188, 190
IFC. *See* International Finance Corporation (IFC)
IFI, 204, 208, 209
Ijārah, 160, 174
insolvency, 137
insurance, 165, 174
interest rate risk, 122
internal rate of return, 139

International Finance Corporation (IFC), 40,
   41, 43, 58, 64, 117, 122, 146, 176, 178,
   179, 193, 208, 209, 222
IRR, 86, 133, 139, 209
Istisnā, 160

James F. Oyster Bilingual Elementary School,
   50, 54
Jozini Tiger Lodge, 47, 65

land, xv, 4, 8, 15–25, 29, 39, 42, 60, 71, 72,
   75, 93, 96, 98
land value capture, 4, 15, 17
lease, 71, 198, 209, 210, 217
legal framework, 25
lending, 200
limited recourse financing, 108
LLCR. *See* loan life cover ratio (LLCR)
loan life cover ratio (LLCR), 135, 137–139
local government, 25

mezzanine, 9, 105, 111, 112
monitoring, reporting and verification, 83,
   84, 211
MRV, *See* monitoring, reporting and
   verification
mudārabah, 160
Multilateral Investment Guarantee Agency, 174
murābahah, 160
mushārakah, 160, 163, 174

negative carry, 110
net present value (NPV), 139, 205, 212
NGO, 212
NPV. *See* net present value (NPV)

O&M, 212
off-balance sheet, 106
opex, 212, 213

political risk, 120, 214, 218
PPP, 4, 5, 8, 18, 29–32, 35, 38, 40–42, 44–64,
   66–71, 73, 75–79, 85, 88, 89, 114, 115,
   117, 148, 159, 161, 162, 164, 165, 167,
   169, 171, 172, 175, 187, 189, 202, 205,
   209, 213, 214, 216
project financing, 10, 11, 106, 131, 139
project selection, 181
public parking, 61, 63

rate of return, 139, 222
recycling, 40
refinancing, 140, 187
return on equity (ROE), 139, 140, 216, 217
RfP, 215
RFQ, 217
ROE. *See* return on equity (ROE)
ROI, 11, 139, 217
ROR, 139

sponsor support, 132
SPV, 108, 167, 169, 170, 174, 214, 218
step-in rights, 204
subordinated debt, 112
sukūk, 160
syndication, 113

takāful, 160, 174
Tamil Nadu Urban Development Fund, 191
TDR. *See* transferable development right
   (TDR)
TIF, 22, 23, 99
transferable development right (TDR), 22, 73

up zoning, 21, 22
urban redevelopment, 41, 42

value for money, 114

World Bank, 1, 5, 10, 15, 17, 29–32, 34,
   35, 38–47, 49–51, 54–58, 60–64,
   66–69, 75, 76, 78, 88, 89, 91, 94, 95,
   98–100, 111, 117, 146, 148, 149, 159,
   161, 162, 164, 167, 169, 171,172,
   174–177, 186, 191, 193, 201, 205,
   208, 209, 222